Contents

Preface   ix

Acknowledgments   xiii

1. Meaning-Making as a Family Process   1

   Why Study Family Meaning-Making?   1
   Conceptual Frameworks   4
   Assumptions   13
   Definition and Elaboration of Terms   14
   Relevance of the Methodology to the Question   16

2. Past Attempts to Understand Family Meaning-Making   19

   Grief and Meaning   20
   The Process of Meaning-Making   22
   Individual Meaning Construction   29
   Family Stress and Family Meaning-Making   32
   Summary   38

3. Capturing Family Meaning-Making   40

   Techniques of Data Collection   41
   Data Collection   49
   Data Analysis   52
   Verification of the Data   57
   Ethical Considerations   63

Researcher Role and Bias   65
Limitations   66

4. Patterns of Meaning-Making   70

    Introduction to Respondent Families   70
    Overview of Meaning-Making Patterns   71
    Individual Level of Meaning-Making   73
    Couple Level of Meaning-Making   76
    Dyadic Level of Meaning-Making   78
    Family Level of Meaning-Making   81
    Sharing Patterns Within Families   86
    Summary   107

5. Stories, Dreams, Comparing, and Coincidancing   110

    Stories and Dreams   111
    Comparison   118
    "Coincidancing"   125
    Summary   135

6. Characterization and Family Speak   136

    Characterization   136
    "Family Speak"   148
    Summary   157

7. Negative and Ultimate Meanings   159

    Category 1: What the Death Was Not   161
    Category 2: There Is No Sense to Be Made   164
    Category 3: Death Was Unfair or Unjust   169
    Category 4: Philosophical Meanings   176
    Category 5: The Afterlife   181
    Category 6: Religious Meanings   184
    Summary   190

8. Meanings About Death and Family Change   191

    Category 7: The Nature of the Death   191
    Category 8: Attitude of the Deceased Toward Death   202
    Category 9: How the Death Changed the Family   211
    Category 10: Lessons Learned and Truths Realized   220
    Summary   228

Janice Winchester Nadeau

Families
Making
Sense of
Death

UNDERSTANDING
FAMILIES

SAGE Publications
International Educational and Professional Publisher
Thousand Oaks   London   New Delhi

9805010

WB 317

For information:

SAGE Publications, Inc.
2455 Teller Road
Thousand Oaks, California 91320
E-mail: order@sagepub.com

SAGE Publications Ltd.
6 Bonhill Street
London EC2A 4PU
United Kingdom

SAGE Publications India Pvt. Ltd.
M-32 Market
Greater Kailash I
New Delhi 110 048 India

Printed in the United States of America

Library of Congress Cataloging-in-Publication Data

Nadeau, Janice Winchester.
  Families making sense of death / by Janice Winchester Nadeau.
    p. cm. — (Understanding families; v. 10)
    Includes bibliographical references (p.) and index.
    ISBN 0-7619-0265-1 (hardcover: alk. paper). — ISBN 0-7619-0266-X
  (pbk.: alk. paper)
    1. Death—Psychological aspects. 2. Bereavement—Psychological
  aspects. 3. Grief. 4. Family—Psychological aspects. 5. Family
  life surveys. I. Title. II. Series.
  BF789.D4N33 1997
  155.9′37—dc2'1   97-21080

98 99 00 01 02 03 10 9 8 7 6 5 4 3 2 1

Acquiring Editor:	Margaret Zusky
Editorial Assistant:	Corinne Pierce
Production Editor:	Astrid Virding
Production Assistant:	Karen Wiley
Typesetter/Designer:	Andrea D. Swanson
Indexer:	L. Pilar Wyman
Print Buyer:	Anna Chin

9. Looking to the Future   230

   Implications for Theory, Research, and Practice   230
   Summary   242
   Conclusions   245

Epilogue   248
   The Family Literature   249
   The Grief Literature   251
   Advances in Methods and Methodology   255
   Advances in Computerized Data Analysis   257

Appendix   260
   Interview Guidelines   260
   Genograms   262

References   273

Index   278

About the Author   289

This book is dedicated to my mother,
Arleen N. Winchester,
who taught me perseverance,

and to my father,
Ray C. Winchester,
who taught me to be curious
about how things work.

Preface

This book is the result of my nearly lifelong interest in grief. When I was 5 years old, my grandfather died. My grandmother, who lived with us, began telling me what it was like to be alone, how she missed Grandpa's warm hands, and how lonely she was.

When I became a nursing student, I was assigned to the patients who were dying. Later, as an intensive care nurse, I was struck by the barrenness and inadequacy of doing nothing more for grieving families than handing them their loved one's personal belongings in a plastic bag and watching them walk down the hall and out of the hospital. This drew me to hospice nursing, teaching nursing students how to care for the dying, and then to work with surviving family members as a grief counselor.

In developing my role as a grief counselor, I became aware that little is known about family grief. This realization inspired me to go back to graduate school to learn more about families and what they need in times of loss. This book is the result of each of these experiences as they culminated in a qualitative study of family grief that helped me earn a doctorate in family social science at the University of Minnesota.

This book looks at family grief through the lens of family meaning-making and asks how what has been seen can be applied to family phenomena other than bereavement. The book is centered around a study of 10 multigenerational, grieving families. Forty-eight family members were interviewed. Families were located by funeral directors and clergy, who made the initial contacts. Of the 10 family members who died, 1 died accidentally, and the other 9 died of natural causes. All 10 were deaths of adults aged 39 to 91.

I wanted first to learn how family members interact with each other in their effort to make sense of their loss and then to capture the nature of the meanings they construct. Much of what the families told me in the privacy of their homes is quoted verbatim in the pages of this book. What is shared here only scratches the surface of what we need to know about the intricate processes of family construction of reality, but this book provides substantive data from families who can teach us a great deal about family processes.

Although the focus of this book is on a study that I conducted in the early 1990s, it draws heavily on the continued processing of the findings from that study. Most important have been ongoing opportunities to verify my study results with those who come to me for marriage and family therapy. Of nearly equal importance have been the many opportunities to interact with a wide variety of audiences about my findings. I have shared the study locally with groups of grieving families and frontline practitioners; nationally, with family scholars at the Annual Conference of the National Council on Family Relations and with grief scholars at the Annual Conference of the Association for Death Education and Counseling; and internationally, with the International Work Group on Death, Dying, and Bereavement. On each occasion, the responses have both validated my findings and pushed me to think of the data in new and exciting ways. What is found in this book is the result of my ongoing interaction with the data.

This book is intended for anyone with an interest in family grief, but also for those with an interest in how families construct reality in the face of a major family event. The many excerpts reveal interior family life. The book can be appreciated most by reading it in its entirety, but for those who want to "cut to the quick," Chapters 4 through 8 contain the family quotations and the analysis. Chapter 9 has a discussion of how the findings may be used to build theory, conduct future research, and work with families in a variety of practice arenas. The Epilogue reviews theoretical and empirical work that has been done since the study data were first analyzed.

Studying families from a meaning-making perspective has changed the way I see families, both my own and those with whom I work. It has heightened my curiosity about family process and given me a great respect for the resourcefulness of most families to find ways to make sense of serious events that confront them. My hope is that this look at families through the perspective of family meaning-making will be illuminating to you as well.

—Janice Winchester Nadeau

Acknowledgments

I owe a debt of gratitude to more people than can be named in this short space. Some are bound to be overlooked. First, I thank my husband, Leonard Nadeau, for his loving support, willingness to proofread, and patience with this project.

Other family members to whom I am indebted for a variety of reasons include Ellen van Nood, my research assistant and daughter-in-law, whose computer and analytic skills helped make the analysis an exciting adventure. Special thanks go to my son Mark for his on-call computer expertise. Credit goes to my daughter Cindy and her spouse, Brian, who gave their support and provided grandchildren Bonnie, Lori, and Brian Keith to help as junior research assistants. My daughter Laurinda was a good listener when the going got rough, and my son Michael came to help celebrate. My surrogate daughter, Valerie Brown, provided encouragement and acted as a sounding board for some critical ideas.

My deepest gratitude goes to Professor Paul C. Rosenblatt for his loyalty, for many meaningful conversations over the years, and for his confidence in me and in the value of this project.

David M. Klein and Bert N. Adams, as series editors, were immensely helpful in fulfilling their promise to give detailed and careful advice. They consistently challenged me to address important issues. This book would never have come to fruition without their consistent moral support and encouragement.

Anselm Strauss and Juliet Corbin helped during the data analysis by critiquing my coding system and by reacting to my data at the 1992 Conference of the National Council on Family Relations. I am grateful for Anselm's personal letter of encouragement.

Many thanks to people who critiqued parts of the original study: Grif Bates, Terry Peterson, Cara Beams, Pat Spoentgen, Phyllis Owens, Leni de Mik, Sandy Lindell, Sheryl Niebuhr, Jack and Naomi Miller, and Pat and Louie Bartscher. Special thanks go to my doctoral committee: Paul Rosenblatt, Kathryn Rettig, Mariah Snyder, Sheila Corcoran-Perry, William Doherty, and Marlene Stum.

I am much indebted to Jane Gilgun, whose qualitative work group provided a forum for the exploration of my data. Jane's ongoing interest and enthusiasm for my work helped immensely. Colleagues at Minnesota Human Development Consultants deserve recognition for helping make this book possible by reading chapters and by joining in my struggles and celebrations.

Ann Garwick, friend and soulmate, met with me monthly to react to sections of the book and to provide invaluable encouragement. Patricia Zalaznik gave generous support both as a friend and as a library researcher. Tracy Kill, Nancy Hokonson, and Karen Pederson provided technical help that was indispensable.

I thank the Ursuline Sisters and the staff of Villa Maria in Old Frontenac, Minnesota, for providing a retreat where I could write, study, and find solitude and inspiration.

Most of all, I thank the families who participated in the research for their willingness to share the privacy of their grief. Their openness made the project possible.

The research reported in this book was funded by NIH Grant #5F31-NRO6139; a Bush Leadership Fellowship; the Society for the Psychological Study of Social Issues; a Special Dissertation Grant from the University of Minnesota Graduate School; a Mary Ellen McFarland Assistantship from the Department of Family Social Science at the University of Minnesota; a grant from anonymous friends; and a grant from the National Foundation of Funeral Service and the Funeral Directors' Service Association of Greater Metropolitan Chicago.

1

Meaning-Making as a Family Process

Why Study Family Meaning-Making?

Few life events have a greater impact on a family than the death of a family member. Most of what we know about grief is from an individual perspective because most studies focus on individuals. This study investigated the phenomenon of family grief—specifically, how family members interactively make sense of their experience. This interactive process, referred to as *family meaning-making,* is thought to occur in a variety of family events, not only following a death.

As long ago as 1959, Hess and Handel (1959) coined the term *family worlds* to capture the notion of family as a finite province of meaning, having its own consistent logic of knowing that applies within the family world but not outside it. Family researchers studying a variety of family phenomena refer to what they call *shared meaning* or *family meanings.* Sometimes researchers falsely assume they have identified family meanings when only one or two members have been interviewed and very little has been done to collect systemic data.

Although family meanings have been identified as critical in family coping, little is known about the process by which families make meaning or about the meanings themselves. This study asked the question, "What are the patterns of meaning-making in families who have lost a member through death?" Answers were sought by interviewing multiple members of 10 families in which a member had died. What was learned about this theoretically and practically important topic is useful in understanding not only family grief but also many other family phenomena.

Divorce, the birth of a child, adoption, chronic illness, disability, natural disaster, geographic relocation, and family blending are but a few of the events that can cause families to struggle with meaning. Virtually anything that has the potential to upset the family's status quo is likely to invoke meaning-making processes not unlike those identified in this study of bereaved families. For this reason, what was learned about how families make sense of the loss of a family member has a broad range of usefulness throughout the family field.

Knowing more about family meaning will strengthen the conceptual bases for several theories currently used in the family field. Broderick and Smith (1979) noted that family systems theory will develop no more quickly than descriptive data on family structure and process accumulate. This study of family meanings provides a new window into family interaction patterns and the panorama of family life from a systemic point of view. Interest in family meanings grew out of my 20 years of working with grieving families, first as an intensive care nurse, then as a hospice nurse, and now as a family therapist and psychologist. The study was sparked by my observation that when family members became aware that someone in the family was expected to die, they started talking with one another about the death and what it might mean. They said things like, "Well, you couldn't wish Mother to go on living with all the pain she is in." Another family member would add, "Yes, and you know I think she has been trying to die ever since Dad passed away." Efforts to make sense of their experience suggest an attempt to create order out of the chaos they were experiencing and perhaps to gain some sense of control over the uncontrollable.

In some families in which death was expected for some time, the saying of meanings sounded like a litany. Family members would say the same phrases about the death over and over again to each other.

When a person dies, his or her family has a story to tell about the events surrounding the death. Such stories are meaning laden, but few researchers have talked about the presence or significance of these meanings or the interactive processes by which they are constructed.

Sometimes meanings are of an existential nature; that is, they have to do with the meaning and purpose of life itself. More often, meaning statements relate specifically to the death and to what a particular death of a specific person means to the members of his or her family. The meanings then articulated relate to how well families manage after the deaths—how difficult it is for them to go on living without the lost family members. Alfred Adler (1958) said, "Human beings live in the realm of meanings" and "we experience reality always through the meaning we give it; not in itself, but as something interpreted" (p. 1).

It could be argued that a search for meaning comes out of the perturbation caused by a death. The status quo is upset. Existential questions are raised. The struggle to find answers to these existential questions, which is the search for meaning, is central to the grieving process. In the families who inspired this study, the ability to attach meaning and to share these meanings within the families and with others greatly affected how the families coped.

An example of what this study attempted to investigate comes from a discussion about meaning with a group of students prior to the study's inception. One foreign student, whose mother had recently died, said he needed to believe that his family had done all that was possible for his dying mother. He needed to hear his father say so, over and over, each time they talked long-distance. He described his actions as "constructing my meaning about her death." His belief that everything possible was being done for his mother helped him cope with losing her. Family meaning was being created as various members of his family talked long-distance across continents.

What was learned in the design of the study and in early interviews heightened awareness of meanings in my clinical practice. It became apparent that meanings are important factors in most, if not all, problems that families may present in therapy. It became important to listen more carefully for meanings, to notice how meanings were being constructed, to watch for discrepant meanings among family members, and to notice how particular meanings played out in the lives of the people who constructed them. For instance, in one divorcing couple, the husband, who had come to realize that he was gay, told his wife that the reason he was leaving her was her inability to satisfy him sexually. She accepted his meaning and believed that the demise of their marriage was because of her failure, rather than his sexual preference. Much of her distress during the divorcing process was caused by her feelings of inadequacy and failure as a sexual partner. Much of her therapy was focused on reconstructing her meaning system to include alternative meanings that were not as detrimental to her sense of self.

In one family, a husband and wife were trying to join their children from previous marriages. Discrepant family meanings were a problem. The husband's meaning was that a "good" husband would take over as the disciplinarian of his new wife's children. The wife's children insisted that he had no business disciplining them. The husband and wife believed that she should be willing to turn the discipline over to her new spouse, but she could not and agreed, in part, with her children, that he had no business disciplining them. Help consisted of working with family meanings in a way that construed the stepfather as a consultant to his wife in regard to parenting her children, the stepmother as a consultant to him in regard to parenting his children, and the biological parent being responsible for discipline in each case.

Why study family meaning-making? Understanding the process of meaning-making will lead to new theories about families, improve family research methods, and help family therapists intervene effectively in ways that respect the subjectivities of their client families regardless of the problem the family presents. The process of family meaning-making, then, is of theoretical and practical importance well beyond the realm of family bereavement.

Conceptual Frameworks

The major conceptual frameworks on which this study was based are symbolic interaction theory and family systems theory. Both frameworks are discussed briefly as they apply to the study of meaning-making in family bereavement.

SYMBOLIC INTERACTION THEORY

Symbolic interaction is a theoretical orientation that grew out of the philosophical writings of James (1890), Cooley (1902, 1909), Dewey (1922), and Mead (1932, 1934, 1936, 1938). *Symbolic interaction theory* has been identified by family scholars as a useful theory in understanding a variety of family phenomena. It is useful because, unlike most other family theories, it emphasizes mental phenomena, or *mentalistic variables* (Burr, Leigh, Day, & Constantine, 1979, p. 47). *Symbolic interactionism* includes the assumption that humans live in a symbolic environment as well as a physical environment and that they acquire complex sets of mental symbols (Rose, 1962). Symbolic interaction theory reflects Thomas's (1923) belief that if people define situations as real, they are real in their consequences. If Thomas was correct, we can expect to find a connection between how a family construes a particular event—be it death, a divorce, chronic illness, or any other event—and how the family responds following the event.

One way in which symbolic interaction theory has been explicated is by comparing it with psychoanalytic theory. Theorists of the interaction school argue against the psychoanalytic notion that some phenomena have universal symbolic meanings. Instead, interactionists posit that meanings of various phenomena vary from person to person, from situation to situation, and are subject to historical time and culture (Burr et al., 1979). Rosenblatt and Fischer (in an early draft of their chapter in Boss et al., 1993), noted: "From a symbolic interactionist's perspective it is less important to know whether or not an event actually happened than whether or not people believe it happened, because all interaction emerges from the meanings with which people imbue events" (p. 5). In comparison with psychoanalytic thought, the symbolic interaction view assumes that behavior is influenced by the meaning of the ideas in the mind, and not by instincts, libidinal energy, needs, drives, or forces (Burr et al., 1979).

As symbolic interaction theory continued to evolve as a viable family theory, Berger and Luckmann's influential work *The Social Construction of Reality* (1966) came on the scene. It was a treatise written with the modest goal of righting the field known as the "sociology of knowledge." Because of its language and theoretical density, it had its greatest appeal mainly to other, sophisticated, sociological theorists.

By the time the current study was designed in the early 1990s, Berger and Luckmann's treatise had been fairly well integrated into the work of other scholars and researchers. Those integrators of Berger and Luckmann's work, such as Burr et al. (1979), informed this study. The following remarks refer, however, to Berger and Luck-mann's original work.

Much of Berger and Luckmann's (1966) theorizing was an elabo-ration of what they referred to as "the essential dialectic of society" based on two propositions. The first proposition was "society exists only as individuals are conscious of it"; the second was "individual consciousness is socially determined" (p. 78). Of greatest relevance to the study of family meanings was Berger and Luckmann's contention that reality is socially defined but that the definitions are always embodied in concrete individuals and groups of individuals. Families may be construed as small groups who socially create their own reality, their own *family world,* as Hess and Handel (1959) called it.

Berger and Luckmann (1966) identified multiple realities. They spoke of everyday reality as *paramount reality* into which marginal realities must be integrated, death being identified as the most impor-tant marginal reality. Death constitutes a crisis situation, they said, the integration of which requires procedures somewhat different from those used to integrate other everyday (paramount) realities. Proce-dures for reality maintenance in crisis situations must be more explicit and more intense than those required to integrate paramount reality. Sometimes, in crisis situations, ritual techniques are brought into play. These ritual techniques may be improvised by individuals but usually are set up by society, which recognizes the risk of the breakdown of reality in such times.

Death-related rituals come quickly to mind as socially prescribed reality-maintaining procedures. We can expect such rituals to be meaning laden. Indeed, asking families what funeral rituals they observed elicited many meanings.

Berger and Luckmann (1966) identified verbal conversation as the most important vehicle of *reality maintenance.* In describing the ways in which conversation maintains reality, they came close to describing the interactive processes by which family members might make sense of their experience.

Berger and Luckmann (1966) suggested that one's everyday life could be viewed as the working away of a conversational apparatus that ongoingly maintains, modifies, and reconstructs one's subjective reality. They contended that significant others are the most important players in reality maintenance and that conversation means mainly that people speak with each other. They did not deny the "rich aura of non-verbal communication" that surrounds speech, but rather assigned speech a "privileged position" in the total conversational apparatus.

"Generally speaking, the conversational apparatus maintains reality by 'talking through' various elements of experience and allocates them a definite place in the real world" (Berger & Luckmann, 1966, p. 153). One could learn about how this process occurs, it would seem, by listening to family conversation and by asking family members what they say to each other when the researcher is not present. Both approaches were used in this study.

One question relevant to the conceptualization of this study was why meaning-making, or what Berger and Luckmann (1966) called *reality construction,* occurs. What drives reality construction at the time of crisis, whether it is a death in the family or some other crisis? Berger and Luckmann emphasized that "*all* social order is precarious" and that "*all* societies are constructions in the face of chaos" (p. 103). Institutional order keeps chaos at bay, they said, and the experience of death is the greatest threat to institutional order:

> The experience of the death of others and, subsequently, the anticipation of one's own death posit the marginal situation par excellence for the individual. Needless to elaborate, death also posits the most terrifying threat to the taken-for-granted realities of everyday life. The integration of death within the paramount reality of social existence is, therefore, of the greatest importance for any institutional order. This legitimation of death is, consequently, one of the most important fruits of symbolic universes . . . all legitimations must enable the individual to go on living in society after the death of significant others and to anticipate his own death with, at the very least, terror sufficiently mitigated so as not to paralyze the continued performance of the routines of everyday life. It may readily be seen that such legitimation is difficult to achieve short of integrating the phenomenon of death within a symbolic universe. . . . [I]t is in the legitimation of death that the transcending potency of symbolic universes manifests itself most clearly, and the fundamental terror-assuaging character of the ultimate legitimations of the paramount reality of everyday life is revealed. (p. 101)

Death and the threat of death drive the process of meaning-making by their power to upset our sense of order. People want to get back to the order and security of everyday life. Making sense of the experience of death reduces the terror by allowing a return to everyday reality. Berger and Luckmann's (1966) notion that "everyday reality is ongoingly reaffirmed in the individual's interactions with others" (p. 150) provides a framework for thinking about the interactive processes by which individuals and families become able to integrate the marginal reality of a death into their paramount reality.

Berger and Luckmann (1966) delineated the processes by which the symbolic universe gets maintained, but they stopped short of speculating about what the construction processes might be within groups such as families.

This study did just that.

Berger and Luckmann (1966) theorized that reality maintenance, modification, and reconstruction occur, but they did not theorize how one would recognize these processes in the everyday conversation of families. They theorized about the interaction between individuals and society but not about the interactive processes by which family conversations help integrate marginal realities. They also did not identify what kinds of meanings might make up the new reality constructed in a time of crisis. This study set out to describe the reality-making conversation itself, asking how family members do it and what the realities they construct are.

Practically speaking, what we can take from Berger and Luckmann's theorizing is that reality is constructed in family groups through the use of conversation. At times of crisis, we can expect that verbal interactions aimed at reality maintenance will be more explicit and intense and may draw on ritual procedures. Indeed, that is what was found to be the case.

In addition to Berger and Luckmann's (1966) treatise, several middle-range theories, developed within the interactionist point of view, informed the current study. The two most helpful were the definition of the situation and the definition of self. The *definition of the situation* refers to the subjective meaning that a particular situation has to a person (Burr et al., 1979). According to Burr et al., if several people witness the same situation, they may all define it somewhat differently. Furthermore, how they define the situation will determine the effects of the situation in their lives. Proposition 1 of symbolic interaction theory states, "The definitions of situations influence the effects of those situations in such a way that the effect tends to be congruent with the definition" (Burr et al., 1979, p. 64). The notion of definition of the situation has been applied to family stress reactions.

The earliest research on family stress revealed that the definition that families gave to the seriousness of stressful events influenced the impact the events tended to have (Burr et al., 1979). What we can take from this line of thinking is that it is important to pay attention not only to the processes by which meaning is constructed in families but also to the meanings themselves. For instance, it stands to reason that the family who construe a move to a new community as a way to have more of what is important to them will react differently from the family who construe a move as losing most of what they hold dear. The meanings themselves are important because they have a direct effect on family outcomes, whether we are talking about bereavement, divorce, chronic illness, family restructuring, or any other family event.

Burr et al. (1979) argued that attention to definitional processes in past studies was lacking. "It may be," they contended, "that much more of the variance in the dependent variables could be accounted for by focusing on the definitional variables as the most direct causes and identifying additional factors that influence the definitional processes" (p. 66).

Boss (1987), writing about work done in the area of family stress, noted a dearth of research on perception of the stressful event, and she attributed the lack of emphasis on perceptual variables to the fact that such study requires a focus on qualitative variables. Boss's contention was that researchers in the past tended to shy away from the study of qualitative variables.

This study was an attempt to examine qualitatively the phenomenon of family meaning-making, or what some interactionists might call definition of the situation.

Burr et al. (1979) suggested the study of various factors that influence the definitional process—that is, how sense is made of some family event. One factor particularly relevant to the study of family meaning-making following a death is the way individuals' definitions of situations are influenced by others. Definitions are not generated in a vacuum (Burr et al., 1979).

Burr, referring to the work of Rose (1962), one of the early thinkers in the interactionist school, noted that through communication of symbols, individuals can learn many meanings and values from others. Learning takes place in the family context. Perceptions of generalized and significant others and the nature of the social institutions in which a person lives are two important factors in the acquisition of definitions (Burr et al., 1979). The interactionist approach strives to interpret family phenomena in terms of processes internal to the family.

In addition to definition-of-situation theories, one other interactionist theory useful to this study was *definition of self.* According to Stryker (1972), the definition of self is a process by which the individual defines him- or herself in terms of socially recognized categories and their corresponding roles, roles that imply relationships to others.

Self is the way one describes one's relationships to others in social process (Stryker, 1972). The self process is ongoing, ever changing, and dynamic (Burr et al., 1979). It is dependent on interactions with significant others. This line of theorizing is useful in understanding how family members are affected by a death. When family relationships are severed by the death of a family member, the contribution that the deceased made to the identities of other family members by interacting with them is lost. The process of redefinition of self occurs for each member. Meanings related to the death may reflect how members experience themselves differently.

One person in a prestudy conversation talked about how she had to find out who she was because her only two siblings were dead. In her words, "It was like coming out from under their cloud into the sun." As this quote implies, definition of self is closely linked to shifting roles, and symbolic interaction theory includes relatively well developed concepts and propositions related to roles, including role transitions typical of those occurring in the family following the loss of a family member.

Symbolic interaction theory has been used in previous grief studies. Rosenblatt (1983), in a study of 19th-century diarists, demonstrated its usefulness. He noted that symbolic interaction theory deals with the importance of others in defining ourselves and our situations. When somebody important to us dies, we lose definitions of self and situations that came out of interaction with that person. Rosenblatt also noted that although one's history of interaction is important, it is the day-to-day interactions that are crucial. When a family member dies, the day-to-day interactions are lost. This study found many meanings that defined death and equally as many that reflected new or shifting self definitions.

FAMILY SYSTEMS THEORY

The second conceptual framework that underlies this study is *family systems theory*. It is highly compatible with symbolic inter-action theory. In fact, some theorists argue that symbolic interaction theory can be completely absorbed into general systems theory (e.g., Buckley, 1967). A *system,* according to Hall and Fagan's (1956) most quoted definition, is "a set of objects together with relationships between the objects and their attributes" (p. 18). Family systems theory is an adaptation of general systems theory as it applies to the family as a system. Muxen (1991) described family systems theory as "providing a view of the family as a set of intimately connected people who are mutually influential on each other in some way, and whose relationships evolve over time interactively with each other as well as with past, present, and anticipated future contexts" (p. 16).

Several systems concepts and systems ways of thinking about fami-lies have relevance in the study of meaning in grieving families. The systems framework provides the concepts necessary for describing the structural changes that occur in the family following a death—namely, changes in roles, rules, and boundaries. Constantine (1986) defined *structure* as "the sum total of the interrelationships among elements of a system, including membership in the system and the boundary between the system and its environment" (p. 52). *Roles* are the expec-tations attached to given positions. This includes family positions, such as mother (Stryker, 1972). *Rules* are prescriptions for familial responses to a wide range of possible inputs (Broderick & Smith, 1979). These "prescriptions" may be spoken or merely understood. *Boundaries* are those things that delineate the elements belonging to the system in question and those belonging to its environment (Broderick & Smith, 1979).

Family restructuring in systems terms means changing family roles, rules, and boundaries. It has often been noted, according to Broderick and Smith (1979), that adding or subtracting even a single member of a family has dramatic implications for the structure of the family. The meanings that families attach to the death may both influence, and be influenced by, structural changes in the family. Not only are there new meanings to be made related to the death, but there are also fewer members to make them.

One systems concept, boundaries, bears further elaboration. As mentioned above, a boundary delineates the elements belonging to the system from those belonging to the environment (Broderick & Smith, 1979). It makes sense to select a boundary such that the level of interaction within the boundary is greater than the level outside the boundary or outside the system of interest. In the family system, boundary maintenance is not arbitrarily or passively determined, but rather requires family energy to maintain (Kantor & Lehr, 1975). The concept of family boundary is extended to boundaries around subgroups within families. Boundaries are described in terms of being open or closed.

An important consideration in this study was the relationship between family meaning-making and family structure. A given family's openness or closedness to outside meanings or to each other's meanings was thought of in systems terms. *Openness* was construed as a willingness to engage in meaning-making with others. Family systems thinking was useful in conceptualizing how a family's meaning-making process was influenced by the absence or presence of a particular member, including the one who had died.

In addition to the concepts of roles, rules, and boundaries, systems theories about change are useful in family grief studies. One contribution from systems theory noted by Rosenblatt (1983) is the notion that families often resist change, even in instances when they ostensibly seek change. The family systems term for maintaining family processes as they were is *homeostasis;* the family systems term for maintaining family structure as it was is *morphostasis.* Both terms describe processes that diminish deviation from existing values or established goals (Constantine, 1986). This tendency to resist change was evident in Rosenblatt's study (1983) in the diarists' wanting to maintain things as they were before the loss.

In the proposal-writing stage of the current study, an example of how families resist change was evident in a conversation with a widowed friend. She shared her desire to keep her spouse "alive" by frequently talking with her family about what he would like or not like or what he would say to his grandchildren on a day-to-day basis if he were alive. Meaning statements shared by respondents in this study illustrated the tendency to resist change as it was foisted on them by a death of one of their relatives.

Closely related to family resistance is the question of what it takes to cause a change in a given family. Systems thinking includes the view that most families exist in some type of homeostatic balance and that the death of a family member will unbalance the system and cause the family to experience discomfort of varying degrees (Worden, 1982). In this study, some of the meanings that families constructed were expressions of their discomfort at being unbalanced, and some had to do with their efforts to regain balance. Hence, family systems concepts were useful in describing what was found, mostly because they provided ways to talk about how structure and meaning-making interact. Systems concepts are also useful in generalizing what was learned about family meaning-making following death to family meaning-making following other family events that involve alterations in family structure, such as divorce, adoption, birth, or blending of families.

Assumptions

The following assumptions underlie this research:

- "Humans live in a symbolic environment as well as a physical environment, and they acquire complex sets of mental symbols" (Rose, 1962, pp. 5-6).
- "One learns nearly all symbols through interaction with other people, specifically, members of the family, and, therefore, most symbols can be thought of as common or shared meanings and values" (Schvaneveldt, 1981, pp. 109-110).
- "If [people] define situations as real, they are real in their consequences" (Thomas, quoted in Burr et al., 1979, p. 64).
- "[T]he most fruitful area to study if one wants to understand humans is the beliefs and values that individuals get from interacting with others" (Burr et al., 1979, p. 48).
- Families have the ability to construct meaning.
- Both individual and family meanings exist.

- Most families are capable of communicating to an outsider at least some of the meanings they attach to the death of a family member.
- Families who have lost a family member are in the process of constructing new meanings that are critical to the grieving process.
- The meanings that people come to as they act, speak, feel, and think in and about their families are crucial data (Rosenblatt & Fischer, in an early draft of their chapter in Boss et al., 1993).
- Any change in a part of the family system affects the entire family system.

Definition and Elaboration of Terms

Terms commonly used in this study are defined as follows: *Meanings* are the cognitive representations of family members, constructed in the context of the family, that symbolically represent various elements of reality. Meanings are the products of interactions with others and are influenced by the context in which they occur, including the influence of society, culture, and historical time.

Taylor (1983) studied mental constructions in relation to traumatic events. She used *meaning* in a way that was congruent with the definition above and elaborated on the term as it might be used in relation to making sense of a particular event. *Meaning* was defined by Taylor as

> an effort to understand the event: why it happened and what impact it had. The search for meaning attempts to answer the question, What is the significance of the event? Meaning is also reflected in the answer to the question, What does my life mean now? (p. 1161)

Important to this study was Taylor's notion that not all meanings are positive because not everyone can construe positive meanings from traumatic experiences. Some respondents in the current study expressed negative meanings, particularly those whose loved ones died traumatic deaths.

The term *meaning* and synonyms for it have been used in the sociology literature in several ways that are consistent with the use of the term in this study. Some of these provided helpful elaborations. Lofland and Lofland (1984), who discussed meanings from a social analysis perspective, described meanings as "linguistic categories that make up the participants' views of reality and with which they define their own and others' actions" (p. 70). Meanings, according to these authors, may also be referred to by social analysts as *culture, norms, understandings, social reality, definitions of the situation, typifications, ideology, beliefs, worldviews, perspectives,* or *stereotypes.* In this study, *meaning* is used as a broad term under which these and similar terms are subsumed.

Some meanings respondents were unable to articulate directly. Lofland and Lofland (1984) pointed out that some of the most important meanings employed in a setting are unrecognized as such by the participants and that one key job of the social analyst is to articulate such latent meanings. Lofland and Lofland called these meanings *latent typifications.* In this study, the notion that such meanings exist helped direct the interviewing so that when respondents seemed unable to articulate an implicit meaning, the interviewer was encouraged to "guess" at what might be meant, seeking confirmation or disconfirmation from respondents at the time. Other latent typifications did not become apparent until transcripts were analyzed. They are identified in the findings chapters.

To study meanings related to a family member's death, a term was also needed to describe the process by which meanings are constructed. In the literature, the process of making sense of experience is referred to variously as *definition of the situation, construction of reality, the attachment of meaning,* and *meaning-making.* During this study, *meaning-making* emerged as the easiest term to articulate and the most easily understood by those with an interest in family bereavement who were not necessarily family scholars or symbolic interactionists. *Meaning-making* was used by Bruner in his 1990 book *Acts of Meaning.* The way *meaning-making* is used in this study is an adaptation of the way Schvaneveldt (1981) defined *definition of the situation.* In this study, *meaning-making* is defined as the social act whereby an actor interprets stimuli in a setting and represents the situation to him- or herself in symbolic terms. *Family meaning-making* is defined as the social act whereby family members interpret stimuli in the context of the family and represent the situation to themselves and each other in symbolic terms.

Meaning-making in this study included making meanings of all types, from the most substantive to the most abstract. Appraisal statements such as "My son's death was the most difficult I have faced in my life" would constitute meaning-making, but meaning-making is not limited to appraisal. Nor is the notion of meaning-making as used in this study synonymous with a search for meaning or purpose in life, as Frankl (1959) used the expression. Meanings constructed by individuals and families in relation to a death may include a sense of purpose in life, but meaning-making would also include negative meanings such as that there is no sense to be made and that life is purposeless.

Family in this study was defined according to Waller and Hill's (1951) definition: "The family is a number of human lives not only mixed together but compounded with one another" (p. 5). This definition emphasizes the interactive dimension of family life that is congruent with symbolic interaction theory and supports the notion of how change in any part of a system affects the entire system. Operational definitions are discussed in the methodology section.

Relevance of the Methodology to the Question

The nature of the research question called for qualitative family research methods. As Lofland and Lofland (1984) commented, "If you are asking 'what are the causes?' of a given outcome, you are asking a quantitative question . . . if you are asking 'how did this build up, how did it happen? . . . you are proposing a qualitative process" (p. 108). Rosenblatt and Fischer (1993) noted, "Qualitative family research methods are most useful when one wants answers to theoretical questions about meanings, understandings, perceptions and other subjectivities in and about families" (p. 18).

The goal was to reveal as much as possible about the meanings that families attach to the death of family members. One might think of the research process chosen as a gravestone rubbing in which the challenge was to get as accurate an impression of the underlying patterns as possible. Tracing family patterns of meaning-making necessitated intensive individual, couple, and family interviewing in ways that would reveal the subtleties and intricacies of family processes not yet well documented. Qualitative methods provided the best means of accomplishing the goal.

Other researchers have presented arguments in favor of qualitative methods for the study of such human phenomena as family meanings. Van Manen (1990) contended:

> The preferred method for human science involves description, interpretation, and self-reflective or critical analysis. Whereas natural science tends to taxonomize natural phenomena and causally or probabilistically explain the behavior of things, human science aims at explicating the meaning of human phenomena and at understanding the lived structures of meanings. (p. 4)

Boss (1987), commenting on the error of imposing our own contexts on families, argued that the phenomenological approach is helpful in preventing this error precisely because it allows us to focus on the family's meaning and perception of the stressful event. McLain and Weigert (1979) pointed out that the "family must be approached as it appears in the consciousness of actors, as it is experienced" (p. 171). Rosenblatt and Fischer (1993) noted that although family qualitative methods vary greatly, all approaches have in common a focus on meanings and other subjectivities related to families.

There is a good fit between the major assumptions of qualitative family research and this study. Rosenblatt and Fischer (1993) identified three assumptions common to qualitative family research. First, the focus of research should be on the family, and not the individual, no matter how family is defined in a given study. Second, the meanings that people come to as they act, speak, feel, and think in and about their families are critically important data. Third, the data collected in qualitative family research consists of the details and idiosyncracies of what people communicate about their families and about themselves in their families. In this study, family accounts of the death of a family member were collected, treated as crucial data, and an attempt was made to analyze and report the data in ways that preserve the details and idiosyncracies of individual families.

The strategies of qualitative family research are useful in studying family grief because they help in understanding family systems phenomena and because they enable sensitive exploration of the multiple viewpoints of family members so that the system can be characterized in terms of patterns of congruence and incongruence among family members (Rosenblatt & Fischer, 1993). In this study, interviewing respondents separately and together at multiple systems levels revealed patterns of meaning attachment, family structure, family communication patterns, and other family dynamics related to grief.

In addition to helping reveal family systems phenomena, qualitative family research methods are useful for studying sensitive issues that would be out of the reach of nonqualitative approaches (Rosenblatt & Fischer, 1993). Techniques like intensive interviewing, because of the time spent and the intensity of the interview process, are more likely to result in rapport with respondents and to encourage the nondefensive sharing of private matters. Because of the sensitive nature of family grief, intensive interviewing of multiple family members became the major data collection technique used in the study.

Lofland and Lofland (1984) saw qualitative research as preliminary to quantitative work. Quantitative researchers and theorists may turn to qualitative studies to gain a sense of what is going on and what variables they ought to investigate. Although a fair number of studies have been done on the attachment of meaning to potentially hazardous events such as victimization, disability, and chronic illness, little has been done in regard to bereavement per se (Boss, 1987; Lazarus, 1966; Patterson, 1988; Reiss, 1981; Taylor, 1983; Thompson, 1985). By studying the meanings attached to the death of a family member, important features of family meaning-making were identified. These findings expand what is known about family grief and suggest ways that families may make meaning of such other family phenomena as divorce, disability, chronic illness, disasters, birth, adoption, economic distress, and blending families.

Lofland and Lofland (1984) identified meanings as the most fundamental unit of social analysis. They contended that meanings "telescope" into higher levels of social structure. Therefore, as was expected, the study of meanings revealed much about higher social structures such as roles and relationships, which are also of interest in the study of all family phenomena.

The qualitative approaches used in this study included grounded theory as described by Glaser and Strauss (1967) and Strauss and Corbin (1990) and the technique of intensive interviewing as developed by Lofland and Lofland (1984). These methods are quite compatible with the conceptual frameworks of symbolic interaction theory and systems theory that underlie the study. Methodology and research techniques are described in more detail in Chapter 3.

2

Past Attempts to Understand Family Meaning-Making

When this study was designed, there were very few references to studies in which the relationship among families, grief, and meanings had been examined. Between the time this research was conducted and the writing of this book, a few relevant studies were done. They were not available at the time this study was being planned, however, and it would be misleading to include them here. The more recent studies are reviewed in the Epilogue. There is one exception: References to Rosenblatt and Fischer's work came from an early draft that was available when this study was being designed; it is cited elsewhere in this book under its 1993 publication date.

Researchers studying family grief may have tipped their hats to the matter of meaning, but few, if any, had studied the interactive processes by which families make sense of losing a family member through death. Before reviewing the few studies that were helpful, I must make a point about whether it is theoretically sound to do literature searches in qualitative studies. Review panelists on academic committees or research review boards may require a traditional search of the literature, but at least some qualitative researchers warn against searching the literature prior to conducting a study. Babbie (1983) speaks for those who advise against a literature review. He argues that library research should be *ignored* in field studies. The danger, he contends, is that the researcher will unconsciously observe only that which she or he expects to find. Babbie calls it *selective perception*. Babbie's point might have the most validity when researchers are studying something entirely new to them. If, however, the researchers have been studying the same or similar phenomena for any length of time, as was the case in this study, it may have been impossible to avoid some degree of selective perception. Furthermore, failure to search the literature could result in repeating mistakes or missing an opportunity to build on work already done. For this study, the research was reviewed, and the lack of relevant studies solidified my resolve to study how grieving families make sense of their loss.

Only one study was found that used qualitative methods to investigate the attachment of meaning in grieving families: a 1987 Canadian study by Davies. She had used methods of grounded theory to study families' responses to the death of a child and the meanings they attach to the child's belongings and room. She did not look at the meaning-making process, however. Some researchers, such as Reiss (1981), had looked at the process by which families construct reality, but neither Reiss nor others had studied the construction of reality by grieving families. Some, like Taylor (1983), Thompson (1985), and Thompson and Janigian (1988), had looked at how individuals make sense of traumatic events but had not studied how family members do so interactively.

The literature review that follows focuses on the literature that was available at the time the study was conducted. It is divided by headings according to the varied areas from which it was drawn. It begins with the studies of grief and meaning most like the current study, moves to studies that address the question of individual versus family meanings, discusses studies about meaning and individual grief, and concludes with family stress studies that were helpful.

Grief and Meaning

As mentioned above, only one study, Davies (1987), investigated meanings in grieving families by using qualitative methods. Using grounded theory and a systems perspective, Davies studied 34 families in which a child had died. Davies focused on how families handled the clothing, mementos, and room of the deceased child. She hypothesized that the child's belongings serve as memories with meanings that vary among family members and that the discrepant meanings affect bereavement in a negative way. Although Davies's report lacked a clear definition of *meanings,* her discussion of the relationship between individual and family meanings was useful. Davies clearly identified both individual and family meanings in her data, noting that it was not uncommon for one family member to assume that his or her meaning was mutual. She was also successful in using the data to demonstrate how the problem of discrepant individual meanings gets played out in the family. Davies's work was different from the current study in that she related meanings to tangible objects—namely, the deceased child's belongings and room—whereas the current study involved meanings attached to any aspect of the family member's death and the family's experience of it. Furthermore, the focus of the current study was on the processes by which families construct meanings interactively and on classifying the meanings they make. Although something was learned about what occurs when meanings are discrepant among family members, investigating this was not a prime goal of the current study as it was in the Davies study.

Lacking other studies that focused on meanings in grieving families, something was learned from looking at raw data from a previous grief study designed to study the role of social support in determining the health of survivors (Nadeau & Johnson, 1983). This study, which was about surviving spouses, revealed a fair number of unsolicited statements about what the death meant to them. The Nadeau and Johnson study involved 2- to 3-hour interviews with 43 bereaved spouses at 6 months following the death of their spouses and again at 13 months. The following statements made by three widowed respondents were typical:

I am hung up on trying to understand death [respondent said the same thing 6 months later]. I am plagued by the fact that he wanted to talk about something but never got to, but death was peaceful.

I believe she is in Heaven. . . . I am getting closer to my religion now. Death has helped. It makes you wonder how long you want to live. It makes it easier to live. When she was dying, she said she wouldn't have changed anything [this respondent died before the second interview].

I am glad we had our 50th anniversary. . . . I should have died first. . . .
In his last few minutes, the nurse said, "Let him rest." If I had a gun, I
would have shot them.

Statements such as these were made whenever respondents had been
asked open-ended questions. The meanings they had attached seemed to
influence the course of bereavement. Those with negative meanings, such
as "He wanted to talk about something but never got to," seemed to cause
distress to the grieving partner. What was learned from this 1983 spousal
bereavement study was helpful in designing the current study in at least
three ways. The first was to support the notion that the meanings people
attach to the death do affect the course of bereavement, and therefore
studying meanings is important. The second was that the data provided
examples of meaning statements such as those listed above. And the third
was to suggest lines of questioning that might be useful in getting respondents to talk about meanings. The raw data suggested that broad, open-
ended questions would elicit meanings both in answer to the questions
asked and as triggers for telling the family's story about the death.

Neither the Davies (1987) study nor the Nadeau and Johnson (1983)
study focused on the processes by which meanings are attached to family
events. The current study had such an investigation as its main focus. To
search the literature for work of this nature, it was necessary to look to
researchers interested specifically in family processes. The researcher
whose work most closely approximated what was of interest in designing
the current study was David Reiss. In his classic book, *The Family's
Construction of Reality* (1981), Reiss described how 400 families jointly
made sense of a social interaction laboratory assignment, referring to
their process as *reality construction*. Because Reiss's work was helpful on
several counts, including the ongoing family research debate about
individual versus family meanings, his work is presented in the next
section as part of a discussion on the nature of family and individual
meanings.

The Process of Meaning-Making

Davies (1987) did address the fact that both individual and family
meanings were being made in bereaved families. Davies's focus,

however, was more on what happens in the family when meanings are discrepant, rather than on how meanings get constructed. The Nadeau and Johnson (1983) study was not designed to study meanings, and only retrospectively was it helpful in learning about meaning-making and bereavement. Much of what has been written about the attachment of meaning to life events is about how individuals, not families, attach meaning. Individual meaning attachment is sometimes talked about in the context of the family, and sometimes it is not.

Adding to the difficulty of studying individual and family meanings is the problem of terminology. The terms *family meanings* and *shared family meanings* are defined variously from study to study and are conceptually unclear within studies. The question debated by family researchers is whether such things as family meanings exist. Can there be a meaning that is the product of the family unit when, literally, there is no such thing as a family "mind"? Are family meanings nothing more than the constructions of individual family members about which there is more or less agreement within the family? Answering these difficult questions may depend on having better observational methods, or maybe it is always a judgment call. Although this study was not designed to demonstrate whether such things as family meanings exist, the question was germane to the study and was an ever-present issue as data were collected, analyzed, and shared.

No discussion of meaning-making in families would be adequate without a reference to the contribution made by David Reiss (1981). Reiss's model is highly complex, but his comments about the processes of establishing shared meanings and his two major constructs, *the family paradigm* and *the crisis construct,* were particularly useful in conceptualizing this study. Reiss studied family behavior in a social interaction laboratory and extrapolated it to family behavior in the everyday world. He concluded from his studies of 400 families that families each have a set of assumptions about the world in which they live and that, within a given family, assumptions are shared by all family members even if disagreements, conflicts, and differences occur within the family. Reiss coined the term *family paradigm,* which he defined as the family's central organizer. The family paradigm is what determines the family's interaction with its social world and consists of the family's assumptions, constructs, fantasies, and sets or expectations. He contended that families can be distinguished one from another by the differences in their paradigms.

Reiss (1981) explained how the family paradigm gets established. His view of the family is as an integrated group that functions as an information processing unit. Reiss hypothesized that family information processing consists of three phases: (a) obtaining a subset of information from the environment, (b) categorizing and interpreting the information, and (c) transmitting it within the family. Data may be gathered by one individual for the family, or each member may gather and interpret data. An intrafamily transmission is necessary, Reiss contended, if the family is to acquire shared signals, which some families do acquire and some do not. Reiss noted that the gathering and interpreting of information are processes carried out by individuals. They become a family matter as the family builds up a collective view or schema of its informational world. One can hear the problem-solving nature of what Reiss required of his families and wonder whether losing a family member constitutes a problem to solve. An important question is whether an extrapolation can be reasonably made from families in the lab to grieving families in a natural setting.

The part of Reiss's (1981) work that relates most closely to families experiencing death is his development of a family construction called the *crisis construct*. He described the crisis construct in the following way:

> Serious family crisis is likely to occur in response to two universal categories of human suffering: prolonged illness and death. The family in acute crisis is disorganized and not experiencing themselves as a unit, but rather as a collection of individuals. The path to recovery or reorganization of the family begins with the crisis construct, a new form of construct for the family which realizes—at some level—that it is in crisis and begins to develop some shared concept of that crisis. (p. 189)

The crisis construct is an implicitly shared conception of the family process itself. Reiss theorized that it is different from other family constructs in three ways. First, it has little to do with the family's position in the social world as the family's everyday constructs do, but rather focuses on the family itself and includes some percept of its disorganization. Second, the crisis construct is likely to be cut off from previous systems of explanation and meaning because these have been destroyed by the crisis. Third, the crisis construct may involve outsiders entering the family and influencing the family's experience of itself. The crisis construct makes it possible for families to change. Reiss indicated that the term *crisis construct* is meant to embrace what Hill (1958) and others have referred to as the "family's definition of the event" (p. 391). Reiss contended that the crisis construct is far less cognitive than the term would seem to imply in that it includes "deeply emotional responses organized as much by fantasy and longing as by observations and rational inference" (p. 392). The crisis construct constitutes a basis for family reorganization.

The way Reiss (1981) talked about "two templates of family reorganization" is as close as he gets to how family meanings might affect the course of bereavement. Family reorganization following crisis, Reiss explained, involves action on the part of the collection of individuals, which is now the family. One of two patterns of reorganization, which Reiss called *templates of reorganization,* is chosen. One template is recognition and growth through experience. This involves reorganization through the acquisition of new experience, knowledge, and skills. The second template, and the one that deals with family meanings, is reorganization by revelation and solidity through meaning. In Reiss's words:

> The central characteristic of this pattern is that the chaos experienced by the family—now a collection of individuals—is transcended by a rich and personal meaning attached to the crisis events. The family becomes involved in decoding the symbolic meaning of the crisis and the subsequent disorganization. The group strives for the emergence of a sense of solidity around a common perception of the revealed significance in the crisis. (pp. 193-194)

Reiss used the birth and death of a child with severe birth defects as an example of a family crisis and pointed to the family's tendency to see the event as "preordained" as their meaning (p. 194). He went on to say that it is not unusual for families who choose the revelation template to single out a circumscribed part of the total stress situation and give it special attention. It is important to note, he said, that whether a family chooses reorganization by experience or reorganization by revelation, they may or may not experience themselves as a family unit. Either pattern may lead to the family progressively pulling apart and members isolating from one another. Reiss typified families on the basis of which template of reorganization they chose. It is unclear whether he did so heuristically or whether he was reporting observations of real families outside the lab. It seems unlikely that grieving families would be limited to one template or another or that the rich and personal meanings to which Reiss referred would all be positive. Reiss's speculations are revisited in the final chapter of this book, where findings in this study are compared to his constructs.

Several other features of the crisis construct were helpful in the design of this study and bear mentioning. According to Reiss (1981), the crisis construct develops over time and may not be fully accessible to an outsider or to the family itself, especially if the construct is tinged with guilt and shame. Using Reiss's thoughts as a springboard, one could think of meanings that would engender feelings of guilt and shame, meanings such as how the death could have been prevented if someone in the family had acted differently or meanings attached to some unfinished business with the deceased. Being on the alert for respondents' verbal or nonverbal reactions that could be suggestive of feelings of guilt or shame led to more sensitive interviewing and data collection in this study.

The second feature of Reiss's (1981) crisis construct that was helpful in conceptualizing this study was how the crisis construct influences the family paradigm. It is well known that families change in significant ways when a family member dies. Reiss's constructs provided another way to think and talk about the process of family change. According to Reiss, the crisis construct has more to do with a family's immediate response to crisis than does the family paradigm because the latter is temporarily inaccessible. The crisis construct constitutes new ways of family being that, in turn, influence the family paradigm. The family paradigm is a more permanent reorganization around a highly stable set of conceptions of the family's place in the world. As meaning statements were collected from families in the current study, it was helpful to think about whether they were meanings attached specifically to the death event or whether what was being said was more about the families' place in the world.

In relating Reiss's (1981) work to the current study, several issues would seem to warrant further attention. First, we must question whether what Reiss learned from observations of families in the artificial environment of the laboratory are generalizable to the everyday world—specifically, to the experience of a death in the family.

Reiss studied how families process the "informational world" as it was presented to them in the lab. It would seem that we do not as yet have enough empirical data about grieving families to know whether family processes in response to the death of a member are the same as, or different from, the responses to things that accost the family from outside the family boundary. We also do not know whether the family processes that have been shown to obtain in families coping with prolonged illness are the same as in families grieving the loss of a family member. Reiss's theorizing about the crisis construct appeals to one's sense of logic, but his observations were not of grieving families, and when he had a choice of which family scenarios to develop theoretically, he chose prolonged illness, not death.

In addition to the question of generalizability, Reiss (1981) addressed the issue of individual versus family meaning in a way that was useful to consider before collecting data in this study. According to Reiss, the task of gathering information and interpreting that information is done by individuals who then contribute to the "collective" worldview or schema of the family. Reiss said that "insofar as a family does construct a shared schema of the informational world, its members must share at least some of their individual observations and interpretations" (p. 25). If Reiss is accurate, we could expect to hear both individual meanings and family meanings reflecting the family's shared schema, or *constructs,* in Reiss's terminology. In fact, Reiss's descriptions of "revelations" formulated by those families who subscribed to the "revelation and solidity template" bear a great deal of resemblance to the meanings found in studies preliminary to this study and in the pilot interviews. Reiss (1981) summed up his thoughts on individual versus family meanings in the following extract:

> Our conception is that families do develop shared constructs in which all family members believe. A construct may have originated in the strident or impassioned beliefs of a particular individual, but when we see the family, everyone has come to experience and construe the test situation in similar terms. . . . The construct which emerges in the lab, we propose, tells us something about how the family may react to a variety of novel, challenging problems in everyday life. (pp. 66-67)

It remained to be seen whether the way families react in the lab is the way they react in everyday life. It also remained to be seen whether individual and family meanings (constructs) are fashioned in the same way in family bereavement as they are in test situations in the lab. What did seem certain, on the basis of Reiss's (1981) work, was that it would be important to interview families in such a way as to allow sharing and interaction of family members and to capture their interaction in a way that would preserve both the individuality and the communality of their constructions.

Finally, there is the matter of the validity of family members' reports. Three points can be drawn from Reiss's research that pertain to any study of meaning-making in family bereavement. One point is that what families say in private may not match what they say with other family members present. Reiss (1981) reported that, in observations of the Friedkin family, there was "a significant discrepancy between their work together in the public-hypothesis testing phase and their work as individuals on the private inventory" (p. 25). This discrepancy may be because of a discrepancy between private and family meanings, or it may be that the development of their ideas was in process and their constructions changed as they proceeded in the problem-solving process. Following Reiss's line of reasoning, it became apparent that if one wanted to know more about the discrepancy between individual and family meanings, it would be important to interview respondents both alone and in family groupings. The design of the current study included plans to interview respondents both individually and in family groups as a way to get at the discrepancy that Reiss pointed out but did not investigate.

A second point that Reiss (1981) made about the validity of family reports has to do with congruence. Reiss wrote, "It is of course true that if family members share interpretations they will not necessarily believe them" (p. 25). The issue of congruence between what is said and what is believed by respondents is discussed further in the methods chapter, but suffice it to say that this is a problem common to research and is important to consider when findings are interpreted and when studies are designed. It becomes vital to report such things as the presence of others in an interview session, to be alert to nonverbal clues, and to search for internal consistency in the data. Respondents may say what is socially desirable, or they may say what they want to believe.

Reiss's (1981) third point about the validity of family reports has to do with how family members often talk to conceal, rather than to reveal, information from and to one another. What is concealed and what is revealed may be influenced by family dynamics unknown to the researcher. In the current study, interviewing respondents both alone and within family groupings highlighted this feature of family meaning-making and made it possible to make some comparisons of within and between family member meanings.

It can be concluded that although Reiss's work on the family's construction of reality informs the current study in the ways that have been discussed, Reiss saw families in an artificial environment with a contrived challenge. The families he saw had not experienced a death in the family. It is not clear that the methods used by the lab families in the "construction of reality," as Reiss described it, are used by grieving families. What was taken from Reiss's work was the notion that families attempt to reorganize by attaching meaning to aspects of crisis situations; that there may be a difference between meanings attached directly to a given event and the longer term, more stable meanings; that both individual and family meanings exist at least in families who share; and that certain important validity issues are associated with family reports. As has been pointed out, at the time this study was designed, neither Reiss nor any other family researchers had published works on the actual process by which families make sense of traumatic events, nor had they classified the types of meanings that were made. It became necessary to turn to studies outside the family literature on how individuals construct meaning. In the following section, studies that looked at meaning-making by individuals following a traumatic event are reviewed.

Individual Meaning Construction

The work of Thompson and Janigian (1988) bears some similarity to the work of Reiss in that they see individuals having life schemes that are upset by severely negative events. In their system of explanation, this upset, which consists of losing one's sense of order and purpose, initiates a "search for meaning." The search for meaning was defined by Thompson and Janigian as a "process of changing the life scheme, or one's perception of the event so that feelings of order and purpose are restored" (p. 260). What Thompson and Janigian referred to as the *life scheme* of the individual has a strong resemblance to what Reiss called the *family paradigm*. The life scheme "is a cognitive representation of one's life, much like a story, which organizes one's perspectives on the world and oneself, goals one wishes to attain, and events that are relevant to those goals" (p. 260). It is the individual's conception of her or his place in the world, just as Reiss's family paradigm is the family's conception of its place in the world. Both the life scheme and the family paradigm are highly stable but may be upset by major trauma. Reiss described what occurs in response to the trauma as the construction of the *crisis construct*; Thompson and Janigian described how the upset initiates "a search for meaning." Both have to do with the creation of new meanings in response to traumatic events, as does the current study.

Thompson and Janigian (1988) developed a theoretical framework about life schemes that they said will elucidate what is meant by the search for meaning following traumatic events. Their framework is useful in relation to the study of family meanings in that it adds credence to the importance of meanings in relation to traumatic events of any kind and distinguishes between two types of meaning: implicit meaning and found meaning. They define *implicit meaning* as "the individual's assessment of how threatening or benign a potentially stressful situation is" (p. 79). The situation may be appraised as being a threat, a challenge, or benign. Thompson and Janigian's contention is that any event has implicit meaning to the people undergoing it and that therefore there is no need to search for this type of meaning because it already exists. It is difficult to determine exactly what is meant by implicit meaning from Thompson and Janigian's brief description, but one could speculate that, in their scheme, implicit meanings are more like what others (Lazarus, 1966; Patterson, 1988) have called *appraisal meanings*. Implicit meanings may be thought of as the result of a somewhat reflexive evaluation of the level of threat, rather than the more transcendent meanings that are discovered over time. Thompson and Janigian focused on the latter and were much clearer about what they meant by found meaning than they were about implicit meaning.

Found meaning, by contrast, according to Thompson and Janigian (1988), results from a search for meaningfulness in the experience. One important aspect of found meaning is that it is teleological; that is, meaningful events are those that have some purpose or reason for being. In the Thompson and Janigian view, the search for meaning is initiated when a person's life scheme no longer provides a sense of order or a sense of purpose or both. Traumatic life events, they proposed, are likely to call into question the validity of world- and self-views. A sense of meaning may be found by changing one's life scheme or by changing one's perception of the event. The examples that Thompson and Janigian gave of life events that can upset one's life scheme are disease, accidents, crime, and financial hardship. They referred frequently to the experience of victimization.

Thompson and Janigian's work (1988) was helpful to the design of this study because they, like Reiss (1981), theorized that certain events in life call for a search for meaning or a shifting of long-term, more stable meanings or both. Although they did not mention death of a family member as a traumatic event, it is safe to assume that such an event would also call for shifts in current meanings and for the construction of new meanings. Indeed, noticing how family members try to make sense of the loss of a loved one was what triggered my interest in family meaning-making in the first place.

Thompson and Janigian (1988) were helpful in that they, like Reiss (1981), identified different types or classifications of meanings. Reiss identified those that were part of the crisis construct and those that were part of the family paradigm. Thompson and Janigian identified implicit meanings and found meanings. Davies (1987) identified the more substantive meanings, meanings attached to the belongings of deceased children, and did not identify meanings that could be thought of as more abstract or more transcendent meanings. One could con-clude from these studies that it would be wise to listen for a wide range of meanings and not limit data collection to either the mundane or the sublime.

To conclude this section, suffice it to say that neither Reiss (1981) nor Thompson and Janigian (1988) directly addressed the case of death in the family. Reiss mentioned loss of a family member but did not consider whether it may be different from dealing with other traumas, nor did he study how bereaved families construct reality. Thompson and Janigian used instances of victimization, such as dis-ease, accident, crime, or financial hardship, as exemplars of "traumatic events" to which they referred throughout their explanation of how individuals attach meaning. They did not include the death of a family member in their list of traumatic events. What had not been studied was how bereaved families make sense of the death of a family member and how they do so interactively. Meaning-making in family grief needed to be studied in the context in which it occurs and as a phenomenon in its own right.

Although the literature on individual meanings is informative, the focus in this study is on family meanings. One area of the research literature in which studies of how families make sense of their experience could be found: the family stress literature. Some family stress researchers refer to the variables that were of interest in designing this study as *perceptual variables,* the cognitive component of family stress theory. In the following section, areas of the family stress literature that were helpful in the current study are discussed.

Family Stress and Family Meaning-Making

Some important work on family meanings was found in the family stress literature. Because of the extensive research that has been done in the area of family stress, it is a temptation to simply assume that a death can be construed as a major stressor and that, therefore, theories on family stress would apply. One problem with doing so is that, at the time this study was designed, family researchers had not studied the death of family members as a stressor. They had studied families coping with chronic or terminal illness, but there are some important differences. In both chronic and terminal illness, the family is exposed over time to the vicissitudes of illness. Generally, the family has some time during which to struggle with the meaning of changes as they occur or with the meaning of the anticipated death or both. When a family member dies, either expectedly or unexpectedly, the family reacts to an event that occurred in the past. They are no longer anticipating an event. It seems reasonable to expect that these differences might lead to the construction of different meanings and perhaps even to a different meaning-making process. For these reasons, it was not clear whether what we know about families and stress is true of families in bereavement.

Despite the proposed differences between family bereavement and other family stressors, the family stress literature provided some useful ways of thinking about family meanings. Aaron Antonovsky's (1979) work is a good example. Antonovsky's interest in studying the origins of health led him to develop the construct "sense of coherence," which has to do with a person's definition of a stressful situation. In his early work, Antonovsky defined *coherence* as the pervasive, enduring feeling of confidence that environments are predictable and that it is likely that things will work out as well as can reasonably be expected. In his later work, Antonovsky defined *sense of coherence* as the extent to which one sees one's world as comprehensible, manageable, and meaningful (Antonovsky & Sourani, 1988). Antonovsky applied the notion of the individual's sense of coherence to families and developed an instrument to measure "perceived coherence of family life" (p. 79). His hypothesis is that the strength of the family's sense of coherence is associated with adaptation, adaptation being a desired state. Sense of coherence theoretically includes seeing one's world as meaningful, a notion that sounded promising at the time the current study was planned. Unfortunately, questions about seeing the world as meaningful were not included in his family instrument, so clues about how to question families about meanings were not found. Yet, Antonovsky remains one of the few who factor the role of perception into the family stress equation. His work can be thought of as a precursor to studies like the current study, which focus more on the actual process by which families might develop what he calls a sense of coherence.

Others have used and further elaborated Antonovsky's sense of coherence concept in developing models to explain family responses to stressful events. A prime example is the *double ABCX model* (McCubbin & Patterson, 1983), which was based on Hill's (1958) classic *ABCX model* of family response to stress. In the Hill model, the A factor represents the stressor event, interacting with the B factor, which represents the family's resources interacting with the C factor, which represents the family's definition of the event, which produces the X factor, which represents the crisis.

McCubbin and Patterson (1983) elaborated each of the factors, thereafter referring to them as *double factors*. The double C factor subsumes Antonovsky's sense of coherence and was the factor of interest in the design of the current study. As elaborated, the double C factor represented the definition the family makes of the crisis event, as well as what they make of prior strains and the hardships that accompany the crisis event. The double ABCX model was advanced in ways more useful to a study of bereaved families. In an effort to describe the processes by which families cope, the double ABCX model was incorporated into a process model called the *family adjustment and adaptation response model (FAAR)* (Patterson, 1988). In her explication of the FAAR model, Patterson described the double C factor as consisting of two levels of meanings: situational meanings and global meanings. These levels bear a resemblance to Reiss's (1981) crisis construct and family paradigm, respectively. Patterson, like Reiss, grouped meanings according to how attached they were to a given event versus how enduring or abstracted they were. According to Patterson, *situational meanings* are "the family's subjective definition of the demands, their capabilities and of these two factors relative to each other" (p. 221). With the exception of one brief mention of families turning to their religious beliefs for meaning, one gets the impression that situational meanings tend to be more of the appraisal type, originally described by Lazarus (1966). Although meanings of the appraisal type were of interest in the current study, prestudy interviews revealed some meanings that would not fit the category of "situational meanings" as described by Patterson (1988).

The second level of meaning that Patterson (1988) identified, the global meanings, she called the *family schema*. Development of the family schema occurs as individuals acquire, through the processes of assimilation and accommodation (Piaget, 1953), a set of meanings for orienting their internal and external experience (Patterson, 1988). As family members fit together in social space, a social consensus emerges. The family schema comes about, according to Patterson, as the family develops an implicit and shared set of assumptions and meanings about themselves in relation to each other and about their family in relation to systems beyond their boundaries. The family schema is the product of shared social construing and represents "the intersection of individual members' cognitive sets" (p. 223).

The FAAR model, as explicated by Patterson (1988), bears some similarity to the Thompson and Janigian (1988) model, particularly in its use of the term *schema*. Thompson and Janigian studied individuals' schemata, whereas Patterson was more interested in the family's schema. Patterson concluded that the family schema is more stable than situational meanings and that the family schema transcends and influences situational meanings. Again, Reiss's (1981) construct, the family paradigm, comes to mind as another expression of the more global or overarching meanings.

Patterson (1988) also noted that although meanings about demands and capabilities are held individually, many are shared by members of the family. She suggested that when sharing does not occur and meanings are discrepant, intrafamily strains may increase. This line of thinking is consistent with Davies's (1987) finding that discrepant meanings attached to a deceased child's belongings can be problematic for the family. It would be important in any study of meaning-making to notice whether discrepant meanings exist and, if so, whether they are problematic in terms of family dynamics.

The parts of the FAAR model (Patterson, 1988) that were of the greatest help in designing the current study were first and foremost Patterson's (1988) notion of *shared social construing,* which occurs, she postulated, when family members fit together in social space. As vague as it is, this seemed to be the most promising description in the literature of how families make sense of their experience. Patterson's description gives at least a glimpse of what had been observed in the grieving families who inspired this study. Imagining that a social consensus might emerge from the interaction of family members suggested some direction to data collection and supported a tentative plan to use some of the methods of grounded theory to capture and analyze emergent meanings. Also helpful were the notions that meanings might be grouped by levels according to how situationally bound they are or how stable they are over time.

What the FAAR model (1988) did not do was describe in more detail how *social construing* actually occurs in families. Not unlike Berger and Luckmann (1966), who used the term *social construction of reality* three decades ago, Patterson focused on showing that the process of social construing occurs and how it fits into the FAAR model. Many questions remain. If meanings do emerge when family members share social space, what is the process by which this occurs? How would one recognize such a phenomenon? Are there such things as shared meanings? If so, how do family members interact in ways that create shared meanings? How does a family develop an implicit and shared set of assumptions and meanings about themselves in relation to each other and about their family in relation to systems beyond their boundaries, as Patterson postulated they do? What is the effect of discrepant meanings within the family? Perhaps the FAAR model does not go far enough in its delineation of meanings and how families construct them, or perhaps the model is not useful in capturing the complexity of meaning-making in family bereavement.

Shapiro (1989), using the Patterson and McCubbin model of family stress, studied meaning attribution and support group participation in 56 mothers of developmentally delayed children. Although Shapiro's study focused on a family crisis other than death, her quest for meanings is similar in some ways to that in the current study. Shapiro defined the double C factor in her study as the parent's ability to assign meaning to the stressful event. She noted that numerous articles cite the importance of the C factor in relation to positive adaptation but that meaning or purposiveness is rarely mentioned in the research literature. Shapiro contended that meaning attribution should be given more prominence, especially from a religious perspective.

In Shapiro's (1989) study, respondents were asked in an open-ended fashion whether the fact that their children had a disability had any meaning to them. The mothers were asked why this had happened in their lives, and their answers were audiotaped. The interviews were focused on how each mother's sense of meaning had evolved over time. Some meanings attributed to having had a child with a disability were: that she had been chosen by God to receive her child, that the child brought special meaning into her life, that the child brought her special happiness, and that the child helped her understand the meaning of courage. Unlike Davies (1987), Reiss (1981), Taylor (1983), and McCubbin and Patterson (1983), Shapiro distinguished between the appraisal of the event and assignment of meaning to the event. *Appraisal meanings* may be thought of as the result of a somewhat reflexive evaluation of the level of threat the event holds for those involved, rather than the attachment of meanings to the event itself. Although Thompson and Janigian (1988) did not use the word *appraisal,* they distinguished between two categories of meanings not unlike Shapiro's categories. Thompson and Janigian's *implicit meanings,* defined as the individual's assessment of how threatening or benign a situation is, correspond to Shapiro's appraisal meanings. Thompson and Janigian's *found meanings,* defined as the result of a search for meaningfulness in the situation, correspond to Shapiro's meaning of the event category. The point here is that several ways to categorize meanings were found in the literature. Some similarities were found among the categories, but little uniformity. Some categories seemed to encompass meanings like those found in grieving families known before the study; others did not.

Shapiro (1989) further reported that mothers who tended to assign meaning also adopted the coping mode of seeing their children's health condition as a challenge; that is, there was an association between assigning meaning and a positive appraisal. Shapiro reported that the assignment of meaning had correlation with well-being and the use of multiple coping behaviors. Implicit in the way Shapiro discussed meaning assignment were the assumptions that meanings are all positive and that meaning-making is a good thing. Taylor (1983) reminds us that not everyone is able to construe positive meanings.

Shapiro (1989) studied mothers rather than families, and disability rather than death, but her differentiation between appraisal and the attachment of meaning to an event helped clarify these terms. Her examples of meanings helped verify that respondents will share with researchers what events mean to them, and their statements are identifiable in interview data. What Shapiro identified as meaning statements were similar to the meanings shared by members of grieving families who inspired this study. The fact that she did not allow for the attachment of negative meanings is a shortcoming of the Shapiro study.

Although Shapiro's (1989) work helps distinguish between appraisal and the assignment or attachment of meaning to an event, Taylor's (1983) conceptualization of the search for meaning suggests ways to relate meaning-making and attribution. Drawing from a study of 78 women with breast cancer, Taylor developed a theory of cognitive adaptation and argued that the adjustment process centers around three themes: (a) a search for meaning in the experience, (b) an attempt to regain mastery over the event and over life, and (c) an effort to restore self-esteem. The search-for-meaning theme had the most relevance for this study. *Meaning* was described by Taylor as an effort to understand the event, why it happened, and what impact it had. The search for meaning attempts to determine the significance of the event. According to Taylor's theory, meaning is exemplified, but not exclusively determined, by an attributional search for what caused the event to happen. *Attribution theory* maintains that when people are confronted with a threatening event, they make attributions in an effort to understand, predict, and control the situation. Taylor described the women's attributions as "illusory." She reported that, in her breast cancer study, 95% of the women offered some cause for their cancer when, medically, none was known. If Taylor is accurate and her theory is correctly interpreted here, there are meanings that are attributional and meanings that are nonattributional. Taylor noted that the search for meaning involves not only an attempt to understand why the threatening event occurred but also what the implications are for one's life. Taylor noted that not everyone is able to construe positive meaning from the experience but that out of the 78 women with breast cancer, over half reported that the experience of having cancer caused them to reevaluate their lives, noting such things as new attitudes, increased self-knowledge, and a reordering of priorities. Meanings flowing from the reevaluation of life would seem to fall in the "nonattributional" category.

Taylor's (1983) research added to the design of this study a useful elaboration of what meanings are, as discussed in Chapter 1, a distinction between attributional and nonattributional meaning, some examples of nonattributional meanings, and some clues about what to ask respondents to elicit meanings. In addition, Taylor was the only researcher who commented on the fact that not everyone can construe positive meanings, the implication being that some construe negative meanings.

The limitations of Taylor's research were similar to those of most research that studies meanings and the meaning-making process. She focused on individuals, rather than on families, and on coping with disease, rather than with a death in the family.

Summary

In summary, at the time this study was conducted, no other studies could be found that focused on the process and content of family meaning-making in multigenerational families following the loss of a family member. Some studies, however, when taken together, provided guidance. Although Davies's (1987) research of the meanings attached to the belongings of deceased children did not study family meaning-making, it was the one most like the current study. Davies used grounded theory, studied meanings associated with grief, and pointed to the likelihood of trouble in the family when meanings are discordant. Reiss (1981) did study the process of family meaning-making, referring to it as the "family's construction of reality," but he studied families performing tasks in a social interaction laboratory, rather than families experiencing the loss of a family member in natural settings. Thompson (1985) and Thompson and Janigian (1988) studied personal traumas and victimization and identified implicit and found meaning, but they did not study the loss of family members and family process. McCubbin and Patterson (1983) expanded our understanding of family perceptual variables, the C factor of the ABCX family stress model. Patterson (1988), who studied families coping with chronic illness, described how shared global and situational meanings emerge by the process of social construing. Taylor (1983), who studied women with breast cancer, helped identify attributional meanings and pointed out that not all meanings are positive and that not everyone can attach meaning to his or her experience. Shapiro (1989), in her study of mothers who had children with disabilities, helped delineate appraisal meanings as a category of meanings and called for more attention to religious meanings.

This concludes the review of studies that were useful in conceptualizing the current study. The discussion drew on research of phenomena other than grief, and more on individuals as opposed to families. At the time this study was conducted, no one had studied the interactive processes by which multigenerational families make sense of a death in the family, and no one had comprehensively categorized the types of meanings they make. That is what this study set out to do. Ways in which findings in the current study have expanded what is known about family meaning-making in bereavement are presented in subsequent chapters. In the Epilogue, studies that have been conducted since this study was completed are summarized. In the following chapter, methodologies that were helpful in designing the current study are reviewed.

3

Capturing Family Meaning-Making

At the time this study was designed and data were collected, the literature on qualitative research methods was sparse. The last few years have seen a burgeoning of published works on qualitative methods. The following discussion, however, is limited to the methodological works that were available when the current study was conducted. More recent works, which admittedly would have been helpful had they been available at the time, are reviewed in the Epilogue.

This study, though not a pure grounded theory study, was greatly influenced by the methods of grounded theory (Glaser & Strauss, 1967; Strauss & Corbin, 1990). *Grounded theory* is theory that is "discovered" from data systematically obtained from social research. Glaser and Strauss (1967) wrote: "Generating a theory from data means that most hypotheses are systematically worked out in relation to the data during the course of the research. *Generating a theory involves a process of research*" (p. 6). These researchers contrasted grounded theory with theory that is logically deduced from a priori assumptions. They argued that logico-deductive theory can be based on ungrounded assumptions, whereas grounded theory is likely to be better theory because it is based on assumptions inductively developed from the data. The assumptions set forth in Chapter 1 provide a prospective for conducting a study such as this; they do not delineate in advance how family meaning-making takes place or what meanings grieving families are likely to construct. Theories about such matters were allowed to emerge during the course of the study.

Strauss and Corbin's (1990) major position is that generating grounded theory is a way of arriving at theory suited to its supposed uses: to fit, to explain, and to be relevant. It is theory that is understandable to social scientists, students, and lay people. It is phenomenological rather than logical. Grounded theory is derived from data and then is illustrated by examples from the data. Although Glaser and Strauss (1967) emphasized the value of allowing the data to speak for themselves, they also recognized that researchers do not approach reality as a tabula rasa, but rather have a perspective that will help them see relevant data and develop relevant categories. For that reason, they advocated the building of grounded theory upon previously constructed grounded theory.

Using a grounded theory approach in a previous study of death-related phenomena led to the belief that some modification of grounded theory might be useful in studying family meanings related to death. In a study of persons who were terminally ill in a hospice unit, grounded theory methods revealed the unexpected, provocative relationship between walking and dying. The majority of those interviewed identified their desire to be in an upright, walking position. It was as if to be upright was to live, whereas to be prone was to die. Once patients could no longer position themselves upright, they seemed to give up and move inexorably toward death. One man even asked his family to bring in a mechanic's dolly and to hold him upright on it and move him around the room as if he were walking (Nadeau, 1980). Modified grounded theory seems to be well suited to the study of the particulars of people's lives.

Techniques of Data Collection

The major technique used to collect data was intensive interviewing as described by Lofland and Lofland (1984). *Intensive interviewing,* also known as *unstructured interviewing,* is a guided conversation in which the goal is to elicit rich, detailed material that can be used in qualitative analysis. Lofland and Lofland contrasted intensive interviewing with *structured interviewing,* in which the goal is to elicit choices among alternative answers to preconstructed questions on a topic or situation. The intensive interview seeks to discover the informant's experience of a particular topic or situation. In the structured interview, the researcher has a knowledge of what kinds of things exist already and wants to know their frequency or prevalence. In the unstructured interview, the researcher seeks to find out what kinds of things exist in the first place (Lofland & Lofland, 1984). In this study, intensive interviewing was used to discover the process by which families attach meanings to the death event and something about the meanings that are the products of the meaning-making process.

INTERVIEW GUIDELINES

The technique of intensive interviewing involved the use of an interview guide that included 25 areas of interest related to the family's experience of death (see Appendix). The strategy was to approach meaning-rich aspects of the grief experience from different perspectives—hence, the redundancy in the interview guidelines. The guide was not used as a tightly structured set of questions to be asked verbatim, but more as a checklist of areas of interest to be asked about during the interview (Lofland & Lofland, 1984). It is important to note that although the questions are worded for individual interviews, they were adapted for multiple member interviews. In *multiple member interviews,* questions were asked of a couple or group, not of individuals one by one.

Although it is acceptable within the Loflands'(1984) method to alter questions as the interviewing progresses, few changes were indicated, and virtually the same questions were asked in each interview. The interview guidelines were augmented by probes pertinent to each area of interest. A *probe* is a gentle request for more information on something that has not been mentioned directly but that the researcher believes to be important (Lofland & Lofland, 1984). Probes were used in conjunction with most of the guidelines (see examples in the Appendix).

The areas of grief experience that the guidelines attempted to tap were drawn from my experience working with grieving families during the past 20 years as an intensive care nurse, hospice nurse, bereavement researcher, grief therapist, and educator. First drafts of the guidelines were discussed with friends and colleagues, some of whom are in the helping professions. A special effort was made to ask about meanings in ways that lay people could easily understand.

Interview questions were open-ended, exploratory, and sufficiently broad to allow the family members to give their accounts of events surrounding the death. To determine the wording of the initial questions, practice interviews were conducted with widowed acquaintances who were not in the study. These interviews helped in identifying important areas of questioning and revealed that, in general, people did not understand what was meant by the question "What meaning do you give to X's death?" They were, however, able to respond to questions about how or whether they had made sense of their loss. It was also noticeable in these prestudy interviews that respondents made meaning statements just in the course of telling about the death event, how it happened, the funeral rituals, and where they thought the deceased was after he or she died. Once constructed, interview guidelines were circulated to professionals proficient in conducting in-depth interviews. Reviewers were asked to read for content, comprehensibility, and order of questioning. Additional comments were invited. The reviewers were one midwife educator, one psychiatrist, and three marriage and family therapists. Their comments and suggestions were used in revising the original interview questions. The guide was then reviewed by two psychology professors, and a third revision was made. The interview guidelines as they were used in the study are included in the Appendix.

CIRCULAR QUESTIONING

As a way of increasing the amount of systemic data, a research adaptation of the Milan family therapy technique of circular questioning was used. The adaptation of the Milan method (Wright, n.d.) asks the interviewee to speak for absent members of his or her family. Wright described it as "mind reading." The *Milan method of circular questioning,* as it was originally developed as a family therapy method by Selvini, Boscolo, Cecchin, and Prata (Boscolo, Cecchin, Hoffman, & Penn, 1987), is a systemic family therapy technique. During family therapy, the therapist asks one family member in the presence of other family members to say how he or she thinks another might respond to a given question. Family patterns are thereby revealed. The Milan methodology is congruent with the study of meanings because, as a family therapy model, it focuses on meanings in families.

From the beginning of its development, the Milan group took mental artifacts as seriously as behaviors (Boscolo et al., 1987). As a therapy method, it involves asking questions of family members in a circular fashion. By *circularity*, the Milan group means the therapist conducts the investigation on the basis of feedback from the family response to the information solicited. The questioner looks for "openings," or clues dropped by the family in the course of the interview (Boscolo et al., 1987), as a way to proceed with questioning. The purpose of using circular questioning in family therapy is to discover differences over time and differences in relatedness among family members.

The purpose of using adapted circular questioning in research is to increase the systemic nature of the data and to reveal more about family interactions and behaviors than would ordinarily be revealed in an interview with an individual (Wright, n.d.). The purpose of using the Milan method in the current study was to learn more about the meaning systems of the families. Using the research form of the Milan method with individual family members included a line of questioning such as "What beliefs do you hold that relate to _____'s death?" followed by "What beliefs do you think your sister holds?" and then "What beliefs do you think your father holds?" and so on through each of the absent members of the family. Interestingly, using circular questioning in individual interviews revealed nearly as much about family meanings and family dynamics as in some of the conjoint family interviews.

To interview family members in conjoint sessions, a second adaptation of circular questioning was made. In addition to asking individuals in separate interviews to "mind read" absent members, as Wright (n.d.) did, family members interviewed together were asked to "mind read" absent members. Mind reading absent members was an effective stimulus for family interactions and revealed many meaning-making patterns, especially because questions were directed to the family as a whole, rather than to specific individuals.

Family members were not asked to mind-read members who were present because it was thought that to do so might trigger family conflict. To purposely trigger family conflict would cross the line between conducting family research and doing family therapy. Still, because of multiple interviews with some families, it was possible to check the accuracy of the mind reading. When absent members whose minds were read at early interviews were present at later interviews, I could notice, without being intrusive, whether or not minds had been accurately read. What I found is reported in later chapters.

The adapted Milan method could have been used with all the questions in the interview guidelines, but because of time constraints, use was limited to interview questions that asked most directly about meaning. Using circular questioning included asking which family members were most alike and which were most different in the ways they construed the death.

As the study progressed, one other way of using adapted circular questioning was discovered: asking how the deceased would have answered some of the meaning questions. It was not that the meanings given were reliably those of the deceased, but rather their answers revealed more family meaning-making patterns. Family meaning-making patterns were revealed even when respondents said they had no idea how other members, including the deceased, would answer meaning questions.

There were additional benefits to using adapted circular questioning: It supported efforts on the part of the interviewer to stay as neutral as possible—that is, not interject my own meanings; it gave direction to the questioning; and it helped families reveal their meanings by considering differences and similarities among themselves. The neutrality feature came about mainly because, rather than interpreting behavior, the user of circular questioning looks for differences. Because using adapted circular questioning called for asking about missing members, it also increased the multigenerational flavor of the study and gave a better picture of family meaning-making over time.

The risk of using the adapted Milan method of circular questioning was that, as family dynamics were revealed, the boundary between family interviewing and family therapy would become more difficult to maintain. To minimize this effect, the Milan adaptation was used more with the questions eliciting cognitions and less with the questions tending to elicit strong emotions (see the Appendix).

GENOGRAM AND DEMOGRAPHIC DATA

Preceding the use of the interview guidelines, data were collected by drawing a genogram and filling out a 1-page demographic form.

The genogram was used as a first step to identify family members and to help determine who would be appropriate to include in the study. Standard symbols were used to indicate relationships among members. Initially, the genogram was used to engage the family in a nonthreatening way and to establish rapport. Throughout the study, the genogram provided a view of the family at a glance and led to more systemic thinking for everyone involved. At the close of the study, the genograms became useful in sharing the findings.

Demographic data were collected on a 1-page form that asked about date and cause of death, relationship to the deceased, and socioeconomic data. The demographic form was combined with the genogram at the start of the interview as a way to put respondents at ease before more sensitive questions were asked. Although the form asked essentially for facts, some respondents began immediately telling their stories.

SELECTING RESPONDENTS

In the purest form of grounded theory, data collection continues until it seems that nothing new is being revealed. Glaser and Strauss (1967) referred to this juncture as *theoretical saturation* and defined it as a point at which no additional data are being found whereby the researcher can develop properties of the category. There was no way to know prior to the study how many interviews might be required to reach theoretical saturation. Because of time and resource constraints, a prestudy minimum was set of 6 families with at least 2 members per family. As it turned out, it was possible to interview 10 families for a total of 48 family members (26 females, 22 males). Interviews were held with 19 individuals, 7 with family groups of 3 to 8 members, 5 with 2 people (siblings or parent-child), and 2 with couples; 15 respondents were interviewed both alone and with other family members.

Despite interviewing more families than the preset minimum and interviewing them in a variety of configurations, theoretical saturation did not occur. Theoretical saturation may have been approached in regard to some common meanings related to the preventability of the death and the attitude of the deceased toward dying, but even in the 9th and 10th family interviews, idiosyncratic meanings continued to emerge. Perhaps including a wider variety of families and types of deaths would eventually yield a finite number of meaning types and meaning-making strategies. Or, perhaps there are as many meanings and ways to create them as there are families who engage in trying to make sense of their experience.

Lofland and Lofland (1984), commenting on the expansiveness and richness of data collected by the method described here, noted that qualitative researchers, sacrificing breadth for depth, typically employ only about 20 to 50 interviews. This study was about in the middle of that range, with 33 interviews totaling 70 hours of audiotape.

SELECTION CRITERIA

Respondents were families found outside the health care system, located mostly by funeral directors and clergy. Families were selected according to the following criteria:

1. *Participants would be a minimum of 3 months past the death.* The 3-month stipulation was chosen to increase the likelihood that the acute phase of grief would have subsided. According to Peretz, the duration of grief is variable; the acute phase should be over within 1 to 2 months (Schoenberg, Carr, Peretz, & Kutscher, 1970). This time line was consistent with my experience in working with grieving families during the 20 years prior to the study.

In the St. John's Bereavement Study (Nadeau & Johnson, 1983), it was noted that, by 6 months, the majority of the 43 widowers studied could articulate meanings to an outsider without undue distress and had fairly well developed meaning systems related to their loss. Three months was chosen as a cutoff date so that respondents would be past the earliest stages of grief yet early meaning-making efforts would not be missed. In this study, the actual range in time since the death was 4.5 months to 21 months.

2. *As many family members as possible would be interviewed, targeting whole households and multiple generations.* This criterion was set to collect as much systemic data as possible. At least two members from each of the 10 families in the study were interviewed,

and in 2 families, 11 members were interviewed. In 5 families, three generations were interviewed, and in 4 families, two generations were interviewed. In one family, only one generation was interviewed. The question of who should be interviewed was determined by asking the family member first contacted which family members comprised the household and whom they saw regularly. Consideration was made as to whether these individuals were available for an interview—that is, lived in town or visited frequently enough to make scheduling an interview possible. It was interesting to notice how much more data was added with each additional family member, particularly if the added members were from a different generation. Even as few as two family members yielded much more systemic data than a single family member even if the two were not willing to be interviewed together. Only one respondent refused to be interviewed with other members of his family. One of his reasons for declining was his fear of offending his sister-in-law; this reason gave data about possible relationships between family dynamics and family meaning-making. One widow, who was the first in her family to be interviewed, went on an extended vacation shortly after her individual interview, so it was never learned whether she would have consented to being interviewed with others. Two of her married children held her partially responsible for their father's death, a meaning they likely would not have shared had she been present.

3. *Participants should be adults.* This criterion was initially translated to mean age 20 or older. It was believed that the grief process experienced by adolescents and children, particularly the cognitive expression of grief, is different enough to warrant different approaches to data collection. As it turned out, one young man, age 18, was included in the study because he was the only available second family member and the only child of the deceased. Minimal data were collected from several other adolescents as they "dropped in" on their mother's individual interview. What was distinctive about their comments in general was that they seemed to be more about the adolescents themselves than were the meanings made by older respondents. One 5-year-old, who had been 3 at the time of her father's death, wanted to be included in the interviewing she had witnessed. She asked the interviewer to her playroom and to sit at a toy table and chair.

Once seated opposite the interviewer, she began to tell about how her father used to take her shopping. In her own way, she was sharing one of her meanings. Not counting this 5-year-old and the two drop-in adolescents from whom bits of data were obtained, the age range was 18 to 74.

LOCATING RESPONDENTS

The respondents resided in several suburbs of a major midwestern city. The majority of families were located through funeral directors, but a few were found by clergy and community program directors. These family finders made the initial contacts with those who met the criteria. A brief description of the study was given over the telephone to families by the persons who had located them, and if they agreed to participate, permission was sought for the interviewer to call. The interviewer (myself) described the study in greater detail, and if the contacts consented, set up appointments.

Finding families was more difficult than first anticipated. Although some professionals agreed to help locate families, their motivation and sense of urgency were, understandably, less than mine. Many families were ruled out by the selection criteria—namely, that more than one member be available for interview and that the death had occurred more than 3 months prior. Once a family had given consent through the initial contact, most followed through with the interviews. In a few instances, it was clear that the respondents had agendas of their own. One confided that he had said yes to the interview because he and his son were not able to talk about their wife's/mother's death and that he thought the interview would facilitate that. Once the interview was over, he became less than enthusiastic about facilitating interviews with the extended family. The protocol called for the initial contact person in the family to help enlist other family members.

Data Collection

Data collection consisted of tape-recording interviews conducted predominantly in the homes of the respondents. One couple was interviewed in a restaurant, two in my home, and one by long-distance telephone call. It was necessary to use a multidirectional microphone to accommodate groups of family members and a recording phone for the telephone interview.

Fifteen of the 48 respondents were interviewed twice, once separately and once together with one or more family members. Four of the 15 were interviewed in a family group first and then individually. Eleven of the 15 were interviewed individually first and then with others. The reason for interviewing respondents both alone and with others was to make comparisons between what was shared individually and what was shared in various family groupings. The reason for alternating the order was to learn which way best facilitated the sharing of meanings. Interviewing family members together before interviewing them separately turned out to be the most productive. Specifics are given in Chapter 4.

Of the 33 respondents interviewed only once, 6 were interviewed alone, 2 were interviewed as a couple, 4 were interviewed in father-son dyads, and 21 were interviewed in family groups of from 3 to 8.

As mentioned above, data collection was accomplished by audio-recording each interview and then transcribing tapes verbatim. During the interview, handwritten notes were made of key thoughts, of questions that needed to be asked later, and of descriptions of respondents' nonverbal communications. Immediately following the interview, a memo was dictated that included my emotional reactions and analytic thoughts, as recommended by Lofland and Lofland (1984). Lofland and Lofland asserted that one should spend as much time immediately studying and analyzing the interview material as was spent in interviewing. The final research report included these bits and pieces of analysis that accumulated in memo form during the data collection process. Memos were coded by using the same process as was used with the interview transcripts and were included in writing packets, which are described below.

In conducting the interviews, it was difficult to judge how much to control the interview process. The issue was how far afield to allow family members to go in their responses. Although the side roads often yielded important data, there were time constraints. As the interview process evolved, it became apparent that the richest data were obtained when the interview was more controlled in the beginning (when questions tended to be more "factual") and then less controlled, with questions more directly connected to meanings. In interviews with multiple family members, time was more of an issue both in terms of length of time required to hear from all members and in terms of cost of transcription. There was always the risk of cutting respondents off from some potentially fruitful side trips. Instances of having done so became apparent during later analyses.

Closely related to the matter of control is the question of how many family members to convene at one time. In this study, the largest family group to be interviewed in one setting was eight. Although meeting with such a large group provided interesting data about interactive meaning-making in large families, it was difficult to hear from all members. The interview was extremely long, more than 3 hours, and it seemed, judging from nonverbal behaviors, that some members were frustrated by the dominance of others and the lack of opportunity to share some things of great importance to them. Interviews with four family members seemed most fruitful; family groups of four seemed to provide adequate sampling of interactive patterns and, at the same time, provided adequate opportunity for each member to be heard. Deciding how large a family group should be probably depends on what one wants to learn. Because this study investigated both the process of meaning-making and the meanings themselves, it was probably best that a variety of family sizes be included.

At the close of interviews with each family, the services of a bereavement counselor, to be paid for by me, were offered. Only one respondent took advantage of the bereavement counselor, and only one meeting took place. The purpose of the follow-up offer was to make certain, to the degree possible, that if strong feelings were stirred up by the interview process, the interviewee would have an opportunity to process those feelings with someone trained in grief support. The bereavement counselor was prepared to assess the future needs of the family and to provide appropriate information for follow-up services as indicated.

In a previous study of 43 surviving spouses (Nadeau & Johnson, 1983), several participants identified the home visit of the researcher as the "most helpful" occurrence during their first 13 months of bereavement. Some cited the seeming disinterest of others in hearing about their grief or the inability to talk about the grief with family members or both as the most difficult part of bereavement. Perhaps the interview itself, without the stigma attached to using mental health services, had given respondents what they needed for support.

In this study, some information was gained about the impact of being interviewed. The 15 respondents who were interviewed twice at least minimally endorsed the interview process by being willing to undergo another round and to enlist the participation of other family members. The one respondent who called the follow-up bereavement counselor indicated that the interview with me had helped her a great deal. Also, the fact that only one respondent made use of the follow-up services could be construed as indicating a lack of distress among other respondents following the interview.

PILOT STUDY

Because of my ongoing opportunities to interview grieving clients in clinical practice and the collaborative way the interview guidelines were developed, a full-scale pilot study did not seem necessary. The interview guidelines were, however, pilot-tested with a family. One main reason for a trial with a family was to practice the use of the Milan method of circular questioning and to practice recording the conversations of multiple family members.

The audio-recording test was uneventful. I found that, by piloting the guidelines, using the modified Milan method with every question would take an unrealistic amount of time. I decided to use the Milan only with questions that pertained most directly to how family members made sense of the death. This proved to be a good decision. The process by which families were interviewed is described in the section on intensive interviewing.

Data Analysis

Data were analyzed by methods greatly influenced by Strauss and Corbin (1990) and, to a lesser degree, by Lofland and Lofland (1984). In each of their methods, analysis evolves during data collection and begins with the first data collected. This means that the processes of data collection and analysis run concurrently and that the final stage of data analysis becomes a time for bringing order to previously developed data analyses (Lofland & Lofland, 1984). In this study, in addition to the memos dictated at the end of each interview, an ongoing analysis file was kept. Entries were dated so that it was possible to track the development of a given idea. Thoughts about relationships between and among categories and methodological considerations were recorded.

When it was time to construct the writing packets, it was possible to draw from the interview data, the memos, and the analysis file by using the Search command of the word processing program. Several computerized data analysis programs available at the time were considered but ruled out because they did not accommodate the large number of categories. Writing packets are described below.

THE FIRST PHASE OF THE STUDY

The first phase of the study preceded the writing of the research proposal and took approximately 6 months. It involved exploring ways of thinking about meaning in families who had lost family members. A journal was kept for recording conversations with grieving family members and helping professionals; responses to readings; and thoughts about family meanings. During daily activities, attention was given to meaning statements made by friends, students, and clients who had lost family members. In addition, the interview data from a previous study of 43 surviving spouses (Nadeau & Johnson, 1983) were examined for meaning statements and clues to the meaning-making process. From this preliminary work, it was possible to speculate about ways that data could be analyzed. Several "schemes" for classifying meanings suggested themselves, but none were as useful or illuminating as those that emerged naturally from content analysis of the data.

OPEN CODING

In the grounded theory approach, the expectation is that categories and subsequent theories "emerge" from the data. Categories are formed by combining like codes. Theorizing evolves by looking at patterns between and among categories. Two types of coding were used: open coding and axial coding. *Open coding* is "the process of breaking down, examining, comparing, conceptualizing, and categorizing data"

TABLE 3.1 Example of Coding

KEY TO FIRST LINE: mp = meaning process codes; family sharing = category; most different = the code; 8a = Person A from Family 8; 43 = transcript page where quote is located.

KEY TO SECOND LINE: 2cd = Persons C and D from Family 2.

mp/family sharing/I'm most different 8a:43
mp/family sharing/no problem discussing 2cd:33
mp/family sharing/not try to convince others 6c:21
mp/family sharing/not in-depth discussions 8a:43
mp/family sharing/not share 6;63, 65, 2cd:44,46,49,78

(Strauss & Corbin, 1990, p. 61). *Axial coding* is "a set of procedures whereby data are put back together in new ways after open coding, by making connections between categories" (Strauss & Corbin, 1990, p. 96). Open coding in this study involved examining line-by-line the transcripts and writing words or phrases as marginalia that were thought to capture what was going on in the text. This was done while simultaneously listening to the audiotaped interviews.

Codes were then taken from the margins of the transcript pages and entered into a Word Perfect 5.1 data file wherein they were listed according to category, code, family, respondent, and transcript page (see Table 3.1 for an example of code list).

For instance, "mp/family sharing/I'm most different 8a:43" indicates that Person A in Family 8 said that, in regard to the category "family sharing," he was the most different. The 43 represents the page on which this reference can be found. The *mp* at the start of the code line indicates that this code is a meaning process code, rather than a meaning statement code. Codes were listed alphabetically under a given category. During the process of coding and while the tape was being replayed, corrections in the transcriptions were made on the hard copy.

Three independent individuals (a research assistant with a BA degree in psychology, and two PhD-level family researchers) reviewed the early codes as a check on the descriptors being used, and several new codes were identified and added to subsequent coding.

Coding was begun by coding some of each type of interview—individual, dyad, small family group, and large family group—to develop the broadest possible code list early in the coding process. After each type was sampled, transcripts were coded as they were completed, regardless of the number of family members involved. Sampling of each type of interview was done to get a sense, early on, of the breadth of the codes. Some codes showed up only in the individual interviews, and some only in the family interviews.

AXIAL CODING

After open coding was completed, Strauss and Corbin's (1990) method of axial coding was used. This method requires the identification of a core category—in this instance, "family meaning-making"—and frames other categories as being in relation to this core category. In conformity with the coding paradigm, categories are grouped according to the following list of headings. Applications to this study have been added in parentheses.

- Causal conditions (the occurrence of a death)
- The phenomenon (felt need to make sense of the death)
- Contextual conditions (who, when, and how of death)
- Intervening conditions (factors that affect meaning-making)
- Action/interaction/or failed action (the process of meaning-making)
- Consequences (the meanings themselves as products of the meaning-making process)

Although this model may suggest causal or linear relationships among the categories, its use was limited in this study to providing a way to group codes into categories and to express their interrelatedness. Without some way to think about grouping codes into categories and about the relatedness among categories, the presentation of data would have been limited to a listing of codes.

ORGANIZING THE CODE BOOK

The first division of the code list separated out those that indicated meanings, coded "M/", from those that indicated the meaning-making process, coded "MP/". Codes were alphabetized and grouped into

categories that were used as the basis for statements about relationships between coded parts of the data according to the axial coding
model described above. Subsequent divisions of the code lists included
a grouping of process codes (MP codes) into categories such as
"sharing patterns," "the systems levels of family meaning-making,"
and "strategies that families used to make meaning." In the axial
coding paradigm, these codes would fall under the "action, interaction, and failed action" heading.

In the category "meaning-making strategies," codes were further
subdivided into different levels of strategies: global, intermediate, and
elemental. Levels of strategies were determined on the basis of how
many words families used to employ them. For example, a *global
strategy,* such as telling the story of how the death occurred, might
take pages of dialogue. An *intermediate strategy,* such as comparing
the death with other deaths, might take a paragraph or two. An
elemental strategy, such as disagreeing with someone about the meaning of the death, might take only a sentence or a phrase. Instances of
the use of each of these strategies were counted. According to the
grounded theory language of Strauss and Corbin (1990), the levels of
strategies such as global, intermediate, or elemental would be considered *properties* of the category "meaning-making strategies," and the
frequency of strategies would be considered a *dimension.*

Distinguishing among levels of strategies was useful in organizing
the data during the early analysis. But the designations of global,
intermediate, and elemental added little meaning in the final reporting
of findings, and strategy levels were dropped.

Another grouping of codes represented factors that seemed to affect
the process of family meaning-making. They were grouped into the
category "meaning-making inhibitors and stimulators." This category
would constitute *intervening conditions* in the language of Strauss and
Corbin's axial coding paradigm.

The codes and categories were outlined and assembled in writing
packets that included related codes from the memos and from the
analysis file. Packets were assembled for each category. For example,
the packet that addressed the meaning-making strategy, comparison,
included all the examples of comparison from the transcripts with
several verbatim, prime examples; comments about comparison from
the memos (dictated immediately after each interview); and thoughts

about comparison from the analysis file that accumulated during the study. Further delineation of some codes was necessary to categorize them. This involved going back to the hard copy of the interview and further specifying the codes.

Another important feature of the coding process was that code lists were made for each interview before they were merged with codes from all previous interviews. This process made three important analytic steps possible: (a) getting a sense of a given interview at a glance, (b) getting a sense of a family at a glance, and (c) making comparisons between and among interviews by comparing code lists. Codes, relationships among codes, relationships among categories, and methods emerged and evolved as the research process progressed.

Verification of the Data

Since this study was completed, much has been written on qualitative methods, including data verification. Works completed since this study are summarized in the Epilogue. The discussion here is limited to the literature that was available at the time this study was designed and conducted.

Rosenblatt and Fischer (1993) contend that the nature of qualitative knowledge and truth can be very different from the nature of nonqualitative knowledge and truth. For this reason, standard methods of establishing validity and reliability are not as applicable in qualitative research as they are in nonqualitative research. Methods applicable in qualitative research are discussed here.

Miles and Huberman (1984) discussed validity in terms of "verification." Verification goes on continuously as data are collected. When a finding begins to take shape, the researcher checks it out with new informants. Validity checks occur when meanings emerging from the data are examined for their plausibility and their confirmability. Otherwise, we are left with interesting stories of what happened, of unknown truth and validity.

Validity can be established in qualitative research, according to Rosenblatt and Fischer (1993), by the internal patterning and coherence of a complex set of interviews without rigorous quantification. Validity analysis involves careful examination of the consistency of data. Cases that deviate from the rest of the data are explored as a check on the validity of the coding and analyses or as sources of additional theorizing (Rosenblatt & Fischer, 1993). For example, in this study, one meaning-making strategy (a category) used by families was comparing (a code) the current death with other deaths in the family. Validity analysis was accomplished by checking all instances of comparison to be certain that making comparisons was indeed a way in which families made sense of their experience.

Babbie (1983) argued for the validity of field research using methods such as those used in this study—that is, comprehensive measurements that tap a depth of meaning that is generally unavailable to surveys and experiments. Babbie identified the potential problem of generalizability that field studies have as being a result of the personal nature of the data. Babbie suggested that the problem is helped by making "comparative evaluations," saying who is more of something than someone else, as opposed to concluding something.

In this study, comparisons were made among families on the basis of the meanings they constructed and the strategies they used. Comparisons were also made among the meanings themselves. Things that could be reasonably counted were counted, and in some instances, frequencies formed the basis for comparisons. The issue of content validity of the interview guide was addressed as part of the discussion of intensive interviewing.

According to Miles and Huberman (1984), validity checks involve ways of verifying data as the analyst proceeds. Verification, the authors say, can be done in two ways. One way can be as brief as having a "fleeting thought," during the analysis, that sends one back to the data for a second look. In this study, fleeting thoughts were responded to by rechecking data throughout the analysis, particularly during coding and again when excerpts were entered into the report of findings. Sections rich in meaning-making activity were examined three times: once to listen for overall themes that would characterize a family, once to code the meanings themselves, and once to code the meaning-making strategies that families used.

The second way of verifying the data suggested by Miles and Huberman (1984) is a more thorough and elaborate process. It involves lengthy argumentation and review with colleagues to develop "intersubjective consensus." Although this study had only one researcher (myself), four other people compared text with codes at various stages of the study: a research assistant with a BA in psychology, two PhD family researchers, and one clergy. About one fourth of the way through the data collection and analysis phase, one of the PhD family researchers with experience in studying family meanings listened to and read a 104-page family interview. Instances of family meaning-making and the appropriateness of the content analysis codes and categories were noted. A very high level of agreement was found regarding the coding scheme and what constituted an instance of meaning-making.

Throughout the study, extensive conversations took place with other family social scientists. During the analysis, conversations took place with members of a qualitative research work group that met monthly. After the code book was constructed and before the writing began, I took advantage of an opportunity to verify the coding system with Strauss and Corbin (1990) at a National Council on Family Relations Annual Conference. Methods used in the study were presented at a National Council on Family Relations Theory Construction and Research Methods workshop, and multiple family scholars made comments and suggestions. Other presentations were made to both family scholars and bereavement specialists, who questioned interpretations and introduced various other ways of viewing the data.

Miles and Huberman (1984) also suggested that data be verified by extensive attempts to replicate findings. In this study, this occurred in two ways: (a) by looking in subsequent interviews for similar findings and (b) by ongoing clinical observation of grieving families.

Babbie (1983) defined *reliability* as a matter of whether a particular technique, applied repeatedly to the same object, would yield the same result. Several of Babbie's suggestions on how to increase reliability were appropriate to this study and were incorporated. One of his suggestions was to ask people only what they know.

Although it is probably true that families have meanings they cannot articulate, an assumption of this study was that they have meanings they can articulate. All 10 families could readily tell the story of the death and what had occurred since. Embedded in their stories were meanings related to the death. They also responded well to open-ended questions about meaning-laden aspects of the death, such as the funeral rituals, family relationships, and where families thought the deceased was after death.

Babbie (1983) also emphasized the importance of asking relevant and clear questions. Evidence for the relevance of the interview questions comes from the fact that questions were derived from informal interviews with people very much like those in the study. Relevance of the data is also supported by the fact that the data were collected expressly for the purpose of investigating meanings in families who experienced a death. This is in contrast with using extant data collected for other purposes. Prior to the inception of the study, clarity of the questions was checked by circulating them to experts in the field, including a psychiatrist and three PhD psychologists in clinical practice. Changes were made as indicated. Because most people are not accustomed to talking in terms of "meanings," interview questions were worded in such a way as to get at meanings by using everyday language. Once interviewing began, clarity was ensured by checking directly with respondents whether the meanings had been heard accurately.

The approach to data collection used in this study was a reliability check in that multiple family members were asked the same questions, together and separately. It is not uncommon in family studies for data collection to be limited to one family member who speaks for the entire family. Sometimes an assumption is made that the questioning has captured family information. In addition to using multiple interviews with multiple family members, the use of the adapted circular questioning method provided yet another way of clarifying meanings as members compared their beliefs with those of other family members, including the deceased.

Two other of Babbie's (1983) suggestions are relevant. One is to ask several questions about the same topic. Although any of the questions asked had the potential for revealing meanings, some questions intentionally triangled meaning-making information. The triangulation included asking families about beliefs and rituals associated with the death, then asking why the death occurred, and then asking how they made sense of the death. For those 15 family members who were interviewed both alone and with other family members present, there was the added benefit of asking the same questions of the same people twice.

Babbie's (1983) second suggestion for ensuring greater reliability is related to the training and practice of the interviewer, particularly as it relates to the ability to collect clear and specific data. My history as a hospice nurse, education as a family therapist, and previous experience conducting research with grieving families were advantageous. This was particularly true in regard to interview skills and tolerance for being in the presence of intense emotional pain.

Moon, Dillon, and Sprenkle (1990) asserted that both reliability and validity are enhanced in qualitative research by the length of time spent interviewing. Length of time spent increases both the "trustworthiness and credibility" of the study (p. 361). In this study, the individual interviews ranged from 1 to 3 hours, with the majority being around 2 hours. The family group interviews ranged from 2 to 3 hours. Family members interviewed twice were engaged in a minimum of 3 hours of interviewing.

Credibility and trustworthiness may also be enhanced by the way findings are reported. Rosenblatt and Fischer (1993) suggested providing the reader with excerpts from the material being analyzed. This tactic not only helps the reader understand the theories and concepts being set forth but also enables the reader to come to some independent judgments about the coding and the researcher's conclusions. This study relied heavily on direct quotes from the respondents. At least one excerpt is given for each analytic point, and in some instances multiple excerpts are given to illustrate subtle distinctions and variations. Contextual information is also given to aid in interpretation of most excerpts.

Probably the most powerful data verification method used in this study was a technique built into the interview strategy. Once it became clear what meanings an individual respondent or a family attached to the death, those meanings were repeated by the interviewer, and respondents were asked directly whether those were accurate. This process provided an opportunity for misinformation and false interpretations to be corrected and, in some instances, led to respondents saying more about what the death had meant to them. The following example is taken from an interview with Toby Miner, a 21-year-old male respondent whose 45-year-old mother died of cancer. He had just been asked whether he was able to make any sense of his mother's death.

Toby   I really haven't done too much with it. I don't know. I guess, you know, it is a tragedy. I guess that's about as far as I can get on it.

Int   And what makes it tragic?

Toby   Well, that she died too young, and I sort of feel cheated, along those lines.

Int   So, she was too young and you feel cheated.

Toby   Yeah, yeah. She was a good person, and there's a lot of jerks in the world.

During the interview, Toby identified several other meanings that he attached to his mother's death. A summary statement was used to reverify Toby's meanings:

Int   So, if I were fortunate enough to be able to sort of peer inside your brain, thinking about this, some of what would be floating around in there would be some thoughts about "I feel cheated. Why did I get so shortchanged here? This is a freak thing, why somebody her age that's got so much to offer when there's all those people, some don't even want to live, and that there is no sense to it." It didn't happen because God said, "Here, I can bring a lot of good if I let this person die." Is that kind of [pause]

Toby   Yeah.

Each of Toby's meanings was verified at the time he shared them and then again in summary form toward the end of the interview.

Although qualitative research does not rely on standard approaches to validity and reliability, there are, nonetheless, some powerful ways to verify the data. In this study, data verification included comparing all instances of a given code with all others, both within and across families; using comparative evaluations; counting what could be counted; taking three looks at the data while theorizing; sharing the analysis with experts; using clear, lay language derived from the bereaved themselves; using multiple questions to get at the same information; interviewing multiple family members intensively in extended interviews; interviewing some members twice; verifying meanings as they were stated; using the skills and training of the interviewer; and generously sharing excerpts with readers.

Ethical Considerations

One ethical issue was related to the notion of informed consent. Qualitative family research interviews can become very intense, and even when people have been warned, they may find themselves saying more or being more emotional than they expected or wanted to (Rosenblatt & Fischer, 1993). In this study, several safeguards were built in. One was an informed consent document that included the warning that strong feelings might be aroused as they talked, and the interviewees were reminded that they could discontinue their participation at any time.

An issue closely related to informed consent is the question of how much information to give participants in advance of the study. On the one hand, the researcher is required to give some explanation, yet on the other hand, telling respondents the complete purpose might lose their participation altogether and affect their behavior (Babbie, 1983). I decided to tell respondents in this study that the topic was how families attempted to make sense of a family member's death. This seemed to be specific enough to give a general idea of what the study was about without setting up respondents to behave or answer in any particular manner.

The vulnerability of respondents was an ethical issue. The precaution was taken to select only those respondents who were 3 months or more from the time of their loss. The assumption was made that respondents were the most vulnerable in the earliest months. A plan that was not needed but that was in place was to abbreviate the interview with anyone who exhibited an extreme grief reaction, to offer him or her a free visit from the grief counselor, and to make a referral for ongoing grief support.

An ethical issue associated with intensive interviewing concerns the role of the interviewer. LaRossa, Bennett, and Gelles (1987) noted that researchers are often perceived as therapists and that participants often believe they are in therapy because the interviewing is nondirective and attempts to get at sensitive areas. These authors found that interviewers were perceived less as therapists when they asked more structured questions and took notes. In this study, an interview guideline was used, and handwritten notes were taken during the interviews.

Confidentiality was a major ethical issue. Confidentiality is sometimes confused with anonymity. *Anonymity,* according to Babbie

(1983), is maintained when the researcher cannot identify a given respondent with a given response. This seldom occurs; therefore, Babbie argued, the term *confidentiality* is the preferred term. It means the researcher can identify the respondent but promises not to do so publicly. Babbie's suggestion, which was followed in this study, was to create a master file with the names and identification numbers or pseudonyms and to use the identification numbers or pseudonyms for reporting data.

Rosenblatt and Fischer (1993) focused on the confidentiality problem related to the reporting of the data, noting in particular the inclusion of verbatim interviews. They warned that revealing family members' accounts of events, feelings, and perspectives may breach confidentiality and create problems in family relations. Family members and others can recognize who said what. Such reporting runs the risk of breaking the "do no harm" rule. It is important to publish quotes in such a way as to disguise the identity of respondents. In this study, noncritical aspects of the stories were changed to disguise the identities of the respondents. LaRossa et al. (1987) saw the major problem as one of balancing the need to penetrate the private, pervasive, and emotional back regions of family life against the tempting, and often easy, violation of a family's privacy and hospitality. The precaution that LaRossa et al. recommended taking, and that was taken in this study, was to hold to the informed consent rule in which respondents are allowed to withdraw from the study at any time or to delimit the areas of discussion.

Another issue related to confidentiality was the question of what to do with private information gleaned from one family member when other family members were subsequently interviewed. As the interviewer, I had to make a conscious effort not to refer to the private comments of any family members previously interviewed. I maintained a questioning format and fashioned questions in such a way as to explore the same content without directly referencing what other members had said. This was an area where the Milan family therapy notion of maintaining a neutral stance with clients was useful.

Finally, an ethical issue pertinent to this study was the matter of ethical obligations to colleagues. Babbie (1983) reminded us that the researcher should know more than anyone else about the shortcomings of the study and make them known to others in the field. Science progresses through honesty and openness, but it is retarded by ego defenses and deception. In the following section, shortcomings of this study are acknowledged.

Researcher Role and Bias

In qualitative research, the researcher is intentionally subjective, and this subjectivity may be handled by making the researcher's role and biases explicit (Moon et al., 1990). Relatively speaking, the role of the researcher in phenomenological research is less involved than in ethnographic research but more involved than in experimental research (Moon et al., 1990). This study, though not purely phenomenological, falls between ethnographic and experimental research in terms of its subjectivity. Exposure to the participants was intense but limited in time to one or two encounters. The intensity of the interviews flowed from the sensitive nature of grief and from the presence of family members who may trigger each other emotionally.

As was noted in Chapter 1, I have worked with grieving families in one capacity or another for more than 20 years. Involvement has included giving direct nursing care to the dying, support to their families, and, for the past 10 years, individual, marriage, and family therapy to people experiencing losses of all kinds. I have also taught both lay people and professionals about issues related to grief and loss in many settings, including professional, national conferences.

My background was both an advantage and a disadvantage in conducting this study. It was an advantage in that, over the years of contact with grieving people, I have had ample opportunity to observe and think about what is important in understanding and helping grieving families. Observations have led to the belief that meanings are important and that what families believe about the death of a family member may be more important than other elements of the grief experience. Years of experience have also led to the belief that, given a supportive environment, most families eventually come to meanings of the loss that allow them to go on with their lives in productive ways; some even grow through the experience of loss.

Another advantage of having been in the field so long and having had training in psychotherapy is having become more comfortable with being in the presence of those who are experiencing intense sadness. Experience has taught me that the bereaved are not asking for someone to "fix" them, but rather to allow them to think and feel what they need to think and feel for as long as necessary. My belief is that the bereaved person's ability to problem solve his or her way through the difficult experience of bereavement "flows" from having done the necessary grief work.

One disadvantage of having worked with grieving people so long is the establishment of preconceived notions about grieving families. One reason why I chose grounded theory was that it takes into account the presence of some preconceptions in the mind of the researcher. One way to counteract the effects of preconceptions is to have some serious onlookers: my academic advisor, the colleagues who judged the match between categories and the data, my research assistant, fellow graduate student researchers with whom monthly meetings occurred, a monthly qualitative research work group, and two clinical supervisors with whom the research was discussed regularly. Also, the interview methods used involved checking things out with respondents during the interview. Despite the precautions taken, I have little doubt that some biases have survived and have influenced interpretations.

Finally, a factor that is both an advantage and a disadvantage is being educated as a marriage and family therapist. Theoretically, being educated in the skill of psychotherapy should help in clearly distinguishing between doing research and doing therapy, but in working with the bereaved, there is a fine line between listening as a researcher and intervening as a therapist. "Lapsing" into therapy can happen insidiously, and it did. In therapy, reframing is used to help people think of their situations in new ways and to facilitate the changes they want to make. In research, getting a picture of what is going on, rather than reframing, is the goal. Getting a picture involves framing, not reframing. Strong interviewing skills were helpful, but maintaining a researcher's stance in the light of the demand characteristics of grieving people meeting in a therapylike environment was, at times, not possible.

Limitations

One limitation of this study is that it was designed and carried out primarily by one researcher (myself). Problems related to this feature were discussed in the reliability and validity section of this chapter. Some limitations of this study are common to most qualitative family research. One common limitation is that qualitative family research is time and labor intensive, necessitating arbitrary limits. Research of this type may require much time in both the data collection phase and the data analysis phase (Rosenblatt & Fischer, 1993). Because transcribed family interviews were used, the data were massive and required large amounts of time for sorting and hypothesizing. The cost in time and money limits the sample size and may raise questions about generalizability in the minds of those accustomed to thinking in terms of quantitative research standards.

The question of generalizability warrants special attention. Babbie (1983) identified three ways that generalizability is a problem in qualitative research. One is the personal nature of the observations and measurements. The more personal the data, the more unlikely it is that others will be found who have the same experience. A second is that qualitative research takes an in-depth view of subject matter, enabling the researcher to reach an unusually comprehensive understanding. Comprehensiveness of understanding reduces generalizability. A third is that one cannot be sure how typical the subjects are. Babbie's solution was that researchers not generalize beyond the observations.

The problems identified by Babbie (1983) assumed that generalizability is important; not all researchers agree. Rosenblatt and Fischer (1993) contended that generalizability of the sample may be less important in qualitative research than in nonqualitative research. In qualitative research, what may be important is showing that some phenomenon exists, developing theory, revealing complexity and richness of the data, and providing illustrations. According to Moon et al. (1990), in qualitative research the focus is on generalizability to theory, as opposed to generalization to populations. Strauss and Corbin (1990) contended that instances of the concepts, not the individuals being studied, need to be sampled. Issues of generalizability continue to be pivotal in the dialogue among qualitative and quantitative researchers.

Rosenblatt and Fischer (1993) pointed out another limitation of qualitative family research: *researcher selectivity* (p. 23). One goal of qualitative family research is to allow respondents close to the phenomenon in question to speak for themselves but to keep the researcher as the person who selects, organizes, interprets, and summarizes the material. But, as these researchers pointed out, less selectivity is still involved in a qualitative study than in most nonqualitative studies. In nonqualitative studies, there is a great deal of selectivity in deciding what to study and no opportunity for the data to "push the researcher to new ideas of what is interesting and important" (Rosenblatt & Fischer, 1993, p. 23). In this study, the "push" was experienced in two ways. In one, specific excerpts chosen to represent certain categories also revealed important subtleties within categories. These subtleties did not usually emerge until several excerpts were compared. In a second, any data even remotely related to meaning-making were coded. This feature of the analysis, for instance, allowed for the emergence of the notion that families make negative meanings as well as positive meanings, the later having been emphasized in the grief literature to date.

Limitations or problems specific to the technique of intensive interviewing identified by Rosenblatt and Fischer (1993) were *selective memory, self-presentation biases,* and *inability or unwillingness to articulate some things.* Interviewing multiple family members was a partial remedy for this group of limitations because it provided an opportunity to tap the memories of more than one family member and increased the likelihood of finding members willing and able to articulate meanings. Individual self-presentation biases became more difficult to maintain when other members of the family were present and members were forced to play to a public audience. However, families may still have worked to maintain family presentation biases in other ways. The fact that groups of family members were interactive in their responses also mediated individual limitations. There were ample opportunities to verify the data both within interviews and, in some instances, with subsequent interviews. Even then, as Rosenblatt and Fischer predicted, some family members were missed; some did not address the same issues; and some did not have the same information. Interviews were not entirely comparable from family member to family member, and characterizing a family from such uneven data was a chore.

Some specific features of this study could be seen as limitations. One feature worth further consideration was the lack of measures over time. The majority of respondents were interviewed only once; some were interviewed twice within a short span of time. For clues about how meanings changed over time, respondents were asked how they thought their meanings had changed since the early weeks of bereavement. Most indicated that although their emotional reactions had changed, their thoughts about the death had remained relatively unchanged. Any study of family meaning-making over time would need to consider how the interview process itself changes the flow of family meaning-making. It may be that interactive interviews with families introduce such a strong influence that subsequent interviews would be more of a measure of the intervention effect than of natural family changes over time. At any rate, how family meanings change over time has not been well documented. In studying meaning change over time, the first step would be to discover what features are important to follow through time. This study was directed more toward the identification of such features.

A final limitation to be mentioned is that, ideally, all respondents would have been interviewed both alone and with other family members; 15 out of 48 were. Reasons for not interviewing everyone more than once include both the unwillingness of some respondents to be interviewed twice and the time and financial constraints of the study. When it was possible to interview respondents both alone and with other family members present, however, much was learned about the differences. Those differences have strong implications for researchers studying any family phenomena and are not limited to the study of family grief.

4

Patterns of Meaning-Making

Introduction to Respondent Families

The following are brief descriptions of the 10 families in the study. Graphic depictions of each family, referred to as *genograms,* give considerably more detail and can be found in the Appendix. Names and noncritical aspects of the family data have been changed to disguise identities. In-laws in each family are given the family name to avoid confusion.

1. *The Mackey Family.* Richard Mackey died at age 71 following cardiac bypass surgery. His wife and daughter were interviewed 5 months after Richard's death.
2. *The Barlow Family.* Vera Barlow died of disputed causes at age 85 after a long illness. Three of Vera's sons and two daughters-in-law were interviewed 6 to 9 months after Vera's death.
3. *The Munson Family.* Claude Munson died of disputed causes at age 72. His wife, two of his sons, two daughters-in-law, and a granddaughter were interviewed. Interviews took place between 10 and 12 months after Claude's death.
4. *The Swan Family.* Julius Swan died of pneumonia at age 91 after spending 12 years in a nursing home. His daughter and granddaughter were interviewed 8 months after Julius's death.

5. *The Smith Family.* Bob Smith died at age 49 of a sudden heart attack. His wife and sister-in-law were interviewed 8 months after Bob's death.

6. *The Primo Family.* Ronnie Primo died at age 39 in an airplane crash. His wife, mother, sister, and eight other family members were interviewed 21 months after Ronnie's death.

7. *The Zeeman Family.* Debbie Zeeman died at age 42 from cancer. Her spouse and her son were interviewed 5 months after Debbie's death.

8. *The Miner Family.* Anne Miner died at age 45 at home after a year-long battle with cancer. Her spouse, father, two children, five siblings, and two in-laws were interviewed 5 months after Anne's death.

9. *The Owens Family.* Irene Owens died at age 85 in a nursing home from "old age." Her son, daughter, and grandson were interviewed 7 months after Irene's death.

10. *The Buchanan Family.* Florence Buchanan died at home at age 84 of "natural causes." Her son and his wife, and her grandson and his wife, were interviewed 9 months after Florence died.

Overview of Meaning-Making Patterns

Families shared their meaning-making process in very interesting ways. As was true of the prestudy interviews, meanings were found embedded in the stories that families told about the death and their experiences since the death. Most family members were able to compare how they thought about the death with how others in the family thought about it. During the interviews, family members interacted with each other in ways that revealed their meaning-making processes.

In this chapter, I demonstrate levels of family meaning-making, specify patterns of meaning congruence within families, and sample other interesting features of family meaning-making. Patterns identified here are pointed out in subsequent chapters as they relate to specific meaning-making strategies and to the meanings that families create. *Meaning-making strategies* are the means or methods by which families construct meaning.

As early as the third interview, Ben Barlow summarized much of what others would say as the study progressed. In response to a question about funeral rituals, Ben said:

Ben   And I think I would have to hitchhike on what Julie said, that it's probably tougher at the church, and in some cases it's probably tougher, you know, maybe later on that day when you are probably by yourself, it might be a tougher thing to deal with. But I guess it all goes back to the person who has died, ah, it has a lot to do with how old that person was, whether they suffered, whether they were happy to die, what the circumstances surrounding it [were], has obviously a lot to do on someone's feelings as to how they feel about that particular death. I think grieving is probably similar, but it's different for different individuals because, depending on what you know about this person, be they friend or relative, determines your thoughts and then your thoughts determine or help you get through this grieving process.

Ben demonstrated how he made meaning by "hitchhiking" his remarks on what his wife said. Although Ben is describing his own individual process, he has gotten to it by comparing and contrasting his experience with his wife's experience. This is an example of the *couple level of meaning-making.*

This quotation also raises the question whether the interview interaction constitutes the making of new meaning or whether it is a reenactment of previous meaning-making. Probably, it is a combination of the two. The point here is that meaning-making is an interactive process and that family interactions create meanings.

At the very end of this excerpt, Ben stated in his own words a main assumption of this study. Ben said that certain factors determine one's thoughts and that then those thoughts determine or help you get through the grieving process. The assumption as it was set forth in Chapter 1 reads, "If [people] define situations as real, they are real in their consequences" (Thomas, in Burr et al., 1979, p. 64). No other respondent was as articulate about the relationship between meanings and grieving as Ben.

Several points need to be addressed before the data are presented further. One point is related to the systems notion that the whole is more than the sum of its parts. In analyzing the data, it seemed important to delineate the actual mechanisms by which families construct their meanings and to classify the meanings they construct. When the data were reduced to mechanisms and meanings, however, some of their flow, color, and texture was lost. Family meaning-making seems to be much like a dance: Only when it is viewed as a whole can its beauty be fully appreciated. An attempt is made to present enough extended meaning-making excerpts to give a sense of the dance even as the individual steps are examined.

A second point to be emphasized is that the study yielded a great deal of information on the emotions of grief that were not analyzed. It was not a goal of the study to collect data on the emotional component of grief because so much is known about grief and emotions. In this study, respondents were asked how they *thought* about the death of someone in their family, rather than about how they *felt*. An attempt was made to tease out their thoughts and then to ask how their thoughts affected their grieving. It was assumed that the emotional expressions of grief convey meaning and that the meanings that people construct affect their emotional states. This interplay between emotion and cognition is explored further as the data are presented.

Finally, it became clear that content and process are essentially inseparable. It takes content to illustrate the process of meaning-making, and process considerations to illustrate the meanings themselves. I decided, therefore, to emphasize the *process* of meaning-making in the early chapters and then to emphasize *content,* the meanings themselves, in the later chapters. As excerpts are presented, they are discussed both in terms of the main point they illustrate and in terms of any other features of meaning-making they may also illustrate.

This chapter, which is the first chapter about the process of meaning-making, includes examples of meaning-making at various systems levels, findings related to family sharing patterns, and findings relevant to the notions of family shared meaning and family consensus. The term *family sharing patterns* pertains to certain action components of family meaning-making, such as whether family members were willing or unwilling to talk with each other about the death. The term *shared meanings* is used to designate those meanings on which two or more, but not all, family members agreed. The term *family consensus* is used to indicate that all family members agreed on a given meaning. The purpose of this chapter is to illustrate the overall patterns in the data.

Individual Level of Meaning-Making

The following passage is from comments made by a highly educated, articulate man, Rafi Miner, whose wife died 9 months after learning she had cancer. Both Rafi and his wife were in their mid-40s at the time of her death. He had been involved in her care at home. The interview took place in the living room, by the window where her bed had been situated during her final illness and death. Her ashes were present in a white box on the buffet behind him. The Yahrzeit light was lit in the window. He described himself as having very different beliefs from those of his wife's family because of religious and educational differences. He was Jewish, and they were Catholic; he had an advanced degree, and most of the family members were blue-collar workers. Despite those differences, he was very close to her family and was the one who later called them together for the family interview.

The passage is from an individual interview done several weeks prior to the family gathering. Earlier in the interview, Rafi had shared his belief that the only way his wife existed beyond her death was in his memory. Rafi had just been asked how this belief affected his grief:

Rafi   Well, I guess it, it probably makes it a little harder for me in some ways because I don't believe that she is anywhere anymore. So I think that, well, now I'm single and she's gone. She's never going to come back. She's not somewhere else watching me, and so I kind of get rational about that. That means that I ought to go on and make other relationships and so on. And I think that, I don't know if you're going to talk about how I've gotten into another relationship that kind of happened even quicker than I even think it ought to have, and I think that if I believe that she was still, that she was in Heaven, it might have been different. I might not have been so quick to allow that to happen. And I think that in a way that might have been better for me because I think it's hurting a lot, and I don't hurt in the same way if there's somebody to hold onto and so on. It's awful confusing because I still have those [inaudible] feelings and . . . .

Int   Yes.

Rafi   I bet that, that probably, that one of the reasons why I let that happen was because of not feeling like she was still alive in any sense. I never thought about that before just now. I can see how that would be a factor. Other than that, well, it's probably a related thing, like a couple weeks ago we did a memory thing in grief group, and I was feeling real out of touch with my memories of Anne, and it just really freaked me out because I don't really, I think that if I don't remember, then she's really gone, and if that's all I have and those memories fade, that's real scary. . . . So I [pause] I'm kind of, I'm kind of hoping for the day when I can have a memory of and just be warm and uplifting with a little fire that I can kind of keep going and put in my pocket and whatever and not hurt a lot [tears]. I haven't gotten there.

The passage above is important because it illustrates how certain meanings associated with the death can cause problems. If he believed that his wife was not anywhere, then there was nothing to keep him from getting involved with someone else before he was really ready. And if his wife lived only in his memory, he reasoned, then to keep her "alive" he must keep his memory of her alive. When he could no longer remember her, then she would be gone. That, he said, was scary.

This passage is also one of the best examples of how the interview itself may have been a meaning-making stimulator. *Meaning-making stimulators* are factors that enhance the process by which families make sense of their experience; *meaning-making inhibitors* are features that impede the process. After answering the question about the effect of his beliefs on how he grieved, Rafi said, "I never thought of that before now." If he had not been interviewed, would he have made that particular meaning? The answer is not known, but it raises issues about the ways even one interview, to say nothing of interviews over time, may alter the meanings that families construct. This factor must be taken into consideration in the analysis.

The excerpt above is important because it is clearly an instance of an individual constructing his personal meaning about his wife's death. It is important to note that he was constructing his personal meaning by comparing his beliefs with the beliefs of his wife and her family. They believed that Anne lived on in some form other than in memory; he believed that she lived on only in memory. An important finding in this study was that meaning-making sometimes takes the form of saying what one does *not* believe. It may be like a culling process in which several possible meanings are considered and discarded, leaving only those that are acceptable to the meaning-maker. This culling may be accomplished by comparing one's beliefs with those of other family members, as Rafi did. *Comparison* is designated in this analysis as a meaning-making strategy and is discussed in the next chapter. Intra-family comparing of meanings is one way the family becomes the context for meaning-making.

Couple Level of Meaning-Making

The next passage is from a couple, Dominic and Joyce Primo, who lost their son-in-law Ronnie in an airplane accident. Ronnie's wife, Rena, the couple's oldest daughter, was left with two daughters, one 3 years old and one 3 weeks old. Dominic and Joyce, the widow's parents, were already highly involved in their children's lives prior to Ronnie's death. This involvement increased after Ronnie's death as Dominic and Joyce moved in with Rena and her daughters. Dominic and Joyce described Ronnie as being more like a son than a son-in-law to them. The excerpt below is from a family interview. In the excerpt, Dominic and Joyce were reviewing events leading up to the accident. Dominic was thinking aloud about whether he could have prevented Ronnie from taking the risk of flying:

Dominic   . . . I kind of wish that I would have, and I might have, you know. I might have later told him that he had, ah, he, having a family, you know, he ought to be more careful of some of the things he did because I think he was ah, ah, [pause]

Joyce   Adventurous.

Dominic   Adventurous. I think he was probably, ah, adventurous and, ah, ah, I see, I didn't know that the [inaudible] that John was a pilot. I really didn't know any of that. Thinking about it now, that it was his good friends. He was a pilot, but he had never flew. It was his very first trip with passengers, you know. Had I known that, I'm sure I would have said to Ronnie something about, you know

Joyce   Except that he would have blown it off when you said it.

Dominic   No, he wouldn't, he probably

Joyce   Yes, he would.

Dominic He would have listened, and he would have probably agreed, but I don't think it would have changed his mind. I mean, I think he would have gone anyway. I think he would have thought about it a little, because when I talked to him, for sure he, you know, he had ah, [had] enough respect for me that he would listen carefully . . .

Dominic Primo expressed his regret that he did not try to stop Ronnie but was in a double bind. If he made the meaning that he could not have stopped Ronnie, he would have to give up the treasured belief that Ronnie respected him and would follow his advice. The couple dynamic appeared as Joyce tried to dispel her husband's guilt. She argued that if Dominic had said, "Don't go," Ronnie would have "blown it off" and gone anyway. The meaning the couple made interactively was that if Dominic had expressed his concern to Ronnie, Ronnie would have listened and agreed that there was a risk, thereby showing respect, but he would have flown anyway. Through their interaction, the couple constructed a meaning that seemed to satisfy competing needs: the need to believe that Ronnie took Dominic seriously, and the need to believe that no matter what Dominic said, Ronnie would have gone. This quotation is a good example of how subsystems within the family create their own meanings.

The implicit meaning held by this family was that Ronnie's death was preventable. Lofland and Lofland (1984) referred to this kind of meaning as a *latent typification* in that the meaning is dependent on the researcher's interpretations, rather than being stated explicitly by respondents. Giving direct expression to such a meaning may have been threatening to this family, especially to Dominic, who thought of himself as a father to Ronnie and the one with enough influence to stop Ronnie from flying.

This excerpt of Dominic and Joyce's interaction also illustrates an important finding that the data repeatedly revealed: Not all meanings are positive. Frankl's (1959) notion of "finding meaning in traumatic events" implies finding positive meaning. In this study, a fair number of negative meanings were found to be attached to the death event. Believing that the death was preventable if someone had acted different-ly is a prime example of a negative meaning. In this case, if Ronnie had decided on his own that the risk was too great or if Dominic could have convinced him not to fly, the death could have been prevented. Nine out of the 10 families had at least one member who believed that the death of the relative was preventable. One widow in her 6th year of bereavement who was not in the study continued to hold the meaning that her husband should not have been taken off life support. To her, his death was preventable.

Dyadic Level of Meaning-Making

The dyadic level includes noncouple groups of two, such as two siblings, mother-daughter, or father-son. The first illustration is from the Miner family, whose oldest daughter, Anne, died at age 45 from cancer. The excerpt is from an interview with Anne's father, George, and her brother Dwight. They were struggling to make sense of her premature death. Eleven members from three generations of this family were interviewed in three separate interviews. This father-son dyad was the last Miner interview. The interviewer is referring to a point earlier in the interview when George had said there was no sense to be made of his daughter's death, but, as was typical of most respondents, he went on to try anyway:

George   . . . I can't, you know. I mean I struggle with me and God. I can't figure out what it accomplished, you know, what unification with family. We're all drawn together and real close. I thought we were pretty tight knit before. But, ah, was that it or, you know, what are we learning from it? Just a sad, angry, bitter experience, you know. And I said from day 1 that it sucks, and that's still the way I feel about it. I think one thing it's done is Anne died very brave and with dignity. I think that makes death easier for me, because I'm going to say to myself, I'm surely, I'd like to do as well as Anne did as well. You know. And I just [pause]

Int   So, in some way she's a model for you as well?

George   Yeah. Because she was such a good person, and I'm sure that everybody that loses somebody will say the same thing. Oh, they were such a good person, but ah, ah, the picture, trying to fit the pieces together, and say, you know. I can't. I don't understand it, you know. And sometimes I say to myself, you're not supposed to. Maybe it's a test of your faith. I'd like to run out on the porch and yell up at God and say, Why? You know but [pause]

George Miner's son Dwight had been listening respectfully to his father. Dwight was then asked whether he had been able to make sense of Anne's death. Dwight had earlier described Anne as being a mother to him as he grew up:

Dwight   Oh, I, you know, I don't think you make sense of it, ah, you know I don't know, you know, you maybe, you know you sometimes, maybe this you think, is a genetic breakdown, you know, I mean. Mom died of cancer of the brain. My sister Anna had a tumor removed at a fairly young age, now

George   The old man's had it. [meaning himself]

Dwight   You know you just, you just wonder if it's, if it's something and it's so totally out of your control really anyway. Um, like Dad says, you have fits of anger.

Int   You do too?

Dwight   Yeah. You know I mean how, how you control them or not control them, I mean I, I don't go into a rage, but I'm sure [my wife] and my kids see some mood changes, um, I do. I do most of my reflecting with myself, you know. You know, try and ask yourself questions, and come up with some answer you can at least live with for awhile. But you know it's just, it's, you know, I mean, you certainly don't, you certainly don't run it off to just a bad break, you know, like Dad says, there may be, maybe it's a test of all of our faith. [Big sigh from George] Maybe it's the test of the family unit in general. Like Dad says, as big families go, we're as close as anybody. There's certainly a lot of caring amongst the brothers and sisters, and, you know, we have our differences too, but I mean I don't think we have relations if we don't talk to each other or we try to avoid each other, stuff like that. I think you try and sort it a little bit at a time, you know. It's going to be a long healing process. For everybody.

Beside giving a sense of how respondents answered the most direct question about meaning, the first part of this passage illustrates how some respondents, particularly those who lost younger members, said there is no sense to be made of the death and then went on to share the meanings they had been considering. As part of the analysis, the notion that there is "no sense to be made" was developed into a category of meaning in its own right and is discussed further in a later chapter as part of the typology of meanings.

In addition to suggesting that "no sense" may be a type of meaning, this passage is also an excellent example of the actual process of meaning-making. For example, several meanings were shared in the presence of other family members. Both Dwight and George recited what they were thinking the meaning might have been. Then they referenced each other's meanings. Dwight referred to his father's suggestion that it may have been a test of the family unit. Also typical of family meaning-making, meanings that seemed to reduce the level of distress were chosen above other possible meanings. Dwight reported that he looked for answers that he could live with, at least for a while.

Dwight and George Miner's interaction provided a good sample of the different types of meanings. George considered whether the death had a God-determined purpose: to unify the family, to provide a model for his own death, or to test his faith. By contrast, Dwight looked for some biological cause by questioning whether the cancer resulted from some genetic defect. Dwight also identified the death of loved ones as being out of our control. His statement that his sister's death was *not* something to be written off as a "bad break" provides an example of the "what the death is not" classification of meanings. It seems that, at least for some, saying what the death was *not* about was a preliminary step in the meaning-making process.

Finally, Dwight's responses exemplify how some respondents claimed their need to make sense of the death on an individual basis yet, in the process of sharing their meanings with the interviewer, referred to other family members' meanings, sometimes adopting the meanings of others as their own. In the Dwight and George excerpt, Dwight references his father's meanings twice: once in relation to how the death may have been a test of their faith and again as he characterized their big family as being as close as anybody else's.

Referencing others' meanings and sometimes adopting them was another way meaning was constructed within families. Even when the most individualistic meaning-making statements were made, the family formed the watershed for the meaning-making that occurred. Some members came to their own meanings by directly agreeing with other members, as Dwight did. Others did so by disagreeing. The matter of how meaning is made within the family context may become clearer as examples from the family level are examined.

Family Level of Meaning-Making

The next excerpt comes from an interview with four members of the Munson family, in which Claude was the member who died. The four in the interview were Claude's sons and their wives. Darren, the oldest, and his wife, Marie, had been interviewed as a couple prior to the interview from which the passage below was derived. Sam and his wife, Deb, had each been interviewed separately. Another sibling, Jeannie, had agreed to be interviewed but changed her mind at the last minute because, as she put it, "I don't want to stir things up again."

Family dynamics were complex. There was a multigenerational pattern of members having disagreements with other members and then not talking to each other for years; such a cut-off had occurred between Jeannie and Darren, predominantly related to alcohol issues. The brothers and their wives believed that Claude had died of alcoholism, whereas their mother and sister gave several other causes of death. Several family members believed that Claude could have lived longer if he had altered his lifestyle. So, in this family, as in the Primo family, who lost a member in an airplane crash, an implicit meaning was that the death was preventable.

One question in the interview guidelines that elicited very active discussions among family members and revealed family meaning making at its best was "Where do you think _____ is now?" The following is the Munson family's response:

Sam   Well, he hung around for a while, and then he's up in Heaven.

Marie   Can I look at what I answered the last time? [laughter]

Int   No, you don't have to be consistent. There's no rule about being consistent. When you say "around for a while," Sam, are, you may have told me this and I've forgotten, like how did you have a sense that there was some period of time when he seemed to be around?

Sam Well, I think his spirit or whatever was around when we were at the hospital yet. And it might even have hung around the valley until the hearse got stuck going up the hill. And that was his goodbye.

Marie He decided to check out.

Sam Yeah.

Int That was his final touch, maybe.

Sam Well, it might have been. I don't know. I don't know that I felt his presence, but I think that's possible.

Int Uh, huh. Any other comments anybody wants to make about that? And you don't have to agree with Sam—whatever you want to, however you want to express your own.

Darren Well, I feel that, that the spirit is with us because I remember very well, and he's had a lot of influence on me, some good and some bad, and you don't care that much about somebody and not have their spirit be with you. But that's where you know, like, he is in the cemetery.

Deb He doesn't have something better to do by now than hang around?

Darren He's always with us because we remember him.

Deb Yeah, but I mean him, actually. [to Darren]

Darren No, he's up there in the cemetery. That's what I think. I mean, I'm sorry.

Deb You don't believe in an afterlife?

Darren Except that we remember him, so his spirit is with us.

Deb I never thought you would have said that.

Darren Really.

Deb I thought you were a real Catholic in the way that you, you would go to purgatory.

Darren That's Catholic enough for me. [laughter]

Deb I thought for sure that would have been your idea. [then to Marie] Do you think the same way?

Marie No, no, not necessarily, but I'm not sure how I do feel. I kind of struggle with that a little bit. Um, 'cause you know I do believe in Heaven and hell, but I don't think that you automatically go to Heaven. I mean, if you've been a shyster and an asshole your whole life, I don't think you automatically go up, you know, and so I'm kinda, I don't know how I feel. I guess I'd just like to pass on that one because I don't know how I feel.

Int	So, you're kind of still thinking about it.
Marie	Yep.
Deb	Do you think there is purgatory, then, if you don't go automatically there then to get reevaluated?
Marie	Yeah, I do. You get a chance to do some things over, I guess. I'm not sure.

This excerpt is a sample of the variety of meanings within a single family. Each of the four Munson family members had something quite different to say in response to the question. Sam saw his dad as hanging around the valley for a while and then going to Heaven. Deb, Sam's wife, thought her father-in-law must have had something more to do than hang around the valley, although she did not specify what else she thought he might have been doing. Marie thought Claude decided to "check out" when the hearse got stuck but was not sure about her beliefs about Heaven, hell, and purgatory. Darren seemed to be the most different in that he thought his father was nowhere except in the cemetery, that Claude lived on only in their memories.

Marie's nonverbals suggested her discomfort with her husband's "non-Catholic" beliefs and with her sister-in-law's probing. It seemed that some of Marie's reluctance to give definitive answers was about not wanting to appear too different from her spouse and yet not too non-Catholic. Furthermore, when interviewed with Darren alone, Marie had been quite vocal about her disdain for Claude and how he had lived his life. With Sam and Deb present, she expressed her disdain obliquely. The above passage contains hints of her anger in her choice of words to describe types that do not get to go directly to Heaven. Perhaps Marie saw Claude as being one of the types needing to go to purgatory, but she could not, or chose not to, construct negative meanings about Claude's death with other family members present. Throughout the study, it was not uncommon for members to share different meanings about the death, depending on who was present.

The excerpt from the four Munson family members is also representative of what was called the *in-law effect* of family meaning-making.

It was found to be a powerful meaning-making stimulator. Seven out of the 10 families had in-laws present in the interviews. In-laws spoke more freely about family matters than did those related by blood. Perhaps, as in-laws, they were less bound by the family rules. Perhaps, because of the gaps in their knowledge about the family, they had legitimate reasons to ask questions. In some instances, perhaps the in-laws' lack of responsibility for past, negative events made it easier for them to talk.

The in-law effect can be seen in Deb's questioning of Darren about his beliefs in regard to the afterlife. She questioned Marie as well, but to a lesser extent. Deb was persistent in her questioning, undeterred by the discomfort shown nonverbally by the rest of the family. Her questioning resulted in an extended discussion of meanings and a revelation of what different members believed.

The in-law effect took other forms in other families; these are noted as instances appear in the interview excerpts. *Stimulators* are factors that acted as enhancers or catalysts in the meaning-making process during the study. Another meaning-making stimulator found in this excerpt is the role of the interviewer and the study itself. The presence of an interviewer can be seen as a stimulator because families, especially those like the Munsons, probably would not have gathered together to discuss the meaning of their loss if not called together by the researcher. Furthermore, any researcher response that introduces thoughts not already mentioned by family members may affect both the meaning-making process and the meanings they make. In the Munson excerpt above, it is possible to see that the process of meaning-making may have been affected when I gave permission to the four members not to agree. The meanings made may have been influenced by my suggestion that the hearse getting stuck may have been Claude's "final touch." Probably, it is impossible to interview without in some way affecting responses. Interview effects, whether they stimulate or inhibit meaning-making, need to be considered in the analysis.

A prime example of an inhibitor of meaning-making found in the Munson family was a lack of contact among family members. This family had intentional cut-offs at four generational levels. This meant that, in each generation, certain family members had no direct contact with certain other family members. This family's way of dealing with conflict had traditionally been to withdraw from each other as Darren and Jeannie had. Even Sam and Darren, the brothers who agreed to be interviewed, had had only one conversation since their father's death, and that conversation had occurred as they passed by each other on a golf course. Without the opportunities to interact with other family members, meaning-making is limited to hearsay and an individual's imaginings about others' meanings.

Another meaning-making inhibitor suggested in this excerpt is a general tendency of members to soft-pedal their meanings when they sense that their meanings are different from those of others. Darren admitted his lack of belief in traditional Catholic values (under pressure from Deb's questioning) but then prefaced a restatement of his belief with, "I'm sorry." His apologetic tone may have been induced by the social pressure that family members exerted on him, pressure to believe either as they did or as they thought he did.

Finally, the Munson family excerpt introduces two more meaning-making strategies: *questioning* and *characterization*. Deb uses questioning to learn what other members of the family believe. It was not uncommon for respondents to ask questions of each other during the interview. Although no family members were asked directly about their motivation for questioning, there was the sense that it was part of their attempt to make sense of the death for themselves. That search may have taken the form of looking for something to believe or to identify what was not believed. As a result of the family interaction, more possible meanings were presented than there would have been without someone asking questions.

The strategy of *characterization* was used as the Munson family remembered together a part of the funeral rituals. Reference was made to the hearse getting stuck going up the hill to the cemetery. One way that families make meaning is by characterizing the deceased. In this family, a joke was made about how "Grandpa" was up to mischief by causing the hearse to get stuck. They imagined he would have been calling the hearse driver a fool and swearing at him. Characterization of the deceased was found in the conversations of all the families in the study.

This concludes the examples of each system level of meaning-making. Other features of family meaning-making only previewed here are developed further in subsequent chapters.

Sharing Patterns Within Families

Interview guidelines that revealed patterns of family sharing included (a) asking families whether they talk among themselves about the death, (b) asking who thinks most similarly and who thinks most differently about the death, and (c) asking what would and what would not be shared with other family members. If respondents said they were unable to share with each other, probes were used to determine what would inhibit them. Use of the Milan method of circular questioning expanded the data to include sharing patterns among family members not present in the interviews. Everything in the transcripts that pertained to patterns of family sharing was coded. The result was several pages of codes that were then grouped into the categories of "family sharing," "shared family meaning," and "family consensus." These three categories form the basis for the analysis that follows.

In family studies, the terms commonly used to describe how families share and whether they agree are vague, at best. Perhaps the ambiguity in word usage is a reflection of ambiguity in thinking about family measures in general. In this analysis, the term *family sharing* is used for the actual *process* of talking among family members about the death. The term *family shared meanings* is used to designate those meanings on which two or more, but not all, family members agreed. The term *family consensus* is used to represent full family agreement. Pure family consensus was not found in this study. Family sharing is discussed first.

FAMILY SHARING

Family sharing is talking about the death. The study had 48 responses to questions about whether family members would talk about the death with each other: 15 responses represented a willingness to talk, 10 responses represented a reluctance to talk, and 23 responses were conditional statements. These numbers do not reflect the numbers of respondents, but rather numbers of responses. Responses that indicated willingness or reluctance to talk are discussed first.

Yes, I Would Share. The first excerpt is from a respondent who claimed a willingness to share anything about her experience of losing a family member. It came from an individual interview with Colleen Barlow, a daughter-in-law of Vera, an elderly woman who had died in a nursing home after a long illness. Colleen was being asked whether she was able to share with other family members:

Int   Are there any parts of what has happened around the death, the death itself, the time leading up to it, the ceremonies, is there any part of that, that you wouldn't want to talk to other family members about?
Colleen No.
Int   You feel whatever you have for a response and thoughts and feelings about it, you could readily share those with anybody in the family?
Colleen Uh huh.
Int   That's how you feel personally?
Colleen Right, yes.

Colleen claimed to be willing to share anything and did not change her answer even when given a chance. It is interesting that at no time in the interview did she share with the interviewer that her mother-in-law had been mentally ill, as other members reported. There was no opportunity to follow Colleen through a family session to observe what she would actually share with other family members, because her husband, Jake, canceled the family session. Perhaps she could talk openly with family members about Vera's mental illness but not with the interviewer.

No, I Would Not Share. Jake represented those who were reluctant to share. He canceled the family interview because he was reluctant to talk about his mother's death with certain family members present. His reluctance was an example of a factor that inhibited meaning-making. Jake had a falling out with his brother's wife some years before Vera's death and had "patched things up" at the funeral. He feared that if he spoke the truth in a family interview, he would surely offend his sister-in-law and lose the ground they had gained. The fear of offending was a fairly common inhibitor of family meaning-making.

Yes, I Will Share; No, I Will Not. Another pattern having to do with willingness to share was a general tendency for respondents to initially claim a high level of willingness; however, with further questioning about specific aspects about the death, they identified some things they would not share with certain family members.

Sometimes the reason for deciding they could not talk had to do with which death was being discussed. Early in the interview, the death being discussed was the one that brought them into the study. Later in the interview, other, more difficult deaths were brought up. It may be that the level of sharing within families is loss specific; that is, members may be willing to talk more about one death than about another. Ben Barlow, quoted in this next passage, was typical in this regard. He was asked whether he would talk with other family members about his mother's death; he answered that he would share with anyone who brought it up:

Int	So, you don't feel as if there is maybe a part of all of this that's really private to you or that is only something that you and Julie would talk about or
Ben	Well, private. I obviously don't run around on a podium and speak of it, but should anybody care to talk about it, that, I have no problem with that. If I did, you wouldn't be sitting right here.
Int	Yes, I guess I should know that, shouldn't I? You wouldn't have said yes to me if you were reluctant to share.
Ben	That's right. So, no, I don't have any problems with sharing that information with anybody who would bring the subject up. But I don't go around talking about it to people.
Int	So, you wouldn't necessarily initiate a conversation about it?
Ben	No.
Int	But if someone showed an interest, you wouldn't hesitate.
Ben	No, I—I again, I would not initiate it, but I certainly wouldn't mind talking about it.

According to other family members, Ben had discussed his mother's death openly with his wife, Julie, and with his brothers, Jake and Tom. Talking about his teenage son's mysterious death was another matter altogether:

Ben   But as far as my, the situation with my son passing away, I [pause], ah, [pause] I'm just, I'm comfortable with it and I, and I have gone through every reason, every thought that I could come up with and other people, from ministers to lay people and [pause], ah, [pause] I have dealt with it and I have dealt with it for a long time. But, I am just not, I guess, I don't know, I guess I don't know if I don't want to share it or I'm just not, I'm just not comfortable talking about it, that's all.

Int   Well, I appreciate that, and I won't force you, not at all. My sense of it is that it has a real different meaning to you than the death of your mother.

Ben   Uh, huh. That would be a fair statement.

Ben described himself as not being comfortable talking about his son's death. He agreed that his son's death had a different meaning than his mother's death. There was some indication later in the interview that Ben had felt responsible for not repairing the car in which his son had died. It seems logical that sharing would be less likely to occur when negative feelings are attached to the death event. Having negative feelings could limit sharing and, by extension, inhibit the making of new meanings with family members.

In addition to being inhibited by negative feelings associated with his son's death, Ben seemed also to be inhibited by the way his wife pressured him to talk about the death. During the interview, he seemed to avoid saying much about the death of his son in her presence. He reported having shared more outside the family. This pressuring of one family member by another is an inhibitor of family meaning-making. The person being pressured may resist any reference to the lost family member. Fewer interactions among members about the death, would mean less chance of family meaning-making.

Another example of how respondents changed their minds about sharing comes from an individual interview with Dominic Primo, who was grieving the loss of his young son-in-law Ronnie, who was killed in an airplane crash. In this passage, Dominic is quite emphatic about his willingness to share with family members and then later qualifies what he has said:

Int   Is there any part of it, any of that that you, uh, would hesitate to share with other family members? Any part of it, particularly the parts that you've said to me today that would be difficult or that you would hesitate to say?

Dominic   No, not at all. No, I don't, ah, I don't think there's anything that ah, you know that I think about . . . that I wouldn't relate to anybody in the family.

Int   Um huh. Do you ever find yourself, and this is a bit of a leading question, I'm going to just identify it as that. Do you ever find yourself keeping some of your thoughts to yourself with the thought that they might make it harder for somebody else if you were to say it out loud?

Dominic   I don't think so. I think you know, we, we talk about Ronnie quite a bit, ah, I don't have to, you know how sometimes there are certain things that come up and ah, . . . where like, ah, you hate to mention [pause] you hate to mention certain things because you think you might offend somebody or you might cause somebody to break down or something like that. I don't think there's anything about Ronnie. I think we have such ah, I have such good memories about him that, ah, the only, ah, the only, ah, one that has a tough time [pause] you know as far as getting real saddened is my wife. She, ah, she can't talk much about Ronnie without just, ah, becoming strictly, you know, uncontrollable, uncontrollable emotionally. I mean, when she thinks about it. Outside of that, I can talk to Karrie and, ah, and Steve doesn't like to talk about it too much. Steve and my wife, my wife kind of breaks down, and gets, you know, and Steve just gets quiet. He doesn't, he's quiet anyway.

Int   Um huh.

Dominic   You know, but as far as talking to Rena or Karrie or, ah, my, my other two sons, you know, I can, ah, talk to them about Ronnie and just different things, and even Steve I can talk about it, and I do. I don't hold back with any of them, but I, but I probably, if I held back with anybody, I probably held back, hold back with my wife a little bit and Steve, only because it seems to me like they are more uncomfortable about it.

It is impossible to know whether Dominic would ever have said what he did about holding back with his wife and son Steve if leading questions had not been asked. Assuming that he would have, then, this is both an example of how respondents tend to say yes and modify their answers later and an example of how family members may be inhibited by their desire to protect other family members from feeling the pain of the loss. This desire to protect others is called *protectionism* and is a meaning-making inhibitor.

Yes, We Will Share. Some respondents maintained throughout the first interview that they were willing to share but failed to do so in subsequent family group interviews. It may have been a matter of social desirability stemming from a belief that families *should* share in such times. Some families might have needed to say they could share to maintain their image of themselves as caring and open. Another possibility is that people responded quickly to the question without carefully thinking through what impact sharing their private thoughts might have, both on others and on themselves. They also might not have realized how much they would reveal before the interview was over.

Valuable insights were gained by comparing what family members said in individual interviews with what they said in family interviews. Fifteen out of 48 respondents were interviewed both individually and with other family members. The most meaningful data came from the Primo family, for which it was possible to interview a family group of four and, within a very few days, follow-up with individual interviews. The four Primo family members were Rena, Ronnie's widow; her parents, Dominic and Joyce; and her sister, Karrie.

Dominic had a concordance rate of more than 50%, meaning that half of his meanings showed up in both interviews. The concordance rate was calculated by dividing the number of meanings appearing in both interviews by the total number of meanings. Rena and Karrie each had a 20% concordance rate; that is, one out of five meanings found in their individual interviews were also found in the family interview. Joyce's concordance rate was only 10%. These data support the notion that the meanings family members offer when they are alone are different from meanings they offer when family members are present.

Differences between individual interviews and meanings from family interviews and the reasons for them are important family data. Differences could have been because of several study characteristics, including the effects of repeated measures. At the time of the individual interviews, Primo family members had already been exposed to both the interview guidelines and the interviewer, as well as to other family members' meanings in the family interview. Time had an effect even though only a few days separated the interviews. Meanings may have changed as members continued to work toward making sense of the death. Some difference may have been that members did not have to compete to be heard in the individual interviews and had more individual attention from the interviewer.

Reasons for some family members having higher concordance rates, as Dominic Primo did, may have to do with how dominant they are in family conversations. Dominant members, like Dominic, may be more likely to have more of their personal meanings heard in family gatherings. It may also be that persons with higher concordance rates have less to hide or are more honest than persons with lower concordance rates.

A correlation may exist between concordance rates and protectionism. Persons with lower concordance rates may tend to hold back some meanings because they fear hurting others, or they sense that their meanings are too different from those of the rest of the family. For example, Joyce Primo, who had the lowest concordance rate, said twice in her individual interview that she thought it was wrong for her daughter to receive insurance money for Ronnie's death. Joyce did not share this meaning in the family session with her daughter present.

Perhaps family rules about politeness and respect caused some members to withhold meanings or to defer to the interpretations of family members judged to be in positions of authority or to be more bereaved. At any rate, differences in meanings shared in the individual and the family interviews were clearly found. Reasons why family members may or may not choose to share with other family members are discussed further in the following section.

Conditions Necessary for Family Sharing

Twenty-three comments were made about conditions under which respondents could or would share. Such comments were more likely to be made by family members who were reluctant to talk with other family members about their loss.

Some respondents claimed from the start to be reluctant to talk with other family members about the death. These respondents gave conditions under which they would share. Each of these conditions is presented in the following paragraphs.

I Would Share If Others Would Listen. Jane Smith was a widow in her 40s whose husband died in his sleep beside her. She characterized her mother and her father-in-law as not talking at all about Bob's death. She is referring to them in this passage:

Int   Could you imagine, for instance, saying what you've said to me in front of your family members?

Jane   If they'd listen, yeah. I mean, I don't have any trouble saying it.

Jane and her sister, Lisa, had a sense that the older generation was not willing to listen or to share. Jane's sharing was mostly with her sister and a friend who had lost her spouse under similar circumstances. She reported that the family had come to her house on the first Christmas after Bob's death and that no one had talked about his death. Although they felt angry and uncared for, both Lisa and Jane also interpreted the older generation's silence as a way of showing respect. Not talking as a show of respect could be construed as a family rule and an inhibitor of family meaning-making because not talking reduces the total number of interactions in which meaning could be created.

I Would Share If I Had Something to Share. Andy Zeeman, an 18-year-old being interviewed with his father, reported that he would be able to share his thoughts about his mother's death but that nothing came to mind. When taken in context, Andy's silence was understandable. Derek Zeeman, his father, cried so hard through most of the interview that, at times, Andy found it difficult to concentrate, and the tape recorder had to be turned off several times while Derek wept. Andy seemed very uncomfortable and perhaps somewhat embarrassed by his father's crying. When drawing the genogram, Andy made it a point to identify himself as being more like the men in the family who do not show their feelings. Andy seemed also to have a sense of his father's fragility, and Andy's behavior suggested that he was attempting to "keep the boat afloat" by being strong and as reserved as his father was emotional. Given his role, it may have been difficult for him to start talking about what his mother's death meant to him.

We Would Share If It Did Not Make Us Uncomfortable. Derek Zeeman, Andy's father, was one of the respondents who said becoming emotionally uncomfortable would keep him from talking about his wife's death. Derek said he could not bear to be present in the room with his mother as she talked about Debbie's death. He gave this as a reason for declining a family interview.

Interestingly, he also was the respondent who had consented to the interview with his son because, as he put it, they had scarcely been able to talk about Debbie's death and the interview might help. When that interview was done, Derek lost interest in arranging subsequent family interviews. It seems important to notice that willingness to share may be dependent on what is being shared and with whom. Derek could talk about Debbie with an interviewer. He could not talk with his son alone, and he could not bear to hear his mother speak of Deb in a family interview.

We Would Share If It Were About Life. Some conditions required for sharing had to do with the content of what would be shared. When the four Buchanan family members were asked 9 months after Florence's death whether they shared their thoughts about her death with each other, Roland, her son, and his wife, Coral, answered this way:

Coral   We shared a lot at the time it happened.
Roland   Yes, but it's always what we did with her.
Int   What about her life?
Roland   Oh, yeah.
Coral   Yeah.

The Buchanans and some other families reported talking more about their loved one's life than they did about the death. Some made sense of the lost member's life as part of making sense of the death. Talking about the person's life nearly always involved characterizing the deceased in some way. *Characterizing* is a strategy used by families as a way of making sense of a death. More examples of characterizations are given in the next chapter.

We Would Share If It Were Positive. Some families put restrictions on the tone of what they shared. In the Owens family, Irene Owens was the family member who had died. Her daughter, Myra, and her son, Randall, and Randall's son, Jeff, were interviewed together. One of their family rules was to put a positive spin on negative things that occurred in the family. In the passage that follows, Myra had just been asked whether her family could share their thoughts about Irene's death:

Myra   I think we would if, I think we would, but it would be on a
        happy note.

The "be happy" rule was enforced in the interview each time Myra cried or said anything about having a difficult time. Her brother would interrupt and say something positive about the death, usually characterizing the deceased as saintlike and the family as having it all together. At the end of the interview, Myra wanted assurance that she had not said anything out of line, anything that would give a false impression. The family was adamant that counseling, even the one-time bereavement follow-up offered as part of the study, would be "the furthest thing from our mind." When Jeff, Myra's nephew, was asked what it was like to have gone through the interview, he answered:

Jeff   Um, for me, I guess it's kind of weird to deal with it, say these
        things, otherwise I wouldn't necessarily come up to Myra or
        my dad and talk to them about Grandma's death and what it
        meant to me and everything else. It feels good to kind of get
        it out, I guess.

One could speculate that if the family rule was not to talk unless one had good things to say, and if Jeff had negative things to say, he would be unlikely to share them. Family rules that disallow sharing are inhibitors of family meaning-making.

We Would Share If It Were Not Negative About the One Who Died.
The next excerpt from Joyce Primo illustrates the condition that what
is said must not reflect poorly on the one who has died. It is reminiscent of the old adage "Do not speak ill of the dead."

Int	Would you be able to express that with the family together or with individual family members?
Joyce	Um. [thoughtful look and pause]
Int	Or would you hold that back some?
Joyce	I would mention it but not elaborate.
Int	Wouldn't be too heavy on it?
Joyce	Right.
Int	Right, yeah. And what would keep you from mentioning it, but not being as heavy on it as you might really feel?
Joyce	Uh, to more or less help defend him.
Int	To defend Ronnie?
Joyce	Um huh.
Int	Say, but not a lot. Would it be some disloyalty or feeling of disloyalty to Ronnie if you were too heavy on that, or not?
Joyce	Yes.
Int	Yes, um huh.
Joyce	Because he wouldn't really deserve that.

Some caution in family sharing may be attributable to the need to
defend or remain loyal to the one who has died, as it was for Joyce.
Whatever the reasons for soft-pedaling beliefs about the death, the net
result would likely be less involvement in family meaning-making and
more private meaning-making. Joyce was clearly bothered by how she
construed Ronnie's death. More engagement in family meaning-making might have helped her construct some less troublesome meanings
or at least become aware that others in the family struggled with the
same, difficult meanings.

*We Would Share If My Meaning Is Not Too Different From That of
Others.* Joyce claimed she was most different from others in her family
when it came to her belief that Ronnie's, her son-in-law's, death could
have been prevented if he had not taken the risk of flying. Reference

is being made here to that particular belief. Joyce had initially said she would share anything, but when she had time to think about what it would be like to share how she attributed Ronnie's death to his risk-taking behavior, she became more cautious. She said she would say what she thought, but not elaborate.

Respondents who would not share because of a sense that their meanings were different from those of other family members also included Rafi, Anne Miner's husband. Rafi participated in the study with his in-laws, his family of origin members being out-of-state and abroad. Rafi was very clear about not sharing some of his thoughts with Anne's family. The following excerpt shows how the question about sharing was asked and how Rafi, 5 months bereaved, responded:

Int   Tell me, are there parts of your reaction or the way, more par-
        ticularly the way you think about Anne's death that you would
        be unlikely to share with the rest of your family? Parts that
        would be yours and that you would hesitate to say to them?

Rafi   I don't talk much to them; I just think she's gone. There's
        nothing left except what we remember. I don't share that with
        them.

Int   So, the part that you told me when I asked you where she was
        and what you think about the part about the afterlife and all
        that, that part you would hesitate?

Rafi   Yeah, I mean, I might have, I might have, you know, I might
        have mentioned it right after, especially when I struggled with
        the other stuff, and I didn't have time for it. I might have said
        something.

Int   Um huh, and what would hold you back?

Rafi   I just don't think that they see it, that they see it that way, and
        I don't need to have a debate about it.

The feature that held Rafi back was his sense that his beliefs were different from those of his wife's family and that he had no desire to debate. Besides religious and cultural differences, Rafi was far more educated than anyone in Anne's family. His connection with his wife's family was more on an emotional level than on an intellectual level. They shared the emotional experience of Anne's dying and death as a close-knit family, but he made a clear distinction about their differences in terms of religious beliefs and other understandings.

Primo family members also expressed a reluctance to talk about the death with others because of a different level of education. As Dominic described it, the more educated sons were reported to have had a reluctance to talk. Dominic described his sons as keeping their beliefs to themselves because they did not think they would be accepted. Perhaps when family members become aware that their beliefs are quite different from those of others in the family, they keep their beliefs to themselves in order to belong and to avoid feelings of rejection. Fear of rejection is another inhibitor of family meaning-making.

An important point should be made about families in which members do not talk with each other about family events. A member who does not share out of a sense that his or her beliefs differ too much from those of the rest of the family may be in a Catch-22 situation. Not sharing because meanings are different maintains the differences. Not sharing precludes being an active player in the family meaning-making process, a process that may reveal individual meanings as not so different and may allow for new meanings to emerge. At the same time, it is clear from the data that expressing a deviant meaning in the family is a risk, one that all family members may be unwilling to take even with support from someone outside the system.

Most families displayed a tendency for members with divergent beliefs to keep them to themselves or to share them only with other family members whose beliefs seemed most like their own. Often, the ones with whom they shared were in coalition or alliance with them, suggesting a relationship between meaning systems and family structure.

Meaning-making may occur within preexisting family subgroups, including alliances and coalitions, and subgroup boundaries may be reinforced by the similarity of the meanings held by members within the group. These subgroups would be more likely to come together in a family interview.

George and Dwight Miner gave reasons why they could not make it to the family interview and asked to be interviewed separately. As they described their daughter's/sister's death, they told how they had felt excluded from care-giving that occurred near the time of Anne's death. They reported waiting together outside Anne's house while other family members were by her side. George and Dwight frequently referenced and agreed with each other's meaning statements. At no point did they compare their meanings with those of other family members.

If this subgroup was the only one to be interviewed, researchers could get a skewed picture of a number of family features, including the level of consensus. Such findings lead to a realization that if one wants to know something about a family as a whole, one must interview not only multiple family members but also multiple family members representing the various subgroups within a family. Otherwise, one's data on the family are likely to be inaccurate.

Finally, one could theorize that, in identifying conditions necessary for sharing to occur, families gave clues to which interventions would be appropriate if grief support services or family therapy were sought. For instance, the Munson family might benefit from help in working through the issues that resulted in cut-offs within the family. The Zeeman family might benefit from help with communications because their communication link, Debbie, had died.

In conclusion, when considering the reporting of conditions under which respondents said they *could* or *would* talk about the death with others in the family, one gets a sense of the complexity of family meaning-making. Certain factors inhibit family meaning-making, whereas others may stimulate it. People within each family subgroup need to be interviewed to get the whole picture.

Comparison of Families' Willingness to Share

To explore the range of family members' willingness to talk with each other about the death, those families most willing to share were compared with those least willing. Of the 10 families interviewed, the Primo and Miner families stand out as being the most willing to talk among themselves about the death of one of their members. It is not surprising that these two families had the most members who were willing to gather together for interviews. Eleven members, including in-laws and three generations, were interviewed in each of these families.

Sharing in the Miner family seemed to be enhanced by their high tolerance for diversity. Sharing was also facilitated by their engagement in many death rituals, including shared home care during the final illness, sitting shivah, and an elaborate funeral service that combined Jewish and Catholic traditions. The Miner family generated a wide variety of meanings. Some members attached meaning to every minor occurrence around the time of the death, whereas others were more reluctant to do so. Meaning-making stimulators in this family included both the use of rituals that gave form and expression to some of the family beliefs, and the family's willingness to tolerate differences.

Primo family members shared as readily as the Miners, but some of their patterns of sharing were quite different from those of the Miners. The 11-member Primo family consisted of a combination of Ronnie's and Rena's families of origin. The two sides of the family interacted on a regular basis before and after Ronnie's death. Two of Rena's siblings and their families lived beside their parents, and a third lived in the same neighborhood. Members worked together in the same businesses. Family gatherings frequently included the deceased's extended family, and Ronnie's wife, Rena, lived with her parents after Ronnie's death.

In contrast with the Miners, the Primo family worked harder to appear more alike in their meanings and were less likely than the Miners to reveal personal meanings they thought might be different from those of other family members. The Primos were more cautious. Whereas differences among members in the Miner family were supported, differences in the Primo family were discouraged. In an individual interview, Joyce Primo, Ronnie's mother-in-law, said all members of the family would agree on the meaning of Ronnie's death, but Dominic, her husband, said they would not all agree. He said their son Steve, who had different beliefs about death because of his education, would see Ronnie's death differently. Sharing meanings among family members was stimulated in the Primo family by the frequency of interaction and inhibited by their family rules to agree to not share meanings they believed could cause others discomfort. Despite the inhibitions, the Primo family shared far more than most families.

The Barlow and Munson families stand out as examples of families in which sharing was minimal. In both families, subgroups did not associate with each other because of past conflicts. Both families seemed to have fears about what would happen if they shared their meanings with each other.

The Barlow family initially said they would meet for an interview that would include two sons of the deceased with their wives. When it came time to schedule the group interview, however, the older brother, Jake, canceled. His fear was that his frankness would antagonize his sister-in-law with whom he had "patched things up" at the time of his mother's funeral. A meaning-making inhibitor operant in this family was the fear that speaking one's mind in the presence of other family members would cause alienation because it had done so in the past.

In the Munson family, splits seemed to be related to alcohol issues: who used and who did not. The daughter, Jeannie, thought to have been closest to the deceased father, Claude, declined to be interviewed. She, like Jake in the Barlow family, had scheduled an interview and then canceled when it was time to meet. The oldest brother, Darren, had denounced his father's lifestyle, particularly his alcohol use, some years before. He had also cut himself off from his sister because of her alcohol use and blamed her for supporting their father in his drinking habit. They all seemed to be cautious as a result of having been hurt in previous family encounters. Multiple family cut-offs occurred in the extended family, meaning that certain family members intentionally had no contact with other family members. The interview that did take place included Darren; his wife, Marie; the youngest sibling, Sam; and his wife, Deb. This subgroup shared the meaning that the death could have been prevented if Claude had been willing to change his lifestyle. In this family, the meaning-making inhibitors could be said to include family dynamics, particularly as they were being played out around the use of alcohol and multigenerational cut-offs.

FAMILY-SHARED MEANINGS

All 10 families gave evidence of at least some agreed-upon meanings related to the deaths. Overall, respondents tended to report in the direction of more agreement than there turned out to be when probes were used or when subsequent members of a family were asked the same questions. In the Mackey family, Jenny, the wife of the deceased, said in an individual interview that everyone in the family saw her husband's death as she did. Jenny's adult daughter, Pam, in an individual interview said her father's death did not mean the same to her as to her mother because their relationships with him were different. In the following quotation, clear differences in meanings were apparent when they were interviewed together. They had just been asked where they saw Richard being now:

Jenny   Well, if what we are taught and I do believe it, that there is a hereafter. That's the biggest thing as far as I'm concerned. And, and, there is a Heaven. And I do believe there is a Heaven and that is where he is. Then I know he is free of pain and, ah, I know that, ah, in Heaven you are happy. You are home with, ah, God, with your Father, however you want to put it, and, ah, as I think I told you, Jan, I don't, people who say well, they're looking after you, they are, I think they are possibly concerned. I don't really know how I feel about that, other than if they are happy, then they cannot see the unhappiness here.

Pam   And that's a little bit where we differ because I still think that he is, I don't think he thinks, I think he's doing whatever he's doing, like nothing. He's forgotten either one of us.

Jenny   Well.

Pam   But he's doing what he's doing, and he does look once in awhile to see how you're doing, and that's how these unique things happen to you that are really very lucky. Things have happened to Mother.

Jenny and Pam were in agreement that a Heaven exists and that Richard had gone there after his death, but they were not in agreement on what that meant in terms of their daily lives. Although Jenny initially reported that she and her daughter had the same meanings connected to Richard's death, it turns out that they disagreed in some important ways. Jenny had made it clear that she did not believe that Richard could be happy in Heaven if he saw their unhappiness. Pam believed that not only did he know what was happening to them but he also intervened in some way. Pam went on to give examples of "lucky" things that had happened to her mother and to herself that she attributed to her father's intervention. It is easy to imagine how these different meanings might result in quite different experiences of grief and how the differences in meanings had the potential to affect family relationships. The comfort that Pam seemed to receive from her sense of her father's ongoing involvement in her life was not being experienced by Jenny. She had decided that it was impossible for her husband to be happy in Heaven if he saw their unhappiness.

The pattern of reporting an exaggerated level of agreement was similar to what was observed in relation to family sharing. Families initially reported higher levels of sharing than they turned out to have, and also reported higher levels of agreement than they actually had. This tendency toward reporting inflated levels of sharing and agreement has important implications for family assessment and is discussed in the final chapter.

The question arises here, as it did in the discussion of sharing patterns, why would families report inflated levels of agreement or shared meaning? The reasons previously mentioned in relation to sharing patterns probably have some relevance: desiring to give socially acceptable answers, responding too hastily, responding to deaths other than the one for which they were included in the study, and revealing more than they had initially intended. In the case of inflated agreement levels, several other possibilities emerged. In some instances, the notion of being in agreement may have mediated against feelings of isolation, not uncommon in bereavement.

Ben Barlow, whose family could be characterized as emotionally distant, expressed his desire for agreement. He is answering the question about whose thoughts were most like his and whose were the most different:

Ben   Again, we're gonna go back to my brother Tom. Uh, I think I'm close to what he would share, but I would not [pause] I guess it's a matter of me saying I would like to think, and that's not right because that to me, it's forcing thought on somebody. But, I would like to think that he would share basically the same thoughts as myself and my brother Jake. And I am, you know, I am confident that [pause] ah [pause] there is some things that we agree upon. But I am not sure as to, again, we talked earlier about would he have liked to have mended some ways with his mother? I don't know.

The notion that Ben wanted the three brothers to be alike in how they construed their mother's death was apparent in this response, as well as elsewhere in the interview. Ben repeatedly compared himself with his brothers. Ben believed it would be good if Tom saw the death as he and Jake did but feared there were some differences because of the conflictual relationship Tom had had with his mother. Both Jake and Ben wanted to bring Tom back into the family fold. Tom was the only member who lived out of state. Living some distance away from the main part of the family could be thought of as an inhibitor of family meaning-making. In some instances, families manage to construct intricate meaning-systems over the telephone and over long distances, but this did not seem to be the case with the Barlow family. Tom's living away seemed to function more as an inhibitor of family meaning-making.

The Barlow family exemplifies an inflated agreement level because of the need to mediate against feelings of isolation. In other instances, inflated reports of agreement resulted from a lack of knowledge of other family members' thoughts about the death. Some seemed genuinely surprised when they heard others' thoughts during the interviews. It typically occurred that when members did not know each other's thoughts about the death, they assumed agreement. Deb Munson looked in amazement at her brother-in-law Darren when he said he did not believe in Heaven. Deb had assumed that because Darren was a Catholic, he would understand Claude's death according to Catholic teachings as she knew them.

Jenny Mackey was surprised to hear that her daughter, Pam, believed that Richard looked down from Heaven and intervened in their lives. Buchanan family members were surprised to hear that Coral had been haunted by a dream in which her mother-in-law was choking as she had at the time of her death. They did not know that one of Coral's meanings was that she had somehow failed as Florence's caretaker by not preventing her from choking. Randall Owens was surprised to learn that his son, Jeff, was pained by the belief that he had not spent enough time with his grandmother before she died. Each of these respondents learned something he or she did not know until the interview. It seems difficult for families who do not talk about the death to reach any level of agreement about the meaning of the death or even to know how others construe the death.

FAMILY CONSENSUS

Family consensus is a troublesome concept. First, the question who makes up the family is of no small import. Second, how can one be sure there is family consensus unless all family members have been interviewed? The four Buchanan family members who were interviewed agreed on the meaning that they gave Gramma a good death, but only one of nine siblings was interviewed. It seems that family consensus would be more likely to occur in small families, but in this study true consensus was not found even in families limited to two members. Even with reports of inflated levels of agreement, this study would suggest that *family consensus*, defined as agreement among all members, is highly unlikely.

Family members may agree in some basic way about certain meanings, but then each member seems to add his or her own twist. This was the case in the Primo family. In the first family interview, there was agreement that Ronnie, the young man who had been killed in an airplane crash, was in Heaven. If the questioning had ended there, agreement could have been assumed. But as the family talked more, the color and variety of each member's meanings surfaced and important differences were revealed. Rena said she saw Heaven as it was portrayed in their 3-year-old's storybooks, where Heaven had gold streets and mansions. Joyce said that although she did not have any particular images of Heaven, she found herself thinking a great deal about Ronnie's being in Heaven. Dominic said that he had no particular image of Heaven either but that he pictured Ronnie as being extremely involved in whatever was going on there. He saw his son-in-law carrying on in a manner similar to how he had in his life. Karrie said that she did not have any particular images of Heaven but that she thought of him as being happy there. Then Karrie said sometimes she had trouble believing in Heaven. These differences seem important because they would likely have a different effect on the course of bereavement, and in this family, with its rules about being alike, believing something different from the rest of the family could be isolating.

The Barlow family was typical of the majority of families in the study in terms of patterns of agreement and disagreement. Vera Barlow had died in a nursing home at age 85 after being ill for a long time. All five family members interviewed agreed that Vera had wanted to die. Colleen, one of Vera's daughters-in-law, summarized the family meanings. She said that the entire family believed Vera wanted to die and that it was time for her to die. She said everyone in the family saw the death the same way; on other matters, however, they disagreed. The differences among them, according to Colleen, were because of the different relationships each had with Vera. Others were in agreement with her on this point.

Both Jake and Ben, two of Vera's sons, reported that the meaning of their mother's death was different for Tom, another brother, because he had been estranged from Vera. Later, when Tom was interviewed, he gave a very different meaning from those of his brothers, which was that he had lost his mother years before when she had started to fail mentally, at which time he had stopped trying to visit her. No one else had construed her death in such a way. Family members who were closer to each other with frequent interactions, opportunities to make meaning, were more alike in the way they construed Vera's death. Ben and his wife, Julie, agreed that it was time for Vera to die, that there was consensus in the family about it, and that her death at that time was for the best.

Julie Barlow said that, as a couple, she and Ben saw the death the same way. But when the question was asked whether they had a sense of the deceased's presence still being with them, Julie announced that they totally disagreed with each other. Julie had a sense that all her deceased relatives, including Vera, were "still with her." Ben did not share Julie's sense of the lost family members still being present. This pattern of families agreeing on some basic meaning, but each member putting a different spin on it, was the most common pattern. As with other families, the Barlows' meanings both converged and diverged.

What can be concluded about shared family meanings and the question of family consensus? First, one must ask who makes up the family. To learn about the level of agreement among family members, each family member must be interviewed. Second, one must ask who agrees with whom about what because the level of agreement varies from meaning to meaning. The data suggest that, in relation to the meaning of a death event, family consensus is unlikely. Some families do not even agree on the so-called facts of the death. In this study, two families gave two different death dates, and one family gave four dates. Two families gave five different causes of the death. If there is a lack of agreement on things as seemingly factual as the date and cause of the death, is it realistic to expect families to agree completely on such complex things as the meaning of a death in the family?

Summary

In summary, the goal of this chapter was to demonstrate some overall patterns of family meaning-making. The chapter began with an introduction to the 10 families in the study. The notion that meanings attached to the death have an effect on the course of bereavement was reiterated as a central theme of the study, and examples from the data were given. Next, an effort was made to demonstrate the levels of family meaning-making. The finding of meaning-making at all systems levels was demonstrated by excerpts of individual, couple, dyadic, and family levels of family meaning-making. The themes that ran through this material included how even individually constructed meanings occur in the family context, how meanings are created reciprocally in couple dyads, and how family subsystems both create and maintain meaning systems.

Throughout the chapter, the more intricate features of the meaning-making process were pointed out as they appeared in selected excerpts. Among the intricate features previewed were the categories of meaning-making stimulators and inhibitors. *Stimulators,* defined as those factors that enhance the family meaning-making process, included family rituals, the in-law effect, tolerance for differences, frequent interactions, and the interview itself. Meaning-making *inhibitors,* those factors that impede family meaning-making, included family rules prohibiting talking about sensitive issues, protectionism, and family dynamics such as family cut-offs. The remainder of the inhibitors and stimulators found in the data are presented in subsequent chapters as they appear in selected excerpts.

The two major categories of the study, "family meaning-making strategies" and "the meanings that families construct," were previewed as they appeared in the excerpts. *Strategies,* defined as the means or methods by which families made sense of their loss, included comparison, characterization, disagreeing, referencing, and questioning. These are developed extensively in the following chapter.

Meaning statements that appeared in the excerpts included death occurred as a test, as a model for others, or to unify the family; the person died because of his or her genes; the deceased is nowhere or is in Heaven looking down; and the deceased wanted to die. The notion that not all meanings are positive was restated. Among the meanings discussed at length was the particularly common and troublesome meaning: the death could have been prevented. It was shown that some families attempt to make sense of their experience by saying what the death did *not* mean. Chapters 7 and 8 are dedicated to a typology of all the meanings found in the study.

The three categories of "family sharing," "family shared meanings," and "family consensus" were explored. *Family sharing* was defined as family members' willingness to talk with each other about the death. Within this category, willingness to share, reluctance to share, and the conditions necessary for sharing were explored in turn. It was pointed out that some members said they are willing to talk with other family members about the death and did so; some said directly that they were not willing to share and gave reasons for why they were not; and some said first that they were willing to share and then either changed their minds or simply failed to do so in subsequent interviews. It was clearly demonstrated that family members have a tendency to overstate their willingness to share. Excerpts were used to suggest that family members' willingness to share with each other about the death may depend on which family death is being discussed, who is present, and whether their meanings are negative or positive.

Information about what conditions are necessary for family members to be able to talk with each other about the loss of their family member was presented as extensive and useful data. The conditions that families identified under which they would share included if others would listen; if they had something to share; if what they had to say would not make them (the speaker) too uncomfortable; if what they had to say was about the lost member's life, rather than his or her death; if what they had to say was positive; if what they had to say was not something bad about the one who had died; and if what they had to say was not too different from what others in the family would say. *Individual concordance rates,* defined as the percentage of meanings a family member expresses both in an individual and a joint interview, were used to suggest that family members may differ in how many of their more personal meanings they are willing to share when other family members are present. It was assumed that any factors that would help family members talk with one another would stimulate family meaning-making and would be a good thing. Furthermore, it was suggested that interventions intended to help bereaved families might be directed at improving conditions necessary for talking about the death with each other.

A comparison was made of the families most willing to talk about the loss of their family member and those least willing. It was shown that families who shared the most had many meaning-making stimulators, such as giving physical care to the person before he or she died, having many family and funeral rituals, being tolerant of diverse points of view, and having frequent interactions. Families who shared the least had many meaning-making inhibitors, such as fragile family ties, previous conflicts including cut-offs, and divergent beliefs.

In discussing matters related to the categories of "family shared meaning" and "consensus," it was shown that *pure consensus,* defined as complete agreement about a given meaning attached to the death, was not found in any of the study families. *Shared meanings,* defined as those meanings on which two or more family members agreed, did occur. It was shown that families seldom turned out to be as much in agreement as they reported to be when first asked. Reasons for initially claiming higher levels were theorized to be social desirability, haste in answering, not knowing how deeply they would share during the interview, and not being aware of others' meanings before joint interviews. Excerpts were used to suggest that families assumed agreement when it was not known; members wanted others to agree and sometimes pressured others within the family to see the death as they themselves saw it. It was shown how differences in meanings can affect family relationships.

In the next four chapters, all the strategies that families in the study used and all the meanings they made, including those previewed in this chapter, are emphasized. Features of family meaning-making such as systems levels, meaning-making stimulators, meaning-making inhibitors, and the interactions among family meaning-making, family structure, and family dynamics are pointed out as they appear in selected excerpts.

5

Stories, Dreams,
Comparing, and Coincidancing

Families use a wide variety of strategies to make sense of the death of a family member. They tell stories. They dream. They compare their loss with others. They make something of so-called coincidences associated with the loss, they characterize the deceased, and they use elementary communication skills in conversations related to the death event. The term *strategy*, as used here, does not mean that study respondents were taken to have made a conscious decision to use certain strategies. Strategies were used spontaneously and automatically.

Strategies such as stories and dreams were more likely to reflect the entirety of a respondent's experience. Stories and dreams were found in long portions of the transcripts.

Strategies such as comparison, "coincidancing," and characterization were found in moderately long portions of the transcripts. *Coincidancing* is a term coined to capture how family members make something of so-called coincidences associated with the death.

Strategies that were more like ordinary communication skills, such as agreeing or disagreeing with each other, referring to each other's meanings, and asking each other questions, tended to deal with specifics of the loss experience and can be found in short parts of the transcript. When families use these simple strategies in conversation, it is called *family speak*.

In this chapter, stories, dreams, comparison, and coincidancing are illustrated. Characterization and family speak are illustrated in Chapter 6. An attempt is made to demonstrate the nature of each strategy and to describe how families used them to make sense of their experience.

Stories and Dreams

Stories and dreams helped create the overall aura around individual families and establish family themes. Among all the strategies that families used, stories and dreams were the most global in scope.

STORIES

In a very real sense, all of what families said in the interviews could be characterized as their "stories." Respondents used storytelling to both construct and rehearse meanings. Since the beginning of time, humans have made sense of their experiences by telling stories. In a National Public Radio broadcast on January 15, 1992, Joseph Campbell noted that telling stories is such an important part of human experience that humans should have been named *Homo narrus,* rather than *Homo sapiens.* Telling stories, Campbell said, distinguishes us from lower forms. Telling stories gives meaning to human experience; stories create order where there is chaos. Few life experiences have greater potential to cause chaos than the death of a loved one. Without exception, the 10 families in this study were eager to tell their stories.

Each family story can be seen as having a theme. In some instances, the theme was what the family wanted others to believe about them as a family. In other instances, themes could be construed as over-arching family meanings about the death event. For instance, the major theme of the Buchanan family story was "We gave Gramma a good death." The message was not found as any particular member's words, but was reflected more in the family's collective meanings and was expressed by way of their overall story. Highlights of their story as it supported their theme are as follows:

- Gramma asked to be taken out of the nursing home.
- We had a family conference to see whether they could care for her at home.

- We brought her home in the van in an easy chair, tied in with a sheet, and called it the "great escape."
- Roland—she called him the "All American Boy"—got up with her every night.
- Coral sacrificed her own needs to give her constant care.
- Gramma was happy from the time she got to our house.
- She never had to go to the hospital.
- All the kids came to see her.
- She was in control to the end.
- People thought we were crazy, but we would do it again.
- She is dead, but we can still see her in her room as we go past.

The Buchanan story had a teleological flow, leading to the conclusion "We gave Gramma a good death." This theme could be construed to be a family meaning. It was jointly constructed and agreed upon.

The role of story in the meaning-making process was most discernable in an interview with Evelyn Munson, a 73-year-old widow whose husband, Claude, had died on the couch while she was preparing his dinner. In the analysis of her 3½-hour interview, it became apparent that her story was made up of substories. Their titles might be "The Illness," "The Dying," "The Funeral," "The Family History," "The Relationship," "The Deceased's Life," and "Surviving the Death." Similar substories were found in most other interviews. At first, some of these stories did not seem to be about the meaning of the death at all, but on further examination, meanings were found embedded in the stories. What follows is an excerpt from Evelyn's substory "The Dying":

Evelyn   Well, see he, uh, he had been on dialysis and they had put, uh, something in his arm . . . I think they call it a shunt. And, uh, so I could always feel that, you could feel the pulse you know. And, uh, so when he was lying down, I looked in there. And, uh . . . it was probably 15 minutes when I looked in there and I . . . [quietly] and I didn't see him breathing. So I went in and I felt that [quietly] and it was cold. So then I felt for that artery there . . . And he was dead. Oh my. [pause]

So [pause] I called, and came and called 911, and I waited and I waited [pause]. So then I called Jeannie, and I said,

"Honey, I think Daddy's gone and I called 911 but they don't come." So, she came and he was gone. Well then, after she had tried to give him, you know, to revive him and everything, it was, he was gone, there was no more bothering him. Uh [pause] then these men came from that fire that night . . . Well, they came with their slickers on and their muddy boots and everything and just came in and they put him down on the floor and they ripped his pajamas and I suddenly came to life and I said, "Don't you dare cut his chest. Don't you dare put a knife on him." [pause] And they looked at me like I was an old witch, but I didn't really care.

The theme of Evelyn's substory in this passage could be thought of as "I protected him." The theme of Evelyn's greater story was that Claude was a good man, greatly damaged in the World War II, but she had remained faithful to him to the end, even protecting him from his supposed rescuers. Data from other family interviews confirmed what was found in Evelyn's transcript. The titles of substories in other interviews were the same or similar. A story line was easier to follow in interviews with individuals than in groups, but even in most of the group interviews, a story line could be found and seemed to support already identifiable themes.

The substory "The Funeral" was one of the more elaborate substories for most families. The following is an excerpt from the Miner family interview, in which Anne's widower, Rafi, tells the substory "The Funeral":

Rafi Um, well, the whole funeral was just really wonderfully beautiful. Linda knew the priest real well, and so he was willing, he was willing to talk with us ahead of time and let us kind of customize it to a certain extent, and it didn't feel really awful. It was really hard to do that. It was definitely Catholic in a Catholic, a very pretty church. We had a pianist and violinist. This pianist had known about Anne before and he even dedicated, ah, a tape that he gave to her. And they were both professionals. They knew wonderful, wonderfully moving stuff at the funeral, so by the time we brought Anne in, everybody was already almost in tears and, ah, and there was this huge outpouring of love from all. We were both in such public positions. Plus, you know, Anne has such a huge family that there was hundreds, literally hundreds of people that came to the wake and that came to the funeral.

The theme suggested in this excerpt is that the family was able to give Anne a funeral that demonstrated how loved she was, or perhaps simply "Anne was loved." The greater family story had as its theme "Anne was a saint." The family told how Anne had dropped out of high school to take care of her mother, worked her way through school later, had been "motherlike" to seven siblings and a helper to her father, raised two children as a single parent, had been a good nurse, created love and respect in her second marriage, and had fought valiantly for her life. Therefore, of all people, she did not deserve to die. The essence of the family meaning was that her death was unfair.

The themes of some other families could be summed up in a few words. The theme of the Owens family was "We are a strong, old, prominent family that takes care of itself and that has no problems with the death of our wonderful mother." The theme of the Swan family was "We are a strong Christian family as compared with others, and we all see our father's/grandfather's death as a blessing for which we are grateful." By contrast, the Munson family theme was "We are a dysfunctional family, and it was Dad's vices that killed him." The Barlow family theme was "Our mother/grandmother wanted to die, but our family structure is too weak to risk revealing to each other our individual differences about the death." The Zeeman family had a kind of "We are lost" theme, suggesting that, without their spouse/mother, they did not know how to live. The Primo family theme was "We are a very close family who loved and admired Ronnie and his fast-track lifestyle even though his risk-takinge behaviors were what led to his death." The Mackey family theme was "I did it my way," a song they identified as their spouse's/ father's theme song. He had chosen to eat high-cholesterol foods and to smoke cigars even if it meant shortening his life, they said.

Story lines were more discernable in the individual interviews. In the couple and family interviews, it seemed that individuals modified their stories as they joined together to construct the family story.

DREAMS

No direct questions about dreams were asked. Reports of dreams were part of the data that respondents seemed compelled to share regardless of what was asked. In 8 of the 10 families, at least one person reported having dreams related to the death. The way respondents talked about dreams led to the speculation that dreams, beside being expressions of emotional pain, may also contribute to the cognitive dimensions of grief—specifically, to help make sense of the death that occurred. People seemed to construct certain meanings by way of their dreams. For instance, Sally, a sister-in-law and childhood friend of Anne Miner, was struggling with where Anne went after her death. Sally reported her dream in the following way:

Sally   Oh, well, Anne came to me in a dream about 2 months after she died and she told me. The dream was on the front steps of my parents' home. Dusty was there, I was there, and I was sitting on the steps. He wasn't a very important part of the dream; he was just there [pause]. And she walked over to me and we walked over towards this metal fence that used to be there, and she appeared there and she looked exactly the way she looked when she married you [pointing to Rafi]. She looked beautiful. She was beautiful, and she had on, not what I would consider heavenly clothes or anything. She had a lot of layered clothing on that was real light and flowing. And it was all shades of cream and beige that Anne had in different times in her life. She always wore cream-colored blouses. But there was a white-haired man who I'd never seen before in my life and who I would never see again. Pure white hair, and she put her hand on my shoulder and told me that, ah, she said to him first that she's ready, and then she said, "I feel more at peace now than I ever have, and it's undescribable. It's okay." And that was it. The dream ended [pause]. It's like prior to that I had woke up every night like 3 in the morning crying; after that, I was at ease with it. And it's like my idea is that she is present with whoever when whoever needs her [pause]. She's present, and she is in completeness, a peace that none of us will understand until the time comes when we'll join her [pause]. Then you know. She's with the gods, and it's not necessarily the gods we all read about and have been taught about. That's where she is.

Sally's meanings included that Anne was available to whoever needed her and that she was now complete and at peace with the gods. Sally's dream typifies not only a way in which meaning is made but also the role that meanings may play in the grieving process. Sally was clear that having gotten to the meanings she found in her dreams put her "at ease." Clearly, certain meanings can result in a lessening of emotional distress.

Anne's brother Dwight also reported a dream. Dwight said he, like his father, George, had wished for a sign from Anne. Dwight construed his dream as the sign he sought. This is how he reported his dream:

Dwight   Ah, you know there again I'm kind of like Dad, you know, give me a sign, you know, and I've dreamt about Anne once real vividly. And it's just been in the last couple of months where we talked, and she said everything is okay and don't worry about it and I'm fine, and you know, I mean, that was just, that was the only time that I have.

Int   But she came to you in that dream?

Dwight   Yes, yes, and she looked good, and she looked healthy and she just, you know, it was, and I woke up and I felt real good, you know, and I had, you know, it was almost kind of like it was a relief. Geeze, I feel better now. You know, Anne told me everything is okay and not to worry about it. She loved us all and missed us all and it was kind of weird, and I haven't dreamt about her since.

The dream, while lodged in the mind of one member and indicating in some way an individual's meanings, became a family affair when it was shared with other members. In some families, reporting dreams may have been a way to share more risky meanings because one is generally not held responsible for dreams. At any rate, dream content became grist for the family meaning-making mill. Other family members referred to Sally's dream, some adopted it as part of their meaning systems, and others, including Anne's father, George, were envious of Sally and Dwight for having had such comforting dreams.

Anne's spouse, Rafi, who had had no dreams of Anne, held that Anne was alive only in memory and not present in the way Sally was describing. He expressed regret that he could not believe that Anne continued to exist in an afterlife and thought his behavior would be different in some important ways if he could believe as Sally believed. Interestingly, even in dreams, the Miner family theme was consistent: "Anne was a saint, available to everyone, even in death."

In several instances, dreams were interpreted as premonitions. Evelyn Munson told how her husband, Claude, had dreamed of his dead mother just before his own death:

Evelyn   . . . that Sunday, before he had his, he said to me, "You know, last night I had a dream about my mom." He said it was so real and I think maybe he kind of knew that he was kind of close. 'Cause he had never told me that he dreamed of her, you know.

Evelyn used her husband's dream to make the meaning that his death was somehow expected—at least that *he* expected it. It seemed to comfort her to know that he had some warning, that he had anticipated his own death. Another dreamer, Rena Primo, dreamed that she had seen her grandfather's face with an aura in her window on the night he had died. The face had appeared to her before she had been told of his death. Such dreams lead to the meaning that death can be announced and is somehow predictable.

In general, dreams that other respondents had were about being with the deceased, doing things with them, and even having contact with them. The data showed a blurring between what people reported as dreams that occurred while they were clearly asleep and "dreamlike" experiences that occurred either on the edge of sleep or clearly during waking hours. Some of these dreamlike experiences consisted of a sense of the deceased's presence still being with them. For instance, Rena, Ronnie Primo's young widow, reported having an experience of her husband's presence while sitting in their bedroom closet to get away from her young children. She had been crying and comforting herself by stroking some of Ronnie's clothing. Suddenly, she felt her husband's hand at the end of one of his shirt sleeves as the shirt hung on a hanger. It was as if, she said, he were "reaching out to comfort me."

Edna Miner, a woman in her early 20s, shared that she had felt her mother come to her as she lay half dozing on the couch. Edna was aware that her brother had received a kiss from their mother just before her death. Edna had not, and she envied her brother. On the day following the death, as Edna dozed, her mother had come to her and kissed her on the cheek and was gone. Stories and dreams were the most global of all the strategies observed, and as such were difficult to sample and to illustrate in excerpts. Meanings connected to the dreams had to be inferred; respondents were not asked how their dreams related to the meanings the death had for them. Whether the meanings suggested here were respondents' actual meanings is not known. What can be said, however, is that stories and dreams are instrumental in the family meaning-making process. Because of the congruence between meanings constructed by way of stories or dreams and meanings constructed through other strategies, story and dream meanings gained in validity.

Comparison

The most common strategy found at the intermediate level of specificity was comparison. The data included 120 instances of respondents making sense of the death by comparing aspects of the death experience with those of other deaths or other life experiences. Also found were 20 different forms of comparison. The most common are exemplified here.

COMPARISON WITH OTHER FAMILY DEATHS

Most comparisons consisted of comparing the current death with other deaths, both inside and outside the family. The properties of the deaths on which most comparisons were made included the age of the deceased, the suddenness of the death, and the cause of the death. The most common form of comparison was a comparison of the current death with past deaths of family members. The following is an example of the most common type. It is from Ben Barlow, who had lost his mother recently and his teenage son many years before:

Ben   And that was again my salvation as far as the getting through from where I was comfortable with my son's dying and my mother's dying. My mother's dying was easier. I think we have discussed why my mother's dying was easier because, hey, the fact that she was an older lady. She had 85 years, as opposed to 18. My son was 18.

The age of the deceased was a factor identified by Ben and many others as an important basis for comparison. In all the data, deaths of younger family members were compared negatively with the deaths of older family members.

In addition to making age comparisons, family members often compared current deaths with other family deaths on the basis of cause and suddenness. The Owens family, like the Barlow family, made frequent comparisons between the current loss of an elderly family member after a long illness and a past, sudden loss of a young member in an accident. The Barlows had lost John, Ben's teenage son, when John and his girlfriend were asphyxiated while parked in his car the night before their senior prom, and Myra Owens lost her 26-year-old son years before in a motorcycle accident. It was not uncommon for respondents to talk about long-past deaths or to answer questions as if they were being asked about these much earlier deaths.

Throughout the study, it seemed clear that deaths of younger members were construed to be worse than deaths of older members. Whether sudden deaths were construed to be worse than less sudden deaths was not clear. Some interviewees thought death was easier to bear when there was a warning; others thought deaths that occurred unexpectedly were easier. Karrie Primo, who had experienced both the sudden death of her brother-in-law and the gradual death of her mother-in-law, talked of how the two deaths compared and how she and her husband disagreed about which had been more difficult:

Karri   Well, Ronnie's death, you know, when I knew my mother-in-law was going to die and I knew that she had the terminal cancer, I had such a harder time with that because she was such an optimistic and energetic and vibrant person. I had a hard time relating to her. I felt so bad for her. I felt much worse for her than I did for myself. I don't think of myself at that point, about what I have to lose and what I'm going to miss and how much I love her. But I just couldn't stop thinking about her, and facing her knowing she was going to die was so hard for me. I thought it was much harder than, um, Ronnie being killed instantly. And I expressed that many times to my husband and my husband didn't think so. He thought it was nicer to be able to say good-bye and tell that person how much you love them and share all those memories, but I saw Ronnie 45 minutes, an hour, before he died, standing out talking to him in the yard, looking up at the sky, saying what a beautiful day it was and I, and I, and um, I'm glad he didn't know except for just a few seconds that he was going to die. I'm glad I didn't have to face him knowing that. That's kind of a cowardly thing probably to say, but I am glad because that's a very difficult thing, although I did get to express the things that I wanted to express to my mother-in-law that I couldn't tell Ronnie.

Because she had had difficulty seeing her mother-in-law die slowly, Karrie was inclined, in at least this stage of her meaning-making process, to think of the sudden death of her brother-in-law as easier. It is important to note that her mother-in-law's death had been within a few months of the interview and that Ronnie's death, the one for which she was in the study, had occurred 21 months before. Using comparison, Karrie argues that sudden death is easier than a more gradual death. But, as she continues, we hear her considering her husband's belief that slower deaths are easier. She reveals both her own uncertainty and the interactive nature of meaning-making. She and her spouse had been comparing the deaths.

In a later interview, Karrie Primo's husband, Tim, made his own comparison of his mother's death with his brother-in-law, Ronnie's, death. Tim used the questions about Ronnie's death to tell what was foremost on his mind: his mother's recent death. He compared their deaths as follows:

Tim   Ah, they were both really hard. I had time to prepare for my mom's, you know, because she gradually died, 11 months. But for a while, we kind of figured she was getting better. And then she just within the 2 months, just 2 months, she just went downhill and then died. So it was a little easier to get ready for it, but then knowing that my dad would be by himself was really hard, you know. But they were both really hard, but Ronnie's, ah, was such a shock to the system and the whole family. This, you know, at least [with mother's] I had plenty of time to talk to my brothers about it and I'd been talking, I'd talked to my dad about it but not as, not like I did with my brothers, you know. So at least got to prepare for it. She planned her own funeral and all of that [pause] and she and

> I had [gotten] to tell her everything I ever wanted to tell her,
> you know, what she meant to me, and how she treated me as
> a kid, and everything like that, you know. Thank her and
> apologize to her and I was, in a way it was easier, you know,
> except it was my mom, which is, I was kind of a momma's
> boy as far as that, because, you know, I was the youngest, you
> know, I think anyway, that's why [teary, pause]. It was gradual,
> and we knew it was coming, and with Ronnie it was such a
> shock, it just knocked you right down.

This quote, in addition to elucidating how comparison was used to make meaning, is also a good example of two other features of family meaning-making. First, this use of comparison is part of Tim's telling of the substory "The Illness." Making comparisons was an integral part of his story, as it was for many respondents. Second, Tim revealed something about family sharing patterns when he reported talking with his brothers and his father about his mother's death but in different ways. Although it is not clear from this excerpt, Tim indicated elsewhere that he felt protective of his dad and therefore would not talk with him about certain things. The term *protectionism* was given to this feature of family meaning-making. In the analysis, protectionism was classified as a meaning-making inhibitor. Other features are discussed as they show up in the excerpts.

Most families, like the Primos, had a previous loss to which they could compare. The shared experience of losing a family member in the past seemed to shape how members made sense of the current loss. The Buchanan family, for instance, had had a very difficult time managing the death of Coral's mother, and by comparison, the death of Roland's mother was construed as wonderful. The Smith family shared the experience of their father's death, which was a painful 2-year process. Comparing it with Bob's sudden death, his wife and sister-in-law were able to agree that, if Bob had to die, the fast way was best. Tom Barlow compared his father's premature death with his mother's late death, concluding that he died too soon and she died too late.

NEGATIVE VERSUS POSITIVE COMPARISONS

Another interesting pattern that emerged was that comparison took both positive and negative forms. A *positive comparison* consisted of citing someone else's bad fortune and concluding that, by comparison, their own situation was not as bad. A *negative comparison* was just the opposite: The respondents cited someone who seemed to have had better fortune and concluded that their own situation was worse. Examples follow. The first positive comparison comes from Jenny Mackey, who referenced the death of a child that had been highly publicized at the time of the study:

Jenny   It's not a difficult thing, but it, ah, you know, I'm such a firm believer, as I say, I think that little 8-year-old girl that was kidnapped and raped and, ah, and all. You know, we never had, ah, Rich and I never had to go through losing a child like that. I mean that would be terrible.

Jenny could be said to be minimizing her own loss by finding someone else whose situation was worse. Or Jenny could also be thought of as using a positive comparison to establish herself in relation to a new reference group, the group made up of all those who have experienced the death of a family member. Among such a group, she could view herself as one of the more lucky ones. For one thing, as she pointed out, she and Rich never had to go through losing a child. Furthermore, his death was not as bad as that of the little girl. Although she did not directly compare the two deaths, the implication was that, compared with the little girl's death, Rich's death was better. Her comparison is positive because the Mackeys' experience was perceived to be better than that of the little girl's family.

George Miner made a positive comparison by citing the difference in the amount of time they had had with Anne, compared with someone lost to sudden death.

George   So, I don't know, but it's like I said, one thing I think about that the nights we had when Anne, then I go back and then I go to that questioning God and then I say, hey, you know, he gave you some quality time with her. [She] was diagnosed in January and took her in September, and we've had all those months to stroke her and love her and support her and let her know how much she was cared for. Where some of these people you read about in the paper they get in their cars and go down to the Tom Thumb and on the way there, they're bang and they're gone.

George cited the advantages his family had over those who experience sudden loss. At another point in the interview, George spoke of reading the obituaries and seeing so many young people in their 30s and 40s. George, like Jenny, seems to have been establishing himself in a new reference group, one made up of older parents who had lost a young adult child.

The study found fewer instances of negative comparisons than positive comparisons, but the negative comparisons were poignant. Jane Smith's 49-year-old husband, Bob, had a heart attack without any warning and died in the bed beside her. This is her negative comparison:

Jane   I get real irritated, as I probably shouldn't. Ah, a [man] in St. Paul who is a little older than Bob just had a heart transplant. He's alive and well and playing tennis, you know. Why him and not Bob? . . . Yeah, it's real tough for me. My boss has an aunt who is 102 years old and vegetating in a nursing home. Why? . . . Ah, you know, there are people out doing dastardly things. I don't know. But it's not going to do me any good to ponder it or worry about it. I'm here and I got to get on.

Jane questioned why Bob, a relatively young man, was dead. She compared her negative outcome with others' positive outcomes. In her new reference group, Jane, rather than compare herself with those worse off as the Mackeys and Miners did, chose to see herself in relation to those who were better off. Perhaps there is a societal ordering of more or less acceptable deaths, and outsiders might agree with Jane that Bob's death was worse than the death of anyone older, especially of a 102-year-old or the death of someone who does "dastardly deeds." Whether negative or positive, comparisons with other people's situations seemed to be used to establish the comparison maker somewhere on a better off/worse off continuum within a new reference group.

INTERACTIVE COMPARISON

Sometimes the use of comparison was interactive. Jenny, a widow, and Pam Mackey, her daughter, had a conversation about whether a comparison could be made between losing Rich and losing family pets.

Pam   Yeah, but we lost, and I'm not saying it's the same thing, but
          we lost how many dogs?

Jenny   Dogs are dogs, and as much as we love them . . .

Pam   Oh, bullshit!

Jenny   No! They were part of the family and felt just as bad, but it
          isn't the same. There is no way I could even compare it. There
          is no way to compare it as far as I'm concerned.

Pam   They were like sisters and brothers to me.

Jenny   It still is a loss. It's very definitely a loss, and they were, any
          dog we had was a member of the family and I don't deny that,
          but it, it's not the same, no way! It's just like, um, losing my
          mother I thought was, I said it before I thought, I hurt as much
          then as I could possibly hurt, and it's not the same at all. It's
          an entirely different loss.

Clearly, there is little consensus between Jenny and Pam as to the
relative difficulty of the death of family pets and Rich. Pam, an only
child, wanted more weight given to the loss of the family pets, which
were like brothers and sisters to her. Jenny refused and added that not
even losing her mother was the same as the loss of her spouse. One
gets the sense that, in cases such as this, losses that have occurred are
ranked. Perhaps the strategy of comparing contributed to rank ordering, and for some, ranking was a part of making sense of the death.

SIMILE AS A FORM OF COMPARISON

One of the more interesting forms of comparison was the *simile:*
respondents saying in so many words that some aspect of the death
was like something else. Karrie Primo compared the death of her
mother-in-law to birth, and she compared the experience of grieving
to labor. Derek Zeeman said the way he felt inside was like a volcano
that needed to erupt every once in a while and added that the interview
had given him an opportunity to do so.

The most elaborate simile came from Leo (in the Primo family),
who had lost Ronnie, his brother-in-law, and two other childhood
friends in the same airplane crash. Leo had also lost his father some
years before. Leo compared the deaths in this way:

Leo   Well, I think I would agree with Renata. It was an accident. It don't seem like, I really don't make sense of it. People live and they die. But like our father's, it seemed like the book was completed, there was a beginning, middle, and end. They died too young. They could have lived longer, had a more . . . completed book. Where Ronnie, ah, died like that, it was like your book, your life, is over right now. You'd have a hard time selling that to people because they expect some closure to it . . .I guess. I guess death is the same no matter how it comes, but yet it seems different.

Leo made meaning by using a simile to capture how his friends' lives were like unfinished books. It seems as if somehow the death of Leo's father served as an anchor point for comparing subsequent deaths.

In summary, comparison was found to be a widely used strategy. Its use varied according to whether comparisons were among deaths or according to features of the death. Sometimes comparisons were made through similes. Comparison was used by family members who drew on shared family experiences of death to make sense of the most recent death. This is one way in which meaning-making occurs in the family context.

"Coincidancing"

When the first families who were interviewed started making something of the "coincidences" that had occurred at and around the time of the death, I decided to ask all subsequent respondents about coincidences. In all, 49 references to coincidences were made: 13 occurred before a family member had died, 10 occurred at the time of the death, 18 occurred after the death, and 8 were not attached to any particular time. Coincidences, whenever they occurred, were referred to variously by family members as "weird," "freaky," or "strange" things that happened.

How to talk with respondents about so-called coincidences was a problem. Many respondents objected to the term. The term *coincidence* suggests a fatalistic view, as in the expression "It was just a coincidence." This interpretation was not in keeping with what most respondents believed. Coral, one of four respondents from the Buchanan family, responded to the use of the term *coincidence* by insisting there was no such thing as coincidence, that everything happened for a reason. Using the term *coincidence* along with a disclaimer that the term was less than ideal seemed to get the point across, and people were able to give their own meanings. The term "coinci*dancing*" was coined to capture the action of grieving people as they used coincidences to construct meanings. The *dancing* part of the term is intended as a play on the active and interactive nature of using coincidences to make sense of a death.

Nine of the 10 families in the study reported at least one coincidence associated with the death, for a total of 49 references. The Owens family, who was characterized earlier as most intent on presenting a good impression, was the only family who did not report at least one coincidence. When asked whether they had noticed any coincidences, at first they did not seem to know what was meant by the question. After a few examples were given, Myra responded to the examples, saying the family would not believe in coincidences because they were a very religious family. In a way, they seemed to be agreeing with Coral Buchanan, who said there are no such things as coincidences. Everything happens for a purpose, they said. Both the Buchanans and the Owenses may have been reacting to the fatalistic connotation the term *coincidence* has. The Buchanans saw coincidences as acts of God; the Owenses said they did not see any coincidences.

The following is a sample of the coincidences that were reported. They are classified according to their salient features.

RELUCTANT COINCIDANCING

Families were asked whether coincidences had occurred and, if so, what they had made of them. Some interesting patterns emerged. Some of the most common features of coincidancing were found in the interview with Ben and Julie Barlow, who had lost Ben's mother, Vera, age 85.

Ben   We got out to the cemetery, and it was a cloudy, overcast day and, believe it or not, the sun for a moment came out during the eulogy, or whatever, at the graveside. And I kept thinking, you know, we're gonna all get soaked, and it didn't start

	raining until everybody got back in their car and Julie made the comment, "Isn't that strange?"
Int	What did you make of it, Ben?
Ben	I just took it rather lightly, I think. I don't think anybody took it really too strongly, but I think there were some, including my wife, thought that it
Julie	[interrupting] Colleen and I did.
Ben	That it was, ah . . .
Julie	You know.
Ben	See, I didn't, not saying it could have been or couldn't have been, I just thought that it was sure nice that it didn't rain.
Int	Uh huh. You had a practical view of it?
Ben	Uh huh. I had a practical view; she had more of a spiritual view.
Julie	We did. It was kind of like the Lord let us have that little bit of sunshine and now we can shed a few little tears because it didn't rain heavy. It was just a few little sprinkles.
Int	Like a light rain?
Julie	Ya, and it's just like, well, you know, now Vera's here with me and everything is [pause] it just seemed like a sign. Colleen and I both felt that way, I mean [trails off]

In this excerpt, we can see how family interactions can occur around a so-called coincidence and can become grist for the family meaning-making mill. The experience of the sun coming out at the graveside was shared by the family, and there was family sharing at the funeral dinner about the meaning of the sun coming out. This is family coincidancing at its best. It is one way families make sense of their loss.

Furthermore, the funeral rituals referenced in the Barlow excerpt can be seen as stimulators of family meaning-making because they gave the family both the shared experience at the graveside and a chance to talk over dinner. The stimulation afforded by funeral rituals was particularly important in this family because of the inhibitory effect of cut-offs among family members that were in effect in more ordinary times. Coincidancing, like comparison, was something the family did spontaneously and automatically, not something they consciously chose from among other possible meaning-making strategies.

Something else can be learned from this particular excerpt. The way Julie and Ben coincidanced gives clues about the interaction between couple dynamics and meaning-making. In some family matters, including Vera's death, there was a certain reciprocity between Ben and Julie. As Julie's meanings tended more toward the irrational, Ben's tended more toward the rational, as if to balance the system. In the quotation above, Julie was quick to interpret the coincidence as a sign from the Lord and as an indication that Vera was there with her. Ben, by contrast, interpreted it as just being "nice" that it did not rain.

Ben's family history may have made it difficult for him to agree with Julie. Ben's mother, Vera, had had a history of debilitating mental illness. Ben's father had died when he was quite young. Ben, Jake, and Tom Barlow each reported doing things to keep their mother grounded in reality. Ben may have seen Julie's more irrational responses as indicators that she was becoming more and more irrational as his mother had. Ben might well have felt the need to rationalize the coincidental events to keep Julie grounded. These data suggest that couple and family dynamics are integral, not tangential, to the meaning-making process.

Not unlike Ben Barlow, Rafi Miner tended to rationalize coincidances. Rafi referred to making something of coincidences as "magical thinking." In an individual interview, Rafi responded in the following way to the question whether he had noticed any coincidences:

Rafi   Well, I'm not big on magical thinking. So, even though there are things that other people have thought of, coincidences like that. I assume that's what you're asking about.

Int   Um huh, yeah.

Rafi   . . . For instance, I'm not sure exactly how my daughter thinks about this, but she got pregnant shortly before Anne died. And she has told me that if it's a girl she's going to name it after her mom. And I believe that she has some magical thinking about that, that somehow it's her mom's spirit going into the next generation, you know, and I told you that her sister Laura has quite blatantly got magical thinking about, just the fact that I use that term, to describe to you what I think about it. Um, but I just, I would never interpret anything that way, you know.

Rafi, like Ben, was able to identify coincidences and report how others in the family used them despite his own reluctance to give coincidences special meaning. Rafi's actions could be cast as an unwillingness to engage in coincidancing, or it may be that resistance on the part of some members may be a necessary part of the coincidance.

In reporting how other members of the family construed coincidences, Rafi identified the meaning that Ann's daughter, Edna, had attached to the coincidence of her pregnancy that began during her mother's final illness. The grief literature is replete with instances of families replacing lost family members, sometimes giving the new member the deceased's name and/or expecting the new member to fill the roles vacated by the lost member. In this study, two coincidental pregnancies commenced near the time of the death, and in one family the attributes of the deceased were powerfully identified in a child who was 3 weeks old at the time her father was killed in an accident.

In the next excerpt, Rafi compared his beliefs with those of other family members, noting that they tended to engage in magical thinking, which he did not. The fact that Rafi presented his interpretation of coincidences to others in the family supports the notion that family dynamics plays a role in the attachment of meanings. Rafi's response may have been simply a reporting of individual differences, but it seems that he, like Ben, was reactive to the extremes of other family members. Rafi's role could have been to represent the rational in a system where other members tended to be irrational in order to balance the system. Other family members readily attached elaborate meanings to coincidences. Rafi resisted.

Rafi continued his response to the coincidence question in a very interesting way. Although he had a personal rule against magical thinking, he still had thoughts about what coincidences might mean:

Rafi   I can't think of anything. I mean it's possible that something would happen and I would, against my better judgment, I would have a thought about, oh, this is weird or this is, is what a coincidence, oh, yeah, I take it back.

Int   Did you come up with one?

Rafi   Right when she died, a whole bunch of stuff broke right at once. The garage door opener broke. The toaster broke. And one of the ovens went out. And the refrigerator broke. It was very strange.

Int   Is it going to take a lot of coincidences to make a believer out of you, Rafi?

Rafi   Well, you know, because when we had the shivah, that crossed
         my mind. It was pretty hard. You know, the refrigerator wasn't
         working and I couldn't get out of the garage. The toaster and
         the oven still hadn't been fixed, but those other things we got
         fixed right away.

Int   Garage, fridge, toaster, and oven all quit. Like what was the
         time line?

Rafi   Oh, geeze, I can't remember. It was an extended time line. It
         might have been over a couple of months or whatever, but
         you kind of compress it all at once. I think that the toaster
         and the garage, no the refrigerator and the garage, were like,
         the guy came to fix the refrigerator the day I was planning the
         funeral. So that was like right in there. And the garage door
         opener was the same thing. I believe it was right when I was
         planning the funeral. It was like right there. The oven was
         maybe a little bit after and the toaster was a little before.

Int   What do you make of it, Rafi? I hear some things that you
         don't make of it. What do you do with it in your head?

Rafi   Oh, I mean that the irrational part of me thinks, oh, well, it's
         just kind of like everything was like, all those mechanical
         things were in mourning [teary-eyed]. I just, you know, basi-
         cally just, I think it was a coincidence. Except it was a pain in
         the ass.

Int   Yes, of course. That certainly is another interpretation, isn't
         it? A little more rational one.

Rafi   Yeah. Yeah. I keep the magical part pretty well in check.

The notion that the household equipment might be in mourning
for Anne elicited great sadness. It was clear that such a meaning had
occurred to Rafi and that such meanings were laden with feelings
regardless of how irrational they were.

COINCIDENCES AS PHYSICAL SYMPTOMS

Some so-called coincidences had to do with family members experiencing physical symptoms. The Primo family provided a prime
example. They reported that some of their members experienced
physical symptoms at the exact time Ronnie was killed. The interview

was with Rena, his widow; her sister, Karrie; and her parents, Dominic and Joyce. The family reported it this way:

Rena	Well, I remember at the time of his death that Karrie was doing my hair and I got sick, in my stomach.
Int	You mean about the time he would have been in the
Rena	The actually, the actual time that he got killed.
Karrie	Yeah, we narrowed down what we were doing, of course, at the time he was killed. It was like 11:57, wasn't it?
Rena	11:58, and I remember it was a couple minutes before 12:00 and you were done with my hair. I said I gotta get going, I just feel sick. I had my kids there, of course. I just related it to queasy stomach after the baby. But I know his sisters and brothers all say the same thing. They all felt
Karrie	Felt the same thing
Rena	You know, at that particular time of day.
Dominic	Is that right?
Joyce	That time of day
Rena	It's really weird.
Int	And what do you make of that, Rena? What do you make of that having happened?
Rena	Um [pause] I don't know. It's just kind of [pause] I don't know, kind of psychic, you know what I mean, something [pause] just something strange.

In a time of disconnection, sharing a physical reaction at the time of death may have brought a sense of connection.

Members of this family were not able to say much about what they made of the coincidental physical symptoms except that the family was perhaps psychic. The implicit meaning was "We are very close; when one hurts, we all hurt." In subsequent interviews, other Primo family members also reported having physical symptoms at the time of the death. Interestingly, the parents, Dominic and Joyce, were not privy to the information about the younger generation having had physical symptoms until they heard about it at the interview. This finding underscores the notions that data vary, depending on who is being interviewed, that family meaning-making occurs on all systems levels, and that the interview itself is a meaning-making stimulator. Interestingly, all 11 members of the Primo family coincidanced.

COINCIDENCES AS PREMONITIONS

Another pattern that emerged from the coincidence data was that some coincidental events were construed as premonitory. Some families used coincidancing to construe unexpected deaths as somehow expected. The data show 12 instances in which family members pointed retrospectively to coincidental events that either had warned of the death or provided signs that something was wrong at the actual time of the death. In the previous excerpt, we saw how the Primos construed their physical symptoms as warnings to them. Mark and Barb Buchanan reported leaving a party to make a trip to Mark's parents' house just at the time Gramma was drawing her last breath. Evelyn Munson reported that Claude's dream about his deceased mother meant that he knew he was going to die. Fran Munson thought her brother's prescheduled arrival home from abroad in time for the wake was because of a premonition.

Sometimes coincidences were seen as someone's premonitions that the death was expected, or at least someone knew it was occurring at the time. In the next excerpt of an interview with Lisa and Jane Smith, Lisa is responding to the question whether they had noticed any coincidences. Lisa reported an unusual telephone call and indicated that her mother and father-in-law had not been able to sleep the night of Bob's death:

Lisa   Not personally. My mother said [pause] Bob called the day before. Well [pause] he died after midnight. That day he called Greg and talked to him. He was doing something, making something. It is very rare that he'll call. Jane will call.

Int   So that wasn't a very usual occurrence then, for Greg and Bob to have a conversation?

Lisa   Right.

Int   What do you make of that, either one, either your mother not sleeping or Greg calling?

Lisa   I'm glad that he called and Greg talked to him. I think it was good for Greg, um [pause] I don't think it was maybe a coincidence really that he [trailing off]

Int	Do you think there was any meaning to your mother being awake?
Lisa	Yeah, I think so. I think sometimes she can sense things are wrong that I didn't, that are wrong [pause] somewhere.
Int	. . . What would your mother make of that, or did you hear her say?
Lisa	I think she thought it was a premonition or [that] something was happening. She was more thinking of my great-grand-father, something in the family [pause] she felt something was wrong somewhere. I think I heard Bob's dad say something to that effect too, but I don't remember exactly, but he couldn't sleep that night.
Int	Um . . . Did he make anything of it, or did he just make a statement?
Lisa	Ah, I heard him talking about it, but I didn't listen to exactly what it was. My mom had said that to me when I called her. That I was picking her up when it happened. Ed had said something about it and she said, "I couldn't sleep either."
Int	Um [pause] so we have the two grandparents, the mother and the father on either side, not sleeping well that night?
Lisa	Right.
Int	What do you make of that, those kinds of things, or that in particular?
Lisa	I think it can happen. I think we sometimes sense some-thing . . . I mean, I don't think they're always going to not sleep because something is happening, but maybe when some-thing as close to them as [pause] they can sense that [pause] like a twin can feel when another twin is [trailing off]

The two coincidences here are Bob's unusual call to his brother-in-law and the grandparents not sleeping. In regard to the telephone call, the family may have been searching for any evidence that Bob himself had sensed he was going to die and that had been his reason for calling Greg.

One of the most important meanings found in this study had to do with the attitude of the deceased toward their own demise, particularly that they somehow knew it was coming. The notion that Bob may have sensed death coming was supported by the fact that he had also written a letter about arrangements and left it in his drawer where Jane could not miss it.

Lisa and Jane were not able to say what the coincidental sleepless-ness meant to family members, but the symptoms were labeled as some form of premonition, and their occurrence was shared with other family members. As with the Primo family, the implied meaning was that the family was connected in some way, so when something went wrong with one family member, others sensed it. That which sounded unexpected could be construed by family members as expected, or at least known, in some way, thus increasing their sense of control and lessening the chaos.

COINCIDENCES AS ACTS OF THE DECEASED OR AS ACTS OF GOD

Finally, some respondents took coincidences to mean that either the deceased or God or both were actively involved in affairs around the time of the death. The previously cited example from the Barlow family about the sun shining in the cemetery during Vera's eulogy is a prime example. Julie Barlow said it was brought about by both Vera and the Lord. Linda Miner reported that after she had prayed again and again for God to let her know where her sister Anne was, the song "I'm in Heaven" came on the radio. The Mackey family took the unexplained availability of a previously unavailable cemetery plot as a sign that a Higher Power was involved. Jenny Mackey gave credit to God for a coincidental, very soothing Northern Lights show in the boundary waters at a time when she was feeling saddest. Jane Smith told of finding a letter her husband had left for her in his bureau drawer right when she had been feeling at her wit's end and had gone to their bedroom to cry and escape the crowd at her house. She marveled at the coincidence and construed it to mean that Bob had tried to take care of her.

What can one conclude about coincidancing? Families do use coincidences to make sense of their loss. There is an interaction between coincidancing and family dynamics. What families make of so-called coincidences has consequences for how they grieve. Asking families about coincidences could function as a projective technique of sorts. Coincidences could be thought of as the inkblots on which respondents project their thoughts. In family conversations, coinci-dences, not unlike dreams, become grist for the family meaning-making mill. In this study, family members noticed coincidences together, agreed and disagreed about what they meant, and tried to influence each other to see coincidences in certain ways. Asking bereaved families what they make of coincidences provides a window into the family's meaning system.

Summary

In this chapter, the meaning-making strategies of storytelling, dreaming, comparing, and coincidancing were illustrated. Stories were shown to have themes that reveal family meanings. Dreams dreamed and talked about in the family were shown to be meaning laden. Bereaved families compared their loss with the losses of others in order to make sense of the death and, perhaps, to establish themselves within the reference group of all bereaved. Coincidancing was presented as a strategy used by families to make sense of their loss by projecting meaning onto events coincidental to the death. Emphasis was placed on how certain factors stimulate, and others inhibit, the family meaning process. Examples were given of the interaction between family meaning-making and family dynamics.

In the next chapter, the meaning-making strategies that are discussed include ways families made sense of their loss by characterizing the person who died and by using "family speak," an everyday way of talking.

6

Characterization and Family Speak

Characterization

Another way family members in this study made sense of their loss was by characterizing the deceased. Families talked about who the deceased was as a person, and often how the deceased's character related to the way he or she died. Characterizing the deceased could be thought of as a way of putting the lost member's death into context. No direct questions were asked about how respondents would characterize the deceased. Characterizations were simply shared.

The data show 70 instances of families characterizing the person who had died. The majority of family members tended to say positive things about the deceased. Of the 70 instances of characterization, 60 were positive and 10 were negative. A few seemed to exaggerate the good qualities of the lost member in a manner reminiscent of Helena Lopata's "sanctification of the deceased" (Lopata, 1981). Lopata theorized that making spouses saintly or other-worldly somehow lessened the pain of missing them as real flesh-and-blood beings, justifying and symbolizing the strong feelings of grief.

A major finding was that when the deceased was characterized negatively, a positive characterization almost always followed. It was as if family members felt the need to say something that would neutralize their negative remarks. In some instances, the adage "Never speak ill of the dead" was operative. The use of characterization to make meaning was evident in all the interviews, but it was particularly vivid in the Primo family interviews.

TYPICAL CHARACTERIZATION

The Primo family's struggle was that Ronnie, who had two young children, took the risk of flying with his pilot friend on his first trip with passengers. In the next excerpt, Ronnie's sister-in-law, Karrie, when asked whether she ever talked with Ronnie about death, launched into an extensive characterization of him.

Int   Did you ever talk about death with Ronnie? Do you remember any talks with him?

Karrie   Oh, yes, yes. We talked about death.

Int   Does anything in particular stand out?

Karrie   Well, he said he didn't think he'd ever live to be 50. He said that to me many times. Ronnie was just a real, could be real cocky and real, just real, appear real confident, and, you know, real outgoing and just had such a really fun personality. A person could just take that as, oh, that's kind of a fly-by to me.

Int   Kind of write it off?

Karrie   Yes, and he was being, he was a very, very handsome man and he was very vain. And so it did kind of fit in. He wasn't the type to want to get old, real old and real sick. Had a very little grey hair and was very meticulous about his appearance . . .

Int   Let me see if I am hearing anything here, and maybe I'm not. Is there any way that you think . . . that somehow there was a part of him that would have wanted it that way, or is that not, [pause] I don't mean wishing to die, but I mean

Karrie   [interrupting] No, no, no.

Int   Fit's his style?

Karrie   Absolutely fits his style. It totally fit his style. He wasn't, ah, he wasn't a totally reckless man, totally reckless, but he was a man to take risks, as is Rena. She's that type of person, along with my dad—a risk taker, someone who'd like to, who'd go to Vegas and, you know, play blackjack with some high numbers, who liked to kind of live more in the fast lane. He and Rena are both, Ronnie was like that just like Rena is and, like I said, their personalities were alike in many ways . . . There was, ah, there was a few newspaper articles written about Ronnie afterwards and his friends . . . and my mom and I, we have never, we could never bring ourselves to read the articles yet. I have never read the articles; neither has she. But we just both laughed because we said Ronnie would have loved this. He loved attention. He loved attention. Loved to be the center of attention, loved to be the center of attention. Was a very competitive athlete. He would have loved that, being on the front [page]. If he had to die, he would have liked to have made the front page like he did. Like you said, not that he was suicidal by any means, but he would have liked that drama. Making the front page and having those stories written about him, he would have loved that.

Karrie used the question about discussing death with Ronnie to characterize him. The meaning that Karrie attached to the death by characterizing Ronnie was that if Ronnie had to die, he would have chosen a spectacular, front-page death. Characterization led also to the meaning that, given Ronnie's proclivity for living in the fast lane, taking risks, and never wanting to grow old, one could understand, if not predict, his dramatic, youthful death. Karrie seemed to be attempting to make Ronnie's death more acceptable by construing it as occurring in a way Ronnie would have chosen.

This excerpt is another example of how using probes to delve deeper into respondents' meanings drew the interviewer into the meaning-making process. Here, the probe was directed at Karrie's remark that the way Ronnie died "did kind of fit in." In an attempt to verify her meaning, the notion of "Ronnie's style" was introduced, and Karrie adopted it. An argument could be made that the introduction of this phrase influenced her thinking in some way. It was difficult throughout the study to obtain in-depth, accurate information without becoming somewhat of a co-constructor in the meaning-making process. It was particularly difficult to avoid influencing the meaning-making process while attempting to check out patterns that had begun to emerge in earlier interviews. The interview process, then, must be considered a meaning-making stimulator.

An important meaning-making feature also found in the previous excerpt is the existence of subsystems of meaning-making within families. Karrie reported that she and her mother had talked and laughed about how Ronnie, liking to be the center of attention, would have loved having the story of his death on the front page of the newspaper. Nothing of the kind was mentioned in the family interview, nor were any references made to sharing this meaning when Rena, Ronnie's wife, was present. The notion that Ronnie's death was congruent with his character seemed to be a meaning that belonged to a mother-daughter subsystem, and not to systems that included his widow.

Karrie offered a second, long characterization of Ronnie that gave further evidence of meaning-making subsystems in the Primo family:

Karrie   Yes, things just happen. I think that you can take a lot of steps, just like, you know, a lot of times, a couple of times since this has happened, I've even thought, Ugh, but just for a brief second, because I loved Ronnie so much, and I knew he didn't want to die, but just for brief lapses I thought, ah, Ronnie, that was selfish, that was selfish to take that chance with a 3-week-old baby and a wife and a child. That was selfish, Ronnie. Because he was that type of guy that wanted to do those things to make him feel alive. You know what I mean, a risk taker . . . approaching his midlife time or whatever. You know, just, this was something to go out and do, you know. To challenge the skies or whatever, and not like so much a macho thing, but just an adventurous thing. He had done a lot in his life. He had been in the service. He had had a lot of life experiences. And to me he's the type that just wanted to grab another one. But for a couple brief moments I thought, geeze, Ronnie, that was selfish. You should have thought that, gosh, you know, something could happen. Sure, it's far-fetched. You're more likely to die in a car accident, but it could happen. You know what I mean? I thought that at times, but I quickly put that out of my mind, just because I loved him so much, and I don't want to be, I don't want to be angry at him, and I don't. You know, I knew he didn't want to die.

Int   That would be a thought that you had lingering in your mind as not helpful?

Karrie   Exactly. To me it's, what, what good is that going to do to feel negative, and I would never express that to Rena because I know she's probably already thought that, and I'm sure she's gone through that anger at him. I hope she has, you know, because, and that's not helpful to her, and I really try to be careful about what I say about him and the situation in front of her, because a lot of times people so quickly are equipped to judge and to say things that, that, really, that can really linger a long time if someone was grieving, you know.

Int   Uh huh, so that would be something that you'd kind of keep to yourself?

Karrie   Exactly.

Int   You wouldn't say that out loud, especially in front of Rena.

Karrie   Yeah.

Int   Would you say it in front of other family members?

Karrie   I would say it in front of my parents, yeah. And I'm sure they would agree with me. My dad wanted to talk him out of it.

Karrie characterized Ronnie as being selfish for having taken the risk of flying but could not allow herself to be angry at him, certainly not in front of her sister, his widow. That part of her meaning-making she did with other family members. Karrie's characterization led to the implicit negative meaning that the death was preventable, and what's more, preventable by Ronnie himself.

This meaning-making sequence is a good example of how specific meanings about the death seemed affected by the emotions of bereavement. Negative constructions, such as, "Ronnie was selfish," elicited feelings of anger for Karrie, and not wanting to feel angry, she constructed other meanings, such as how it does no good to be angry and how Ronnie did not want to die. By downplaying the meanings related to Ronnie's selfish character and the preventability of his death, Karrie protected herself from feeling her unwelcome anger. This is how meanings, the way the death is construed, can affect the grieving process.

In the previous passage, it can also be seen how meaning-making occurred at a number of systems levels and consisted of an interaction among family rules, meaning-making strategies, and a variety of inhibitors and stimulators of the meaning-making process. Although this was an individual interview, Karrie referenced the subsystem that included her father, her mother, and herself. Within that subsystem, one meaning was that Ronnie had been selfish to risk flying. Karrie reported that she and her parents shared this meaning but that she would not share it with her sister, Rena. Frequent, daily interactions that Karrie and Rena had with their parents and with each other because of living and working together functioned as meaning-making stimulators.

Within the Primo family's meaning-making systems, some family rules were operative. One rule was that family members should protect one another from sensitive information, a dynamic referred to earlier as *protectionism*. Karrie protected her sister by not saying Ronnie was selfish. Or, Karrie's withholding negative interpretations of Ronnie's behavior may have been governed by family rules favoring a show of respect and politeness. Respect and politeness rules might call for the less bereaved family members to defer to the most bereaved family member, Rena, to allow her to take the lead in discussions of the death and for her meanings to have more weight.

Another family rule that may have been operative in the Primo family and revealed by Karrie in the last excerpt was a rule against feeling negative emotions. Karrie reported that she sometimes felt angry at Ronnie for taking the risk of flying but "quickly put the thought out of her mind." The rationale Karrie gave for disallowing her negative feelings was that it would do no good to feel angry and that she loved Ronnie so much. The implications were (a) because negative feelings do not change things, they are not justified, and (b) that, in this family, one does not have angry feelings toward someone he or she loves. Such family rules would lobby against intrafamily sharing of any negative meanings that members might have constructed and further inhibit the family meaning-making process. By contrast, in families such as the Miner family, whose rules prohibiting negative emotions were not as pronounced, members were more able to share their negative constructions about the death.

Finally, Karrie's characterization of Ronnie serves as an excellent example of how complicated family meaning-making really is, how unlikely it is to be captured by a single model. Meaning-making occurs on a variety of systems levels and involves an interaction of many factors, including family rules, a variety of meaning-making strategies, and inhibitors and stimulators of the meaning-making process. In this study, different subsystems within the families were found to have constructed different meanings, yet the process was so family-bound, so contextual, that it was difficult to think of it as anything other than family meaning-making. Other instances of characterization of the deceased were grouped according to their similarities. Examples from major groups follow.

BALANCING THE FAMILY BY POSITIVE CHARACTERIZATIONS

Although patterns associated with characterization were most pronounced in the Primo family, such patterns were found in other families as well. This next example comes from an interview with Sam Munson, a man in his late 30s who believed that his father had died from complications of alcohol abuse. Toward the end of the interview, when Sam was asked whether he wanted to add anything, he proceeded to characterize his father in the following manner:

Sam   Well, I don't know [pause] the kind of man he was is kind of understated. He was just this, he was just that, or he drank too much, or I mean all these things. I don't think, even among the family members, we don't realize even with his faults what a great guy he was. Just a genuinely great guy. He was opinionated, prejudiced, he could make you realize it, he could turn you the other way and you wouldn't be prejudice after talking to him because he was so blatant. He was just like Archie Bunker. You don't want [pause]

Int   To be like this?

Sam   Right, you just want to be the opposite, a little reverse psychology. But with all the things that he was, he was just a very straightforward, good person. If he liked you, he liked you. If he didn't, he didn't. There was not a lot of b.s. to go with that.

In his characterization, Sam chose, as the majority of respondents did, to highlight Claude's positive traits while minimizing what was negative about him. Several explanations for Sam's positive characterization are possible. The most feasible is that Sam may have felt the need to represent the good things about his father to others because he knew that his brother, Darren, characterized Claude negatively, especially in regard to Claude's lifestyle. Perhaps Sam also was trying to convince himself of his father's good traits as a hedge against his loss of hopes that his father would someday change.

Parkes and Weiss (1983) reported that the bereaved in conflicted relationships have a double loss: the loss of the person and the loss of the possibility that things will one day be resolved. It was not uncommon for family members to attempt to construct positive meanings out of the rubble of negative family circumstances. The meaning that Sam salvaged was that, despite Claude's persistence in an unhealthy lifestyle that had led inexorably to his death, his father was a good man.

Sam's choice to characterize his father positively revealed something more about family meaning-making—namely, how family structure and family meaning-making interact. A reciprocal relationship seemed to exist between family structure and family meaning-making systems in that members were more likely to make meaning with members within preexisting coalitions and alliances than they were with family members outside these coalitions and alliances. Reciprocally, the meanings made within such subsystems helped in maintaining subsystems boundaries. Differences in meanings among subsystems seemed to influence bereavement patterns, so different subsystems grieved differently.

Sam and his wife seemed more at peace with Claude's death because they were able to more positively characterize Claude overall. Darren and his family seemed more distressed as they negatively characterized Claude and blamed him for not choosing to change his lifestyle.

In the next two excerpts, Jake Barlow, like Sam Munson, can be seen to have provided more positive characterizations than did some members of his family. Unlike Sam, however, Jake was able to sway family members toward more positive characterizations. The next excerpt is also an example of how some respondents followed negative characterizations with positive statements about the deceased. Jake Barlow, the oldest of Vera Barlow's three sons and the one who assumed the major responsibility for her affairs, characterized Vera this way:

Jake My mother died. She probably could have lived a little longer had she taken better care of herself. But she didn't. Ah, she wasn't positive. She had a negative attitude in

general and didn't care. Although I don't know how much
of a factor that was in shortening her life, if she'd have had
a different longevity, had she not had cancer, cancer certainly isn't what killed her. Ah, if she had a different attitude,
ah, would that have made any difference? I don't think so.
She got good care, ah, in fact she got great care and, ah, I
think she died of a very natural condition—just plain of old
age. Things just quit working. . . . In her case, she lived to
be 85 years old, and she made the best of it, that she was
capable of making it.

Jake started by characterizing his mother as having a negative
attitude: not caring and not taking care of herself. Toward the end of
the quote, he was more positive, saying she made the best of it. Jake
talked about having examined his mother's private papers and was
impressed with how, despite her limitations, she had devised ways to
survive.

The following excerpt reveals how Jake's youngest brother, Tom,
characterized his mother negatively and how he came to adopt Jake's
positive characterization of her. Tom lived out of state and had very
little contact with his mother in the years preceding her death. It was
clear from interviews with family members that Tom's experience with
his mother had been quite different from that of the other siblings. He
was interviewed by telephone. Because of equipment failure, a few
words were inaudible.

Tom   So he [meaning Jake] would force me to go visit my mother
        [inaudible] and I was rather upset with her. But I always still
        had a problem with my mother because I didn't understand
        why, but, I guess after discussing it with Jake, maybe because
        she didn't know how to deal with you. Now she wasn't a
        very intelligent woman. And, but, I have to give her some
        credit. I mean [inaudible] she was my mother. And that takes
        a lot of work to bring children up.

Tom adopted Jake's meanings about how well their mother had
done, considering her limits, and together they constructed meanings
that included how she would be remembered. This is an excellent
example of how family meaning-making occurs, over time, among
multiple members and over multiple means of communication.

EXCESSIVELY POSITIVE CHARACTERIZATIONS

As mentioned earlier, family members, for a variety of reasons, tended toward positive characterizations of the person who had died. The most obvious explanation is that family members wanted outsiders to think well of their family, a matter of giving a socially desirable answer to the interview questions. This possibility seems the most likely for the Owens family, in which not a single negative word was spoken about the deceased by three family members in 2 ½ hours. As was mentioned before, this family was particularly concerned about its image in the community.

No discussion of characterization of the deceased as a meaning-making strategy would be complete without giving examples of how positive characterization of the deceased was so excessive as to fit Helena Lopata's (1981) description of the phenomenon called *sanctification of the deceased*. Sanctification of the deceased is said to have occurred when the person who has died is described by the bereaved as saintlike or other-worldly.

In this study, sanctification of the deceased occurred in 6 out of the 10 families interviewed. In the Miner family, this pattern emerged most clearly. The way Anne was described suggested a saintlike quality.

Anne was the oldest girl in a family of eight children. Her father told how Anne had dropped out of high school to take care of her mother, who had suffered a disabling heart attack. A younger brother described her as more like his mother than his real mother. He told how she had assumed great responsibility for parenting both him and other younger siblings. The family expressed great pride that she was later able to finish high school and earn a college degree. Her oldest brother expressed regret that Anne would not be there to help him through his own dying process. Anne was praised by several family members for her good work as a professional.

Anne was highly praised by the family for raising two children single-handedly following her divorce. According to accounts from her siblings, after she remarried she continued to be the family organizer, in charge of family rituals and always available to everyone. She even came to her sister-in-law in her mourning dream. Her second husband credited her with teaching him how to love. In the last of three interviews with Anne's family members, her father summed it all up:

George   She never got a break. She worked for all she had. . . . She
was upbeat, optimistic, and didn't complain. . . . She was
brave not to fight death and was loved by many.

In the individual interview, Rafi, Anne's spouse, reacted to how
they all had "sanctified" Anne, noting the implications it had for him
as he attempted to establish new relationships:

Rafi   Part of it, I suppose, is idealization not just on my part but
everybody's part that, you know, how wonderful our relationship was and how wonderful she was and so on. But then
you think about going on from there, you know. And on the
one hand, because I loved her so much and I was so happy
being with her and being in love with her, I don't have any
question that I want to have another relationship like that.
But I think that, I think that I might be kind of critical of
everybody that I relate to because they won't be her. And
somehow that's going to be letting go of that and letting
some other relationship just be itself. It's going to be kind
of hard because it was a really good relationship in a lot of
ways. . . . That's just the way it was.

This excerpt reveals how the meaning given to the death, particularly how the deceased was characterized, affected the course of
bereavement. Rafi noted that his idealization of Anne had made it
difficult for him to have another relationship. Perhaps sanctifying the
deceased plays a protective role, protecting the bereaved from involvement with others: Others could be viewed as "mere mortals" by
comparison and, therefore, unworthy.

It is interesting to note that, in the individual interview above, Rafi
spoke to the effect his idealization of Anne had had on the course of
his bereavement, whereas in the family interview below, he refrained
from mentioning how he was affected and assumed his role as family
sage, calling the family to task for sanctifying Anne.

These two excerpts provide good examples of how individual and
family interviews differed. Meaning-making in family interviews tended
to have more of an interactive nature. More deviant or private
meanings were less likely to be expressed than they were in individual
interviews. A variety of family roles were assumed, and members
tended to play to the family audience as much as, or more than, to the

interviewer. Eight Miner family members were present for the interview from which the following excerpt is taken. Rafi discusses Anne's alleged "sainthood":

Rafi   I think it's interesting that . . . it's probably not very unusual, but I think to a certain extent we've idealized Anne. Anne, we all loved her, but she was not a saint. Or if she was a saint, then saints are not as perfect as what we think they were. You know, I mean, like when you were talking about she was angry you [inaudible] she had a temper. She didn't like people to do, to mess with her, and when she wanted certain things to happen, like if she wanted to go to this movie and not that movie, you went to the one that she wanted you to go to. She was strong-willed and, you know, she could be real bitchy, I mean she always, even went more than once. [family members giggle] And, uh, you know, and she didn't always conduct her life in the best possible way. I mean she, [the] transition from, from her first family to being a single parent to not, to being our family was real messy with lots of pain and lots of angry feelings on everybody's part, so I think that, I don't know. I mean that's not any news to you that we would do that, but I think that's part of, part of it too, that I think that everybody has taken the best of Anne and put their love and all their feelings into that and I think that, that uh, you know, it's just something. [pause] They must really bring back all the other stuff, the times that we were sick of her, or we wished that she would, you know, do something different or whatever. . . . We all had those days. Or the times that she was mad at us, you know, whether we believed it or not.

Rafi's meanings were different in that he was the only one of the 11 family members interviewed to mention any of Anne's negative attributes or behaviors. Rafi's status as in-law may have given him more of an outsider's view, the in-law effect as it was described earlier. This may have resulted in the construction of different meanings. He lacked the childhood interactions with Anne that her siblings had. Rafi may have had greatest latitude to speak his mind if family members saw him as being the most bereaved. It also seems important to consider that Rafi had already begun a new relationship. The new relationship might better be served by less idealization of Anne and the remembering of what was not so positive about her. And because of his new relationship, Rafi may have been less worried about getting along with Anne's family.

Although Rafi reminded family members of Anne's character flaws, it did little to change the way they spoke of her in the remainder of the interview. They did not appear to have adopted Rafi's less positive characterizations, but rather continued to talk of her in saintly terms. The characterization done by the Miner family as a whole led to the agreed-upon meaning that, being a saint, Anne did not deserve to die. This meaning was a major theme in the story of her death. Characterization appeared to be a very useful and common strategy.

When transcripts were examined line by line for the actual mechanisms of family meaning-making, it was seen that family members used ordinary communication skills to make sense of the death. Excerpts of their interactions referred to as *family speak* are discussed next.

"Family Speak"

One of the most important findings in this study was the way families used ordinary conversation to make sense of the death of a family member. When the intricacies of their conversations were analyzed, it was possible to identify and name certain simple communication methods.

When family members used these simple communication methods to make sense of the death, the result was an intricate weaving together of individual threads of meaning. This verbal weaving was dubbed *family speak*. Family speak includes agreeing/disagreeing, referencing, interrupting, echoing, finishing sentences, elaborating, and questioning. Examples of how each of these strategies fits into family speak are given. Occasional references are made to previously introduced meaning-making features, including meaning-making inhibitors and stimulators. Once again, consideration is given to the effect of the interview on the meaning-making process.

AGREEING/DISAGREEING AND REFERENCING

Agreeing/disagreeing was the most commonly found elemental strategy: 48 examples were identified. This strategy typically involved one family member stating what he or she made of a particular aspect of the death, and others agreeing or disagreeing with the speaker.

In an interview with members of the Smith family, Jane, the wife of the deceased; and her sister, Lisa, were asked where they thought Bob was after his death:

Jane   Who knows. I mean, you know, and the more I read about it and the more I think about it, the more unsure I probably am. I would like to think that as soon as you die, somehow your soul or your being ascends or, you know, is somehow with God and things are better. And somewhere I read a long time ago that maybe dying is like when you're a baby in a mother's womb to begin with. You leave that womb and you go to something that you at least think is better, whether it is or not. And that you, hopefully, that's what happens when you die. I don't like to, and I know there is a belief that you, just, when you die, you just lie in the ground until some point in time when there is a Second Coming or something. Maybe that's, who knows. [pause]

Lisa   I totally agree with Jane. I've read a lot and heard so many different views but I can't believe that you're just not somewhere after you die.

The question where the deceased was after death elicited a plethora of death-related meanings from most families. This exchange between Jane and Lisa represents the making of a typical meaning statement and of family members' agreeing. In this case, interviewer questions were asked between responses, but in most instances of agreeing/ disagreeing, this was not the case: One family member would agree or disagree with another without prompting from the interviewer.

The Jane-and-Lisa excerpt represents both the strategy of agreeing and the strategy of *referencing*. Lisa identified Jane as the family member with whom she agreed, and she restated Jane's meaning as she heard it. It was not uncommon for family members to reference each other's meanings. In some instances, statements indicated agreement with the family as a whole; in other instances, with certain subsystems within the family; or as in this case, with one individual. When the person in the room with whom the speaker agreed was identified nonverbally, the interaction did not show up in the transcript; neither did instances of family members nodding their heads in agreement. Agreeing and referencing were not always found in tandem, as was the case in this instance.

The above excerpt is also another example of the relationship between family structure and meaning systems. Family subsystems that existed before the death functioned as satellites of meaning-making after the death. Over the years, Lisa and Jane, as the middle generation and the only children, joined in a well-differentiated alliance. They differentiated themselves clearly from the older generation, from their children, and from their husbands. Their subsystem of meaning included many shared meanings about their childhood, including a shared reality about their father's alcohol abuse and its consequences. Agreement and referencing between Jane and Lisa were reciprocal.

In the excerpt that follows, family dynamics and the strategy of disagreeing can be seen to interact. Disagreeing can be seen as one way in which individual family members differentiate themselves. The interview from which the next excerpt is taken included Steve and Randy Primo and their brother-in-law, Tim.

Using the Milan method, I asked the Primo siblings what they thought the oldest of the brothers, Dale, would say about the meaning of Ronnie's death if he were present. In identifying his own beliefs, Steve said that Ronnie's death had something to do with Ronnie's karma. In this excerpt, the brothers reveal family speak by using the agreement/disagreement strategy:

Int	Anybody care to hazard a guess, if we had Dale here, what he'd say? If I turned to him and I said, "Dale, when you go inside yourself, what would you, what do you think?"
Steve	I think Dale would say exactly the opposite of what I said.
Int	Would he?
Steve	He's Dale.
Tim	I should have seen that coming.
Steve	Once in a while, I think Dale [inaudible] because he was in the parochial school longer he might have to say something [pause]
Int	God's will, you think he might, Dale might?
Steve	Might say something to that.
Int	He wouldn't say *karma*.

Steve   No, he doesn't say *karma*.

Tim   He would have said it was definitely not karma. [laughter] And you're wrong.

Int   So, you two kind of differentiate between each other by being different, right? By saying different things?

Steve   Right. Right. We're exactly polar opposites about just about everything. . . . Oh, I think most of us would be closer to me and my dad, but Dale is, you'd have to know Dale. Dale is

Tim   He's a debater.

Steve   Dale's a debater. If you say white, he says black.

Tim   He can find, usually, a fairly good argument.

Steve   Yeah.

Here, the brothers are quick to set Dale apart as being different. In this family subsystem, being different meant holding more traditional beliefs. It seems that both Dale, as the oldest sibling, and Steve, as the second-oldest sibling, were invested in differentiating themselves from each other.

If family members do disagree in order to differentiate, then family structure could be considered to have a strong influence on the process of meaning-making and vice versa. Under this rubric, developmental needs could be seen as meaning-making stimulators. Members would disagree in order to differentiate from the family, and the meanings introduced as counterpoint would be woven into the fabric of family meaning.

The above excerpt also illustrates how a modified Milan method of circular questioning was used to collect systemic data. Members present were asked to "mind read" how Dale would construe Ronnie's death if he were present. It is not what Dale would have actually said if he were present that is important; rather, it is how the act of asking about Dale revealed more systemic family meaning-making patterns than would have been revealed without asking about absent members.

INTERRUPTING AND ECHOING

Interrupting occurred in most couple and family interviews. *Interrupting* was said to have occurred when one family member's remarks overlapped those of another. Interrupting was found in both its cooperative and uncooperative forms. Whether interrupting is of the cooperative or uncooperative type, according to Tannen (1990), depends on the intention of the interrupter, how the interruption is experienced by the one being interrupted, and the content of the interruption.

In *cooperative interrupting,* what the interrupter says is intended to support or expand what the original speaker has said and is not intended to dominate or derail the conversation. In cooperative interrupting, the words of the interrupter are congruent with those of the original speaker. An example of cooperative interrupting comes from the Primo family interview in which Rena, Ronnie's widow, and her parents, Dominic and Joyce, are discussing previous conversations about death with Ronnie, who died at a young age in an airplane crash. Joyce has just been asked whether she remembers conversations with Ronnie about death:

Joyce	I remember hearing him say that particular phrase. "Oh, I don't think I'm going to get old anyway. I'm going to probably die young." You know, kind of jokingly or whatever, you know, but I remember hearing him say that.
Int	Uh huh. And, Dominic, I saw you nod your head.
Dominic	No, I don't ever remember him talking like that with me, I, ah,
Joyce	He wasn't talking with me, he was saying it in general
Rena	Just in general
Joyce	To the crowd or whatever
Dominic	If he did say it, I didn't
Rena	didn't hear it
Dominic	Didn't hear it, or, you know, or, it didn't register.

First, Rena interrupted Joyce, her mother, and then she interrupted Dominic, her father, to finish part of his sentence. The conversation had a flow as if one person were speaking. At least to an outsider, the overall effect of these interruptions seems to indicate involvement and participation in the process of communication, not derailment or domination.

To learn whether the interruptions were experienced as cooperative, family members would have to have been asked about how they experienced the interruption. It may be that family dialogue has to be looked at in this atomistic way to learn the most about how family meaning-making actually does take place. It might need to include reviewing transcripts with families and asking about motivation and intent.

Echoing also occurred in the last excerpt above. *Echoing* occurred once as Rena echoed her mother's words "in general," and once when Dominic echoed his daughter's words "didn't hear it." Although not as frequently seen as the strategies of agreeing/disagreeing or interrupting, in a dozen or so instances, family members repeated the words of others. Echoing is a way that family members indicate they are attending. It could be viewed as a way of speaking in one voice, hence the term *family speak.*

An example of uncooperative interrupting was found in an interview with Darren Munson and his wife, Marie, in regard to the loss of Darren's father, Claude. Darren was explaining that his father's abuse of food and alcohol destroyed his health, made him unavailable to the family, and was Darren's reason for turning his back on his father when he was a young man:

Darren	So it was that he deserved a good time, and it was all right that her view and mine was just the opposite. It made me real angry that he treated himself that way, and it could have been so much different if he hadn't. He would have been healthy and he could have been closer to, ah, kids, and to me, and, ah, it's really hard when there is somebody you love that much as I did when I was a kid, and you have to reject him and move on to other things. That is not an answer, being [pause] very tough.
Int	Would it be an inaccurate statement to say that there was a way in which he died for you way back then?
Darren	Absolutely.
Int	Or at least that idealized image of him died.
Darren	Yep. Yeah.
Int	So you kind of experienced two deaths?
Darren	Yeah. Yeah.
Marie	That's a great deal of acceptance. Me, I don't know if two deaths are the right words.

Darren   Well, I think they are. [emphatically]
Marie   Somewhere [pause] Well, in a way. In a way.
Darren   Yeah, that's exactly the words I used.

Marie interrupted in an uncooperative manner by breaking into her husband's conversation to disagree with him about whether his early experience of giving up on his father was best described as "a death." It was not uncommon, in the two interviews that involved Marie, for her to express her opinions by reacting to what others said. Although on the surface, the content of Marie's remarks sound congruent, her interruption changed the focus of the conversation from his meanings to her meanings. It may have been that, in changing the focus, Marie was protecting Darren from the emotional distress he had started to show as he spoke of his father. Whatever the motivation, Marie's interruption elicited from Darren the need to reiterate how "two deaths" were "exactly the words" he had used. Neither cooperative interrupting nor uncooperative interrupting seemed to preclude meaning-making, although perhaps it could be argued that the meanings constructed were influenced in some way by the negative or positive tone of the processes used to construct them.

In regard to the Marie and Darren excerpt, it must also be noted again how the interviewer became a player in this couple's meaning-making process. The use of probes, such as the one used here about Darren's having experienced two deaths, always risked introducing thoughts that, if left to themselves, respondents may not have had or, if they had them, would not have expressed them.

If Darren's report is accurate that he had already thought of what had occurred as "two deaths," then using this probe constituted a way of unearthing his deeper meanings. If, however, he had not construed his experience in this way before the interview, then the interviewer could be seen as having changed the course of his meaning-making. As has been noted before, there is a thin boundary between conducting intensive interviews and doing therapy. The challenge is to explore deeper meanings without introducing new meanings. Doing so is not always possible.

FINISHING SENTENCES AND ELABORATING

The next excerpt contains examples of two strategies that constitute family speak: finishing sentences and elaborating. These strategies were not as common as agreeing/disagreeing or interrupting, but a dozen or so of each was found. Finishing sentences and elaborating were each found at least once in most of the family transcripts but were most pronounced in the Primo family. In this particular excerpt, Karrie, Ronnie's sister-in-law; and her mother, Joyce, were responding to the question why Ronnie died:

Joyce	I just think that, we're probably, uh, always tested through-out our lives. And I think that these things happen to, ah, see how
Karrie	Test our faith
Joyce	Test our faith and our strength and courage, you know. I think that way.

Karrie finished her mother's sentence. Her mother echoed her words and elaborated on the original thought. The joint meaning created here was that Ronnie's death occurred to test the family's faith, strength, and courage. By using these strategies, phrases were spliced together as if to create one voice.

Once the splicing had occurred, it was difficult, if not impossible, to tease out individual meanings. The two families in which 11 members were interviewed provided the best data for looking at these strategies. It is difficult to say whether speaking in one voice is as likely to occur in smaller, less enmeshed families. These two families were forced to share scarce airtime both in day-to-day life and in the interview. These families provided prime examples of family speak, using the strategies of finishing sentences for others, echoing, and elaborating.

QUESTIONING

The next excerpt is a continuation of the above excerpt. In this section of the interview, Karrie questions her mother about her beliefs. Questioning appeared as a characteristic element of family speak in several families studied. In this excerpt, the interview question refer-ences Joyce's belief that Ronnie's death happened in order to test the family's faith.

Int	So, if you were to relate that specifically to Ronnie's death, then, that would mean that there is a way in which everyone

	who is having to deal with this, in a sense, is being tested. Am I getting what you mean, or am I off?
Joyce	Yes, I think that's partly it.
Int	Partly it?
Joyce	Right. Ah, ah. Of course, it's accidental but still, still
Karrie	Do you mean God is responsible, Mom?
Joyce	Not responsible, no.
Karrie	But it's part of a greater plan that God has or something?
Dominic	Special plan
Joyce	Yeah, right. When certain times in life, certain people have to be tested. See if they can get through, whatever, I don't know.
Int	[inaudible] [pause] So that's interesting. So that's a little different than what I've heard from Rena and from Karrie. There's an added meaning for you there.
Joyce	Right.

In this exchange, Karrie's question "Do you mean God is responsible?" challenged her mother to clarify her contradictory meanings that God tested the family by causing Ronnie's death and that Ronnie's death was an accident.

The discovery that respondents were able to hold seemingly conflictual meanings raised some interesting points. This finding alerts us, once again, to the advantages of intensive interviewing. A more restrictive format could have required Joyce to make a choice among meanings, with a low likelihood of her unique meanings being among the choices. Subtleties of the process would be lost, and false conclusions might be drawn. Meaning-making, it seems, does not necessarily produce a logically consistent product.

Finally, in regard to this particular excerpt, it is interesting to note that the family was not quick to adopt Joyce's notion of death as a test, but Karrie's questioning had the effect of bringing Joyce's unique meaning into the family meaning-making system. Data such as these support the finding that there are meanings at each system level.

With the exception of the Zeeman family, a variety of elemental strategies were used whenever two or more family members were interviewed at the same time. Derek and Andy Zeeman did not interact during the interview even when Milan interview questions were clearly directed to both of them. Derek Zeeman had confessed to saying yes to the interview because he and his son had not been able to talk with each other about his wife's death. He thought the interview would help.

During the interview, they did not talk with each other. It seems likely that they had been accustomed to communicating through Debbie before she died and that they had not yet developed the skills or willingness to talk with each other directly. It was not that they failed to react to each other—they did, but in an emotionally reactive way. As father became more emotional, son became less. This finding suggests that another meaning-making inhibitor may be the loss of a family member who has acted as the communication channel or switchboard.

Family speak was found throughout the data but was used more by some families than by others. When family speak was used, it was found to interact with a myriad of other factors, such as family dynamics, family structure, other meaning-making strategies, and meaning-making stimulators and inhibitors.

To learn more about how families construct meaning, it may be necessary to look further at the intricacies of family conversation. As intricate meaning-making patterns were examined in excerpts such as these, it seemed that meaning-making was mostly a joint work.

Summary

In summary, families make sense of the death of a member by characterizing that person, usually positively, and by using ordinary ways of conversing, called *family speak*. Characterization focused on the personhood of the deceased and helped put his or her death into context. Characterizations tended to be positive, occurred at various systems levels, were influenced by family rules, interacted with family structures, and affected the emotional responses and behaviors of grief.

Family members were shown to use simple communication methods to make sense of the death. The result was an intricate weaving together of individual threads of meaning to create family meanings. This verbal weaving, called family speak, included agreeing/disagreeing, referencing, interrupting, echoing, finishing sentences, elaborating, and questioning.

The closely woven patterns of family interaction illustrated in this chapter were chosen because they illustrate characterization and family speak. Data such as these support the notion that the construction of meanings is a family process that yields at least some meanings that do not belong to any one individual, but to the family or family subsystem that constructed them.

7

Negative and Ultimate Meanings

Family members shared an abundance of meaning statements. Statements ranged from uncommon meanings like "death is like Santa Claus" to the more commonly heard "death was peaceful." Some meanings were offered in direct response to questions. Many meanings emerged as family members interacted with each other in response to the questions asked. Other meanings were in the stories that families told about the death. Some said there is no sense to be made of their loved one's death but still attempted to make sense of it.

By way of review, *meanings* were defined in this study as cognitive representations, held in the minds of individual family members but constructed interactively within the family as it is influenced by society, culture, and historical time. Meanings are the products of interactions with others and symbolically represent various elements of reality. *Meaning statements* can be thought of as linguistic categories that make up respondents' views of reality (Lofland & Lofland, 1984). The terms *meanings* and *meaning statements* are used interchangeably here.

At the risk of stating the obvious, it is necessary to note that, because the family does not have a voice of its own, all the meanings recorded were in the words of individuals. Some meanings were in *family speak,* the process by which families splice together sentence fragments in such a way as to make individual meanings unidentifiable. A few meanings, such as the notion that the death was preventable, were inferred from things the respondents said. Lofland and Lofland (1984) referred to such inferred meanings as *latent typifications* and encourage their inclusion in analysis.

Before presenting the meaning categories, a few important points are to be made. First, not all meanings that family members attached to the death were positive. Negative meanings occurred in many of the categories and, except for their negative valence, possess the characteristics of the category to which they belong.

Second, in keeping with symbolic interaction theory, not all meanings associated with the death were expressed verbally. Some of what family members made of the death was conveyed nonverbally: by facial expression, by posture, and perhaps most powerfully, by silence. In particular, the Zeemans stood out because of the paucity of their meaning statements. In nearly every count, they came up short. Over the telephone prior to the interview, Derek Zeeman reported not being able to talk with his young adult son about the death of his wife, Debbie. During the interview, they did not interact with each other, yet their silence spoke volumes about the way they were experiencing the loss of Debbie. She had been the communication link between them. Only the meanings that were actually spoken by respondents or that could be inferred from their words are included in this analysis.

Third, several features of the process of meaning-making surfaced while the categories of meaning were being developed. One was that family members often attached seemingly contradictory meanings to the death. Even when the apparent contradictions were pointed out, families held fast to what they had originally said. Contradictions are noted as they are found in this chapter's excerpts.

Another feature of meaning-making that relates to the meaning-making *process* more than to the meaning-making *products* was what respondents said about how particular meanings affected their grief. This information, though not the main intent of the study, seems important, and examples are included as they are associated with particular meanings.

Finally, an unexpected finding was that, in the process of telling about how they made sense of the death, many of the respondents made statements about what the death did *not* mean. It could be argued that such statements do not constitute a real category of meaning because they represent a failure to make meaning, but because "not" statements were so prominent in the data and because they are not known to have been previously described in the literature, they are given the prominence of being their own category. They are discussed as Category 1.

Category 1: What the Death Was Not

Some respondents, while telling what the death meant to them, made statements about what the death did *not* mean. Part of their process of reality construction included ruling out possibilities. Statements about what the death was not are referred to in this discussion as *not statements*. Interestingly, the 17 instances of not statements all came from families in which the death had occurred unexpectedly and in which the deceased was relatively young. Examples of not statements follow.

Jane Smith's 49-year-old husband, Bob, had a heart attack as he slept beside her. He had not been ill. She was awakened by the strange sounds he was making. Later, she described herself as having been immobilized for a time and unable to call 911. Jane answered the question why she thought Bob had died:

Jane   Because his heart gave out. [pause] Why? I think it was just a physical thing. And I don't think, a long time ago, I decided that things don't happen. Day to day, individual things don't happen because God makes them happen. I mean, I don't believe you, that if you have a car accident, it's because you did something wrong and God has decided to punish you. I don't think Bob died because I'm being punished. I don't think Bob died because he is being punished. I think he died because his heart gave out. . . . I don't have this feeling that somebody, that God or somebody, is in control and just comes down and snuffs lives out because he figures it's time for Bob to be someplace else or it's time to punish me.

Jane's meaning-making included that God does *not* use tragedy to punish people and that Bob did *not* die because he was needed elsewhere. She believed, rather, that the cause of Bob's death was physical. His heart gave out. Apparently, Jane was sorting through the various platitudes commonly cited for the cause of death and was ruling them out one by one. Notions about death occurring as a punishment were not uncommon in the data, nor was the idea that God needed the deceased elsewhere.

Like Jane Smith, Paul, a brother-in-law to the deceased in the Miner family, seemed also to make not statements to counteract common platitudes. Eight members of the Miner family were asked how they made sense of Anne's death. Paul drew on his health care background to select certain meanings and to rule out others:

Paul   Exactly, [her death was] the consequence of having an illness that will kill you. It's not God took her because it was her time, she was needed in Heaven. I have a real tough time when I hear that from people. The reason why my son died in a car accident is because God, because God, needed him in Heaven. No, he died because he went through the windshield and he hemorrhaged to death. I see Anne's death as a consequence of an illness that was fatal.

Paul's not statements included that it was *not* that God took Anne because it was her time and she was needed in Heaven. Paul, like Jane Smith, attributed the death to physical reasons: "an illness that was fatal." Sometimes family members agreed with each other's not statements. After Paul made the above statement, Edna, Anne's daughter, agreed with him:

Edna   I don't think it's fair that she died, but I don't think that, you know [pause]. She got sick. I agree with Paul because it's her time to go. I just think it basically happened 'cause, you know, she got cancer, not that, you know. I just, I think all the good she still could have done and that makes me mad, but I don't think she was taken or got it for anything specific thing she did, she just got sick, unfortunately. I can think of a lot of people I'd rather have die than my mom.

As family members commonly did, Edna referenced Paul's meanings and then added her own twist. Edna agreed with Paul's meanings. Her mother died, *not* because it was her time, but because she got sick.

Then Edna built on the collective meaning by adding that she did *not* think Anne got sick for any particular thing she had done. Edna ended with the notion that her mother just got sick and that it was unfortunate. Not statements sometimes preceded, sometimes followed, and sometimes were mixed in with other meaning statements that family members made.

Part of Karrie Primo's meaning-making strategy was to say what she did *not* believe. Karrie made statements in regard to the death of Jackie, her mother-in-law. The Primo family had been selected because of Ronnie's death, but the family used the interview questions to also construct meanings about Jackie's more recent death.

Karrie   I don't believe God was up there and said, "Geeze, we need another retired teacher for the gifted, it's time to pull Jackie." I don't buy that, and I know he [meaning her spouse, Tim] wouldn't either. Other members in my family, um, my brother Steve wouldn't believe that either. Yes, maybe my brother, my brother Dale probably would think more of the trad, the other way. I keep calling it the traditional way. It necessarily probably isn't and, ah, my brother Randy would feel the same way I do too. I don't think he believes that. A lot of people talk like that. And I think a lot of people talk like that because it's an excuse to just do what they want to do. You know, like we all have the idea that God just pulls random numbers out of a hat on who's going to die next. I'll tell you, there's a lot of things I'd be out there doing.

Karrie alluded to some meanings she did not "buy." She said she did *not* believe that God caused deaths to get people He needs and did *not* believe that God pulled random numbers out of a hat.

The Karrie quote is probably an even better example of how families reconstructed meaning, whether together in the same room or not, by comparing their beliefs with each other's. Karrie compared her thoughts with those of her husband, Tim, and her brothers, Steve, Dale, and Randy.

Other respondents made a variety of not statements similar to those quoted above. They each were attached to the death of the family member and included the following: there was *no* master plan, it was *not* a calling to Heaven, there was *no* spiritual meaning, it was *not*

God's plan, it was *not* just a bad break, and death was *not* engineered by God. In some instances, not statements were accompanied by statements about what the death *did* mean. In other instances, what respondents said was limited to not statements.

It is a matter of speculation why the not statements were limited to families in which young, unexpected deaths had occurred. Perhaps existential questions took on more urgency when death occurred at an unexpected time. Perhaps in cases of unexpected deaths of young family members, there is more about which to puzzle. Perhaps certain deaths, like suicides, young deaths, and sudden deaths, beg for explanation. Or maybe there are stages in making sense of a death, and families who have had warning of the impending death have done their *not* phase of the meaning-making process before the death occurs. Families with little warning may not have. At any rate, "not statements" seem to be an important category of the meanings people make. Paying attention to not statements may help us learn more about the meaning-making process itself and better enter into a given family's experience.

Category 2: There Is No Sense to Be Made

Respondents made 60 statements that there is no sense to be made of the death. At least one member from 8 of the 10 families made a statement of this kind. Of the 60 statements in this category, 40 were made by members of the Primo family who were grieving Ronnie, the youngest death in the study. Ronnie's father-in-law, Dominic, when asked how he made sense of Ronnie's death, answered, "I could not make sense of it. . . . I could not logic it out. . . . I could not explain it." Ronnie's brother-in-law Steve expressed somewhat the same idea when he said, "There was no meaning, just karma. . . . It was bad joss."

In most instances, after respondents said there is no meaning to be made, they had tried to make meaning anyway. This was evident in what Ronnie's widow, Rena, said when she was asked whether she was able to make sense of Ronnie's death:

Rena   I don't. It doesn't make any sense to me, so I don't make any
             sense of it. . . . Well, to me it was very senseless. Um, I don't

know. I just, I really, I still, you know, am mad about it, but what's done is done, what are you gonna, you can't bring him back. . . . Well, just the whole situation was, you know, bad, going up in the plane, going with somebody inexperienced, although you know, I may have done the same thing myself. I've flown in a small aircraft, you know, a few times . . . you know, he told me the night before that he was going or, yeah, yeah, the night before. And I had said, "Gosh, you know those small airplanes are, are dangerous," and he said, "Well, you've done it." I said, "Yeah, I know I have," I said, "but, just don't make it a habit" because this was a good front, you know. I thought it could become a habit, you know, go up every Sunday, or just don't make it a habit. He goes, "I won't. I'm just going to do it this one time 'cause I haven't been in an airplane this small."

Rena said there is no sense to be made, but her later expressions of anger suggest that, at some level, one of her meanings was that Ronnie could have prevented the death by not taking the risk of flying. Believing that there is no sense to be made did not preclude attempts to make sense of the death. If one thinks of this meaning as a *latent typification,* in Lofland and Lofland's (1984) language, Ronnie's death was preventable. Construing the death as preventable would likely affect the course of bereavement.

One feature of meaning-making found in connection with meaning statements in the "no sense" category was how sudden deaths of younger people tended to be viewed as more meaningless than the deaths of older members who had been ill for a protracted period of time. An excerpt from the interview with three members of the Primo family reveals this feature:

Rena	I, you can't make sense of that. Just like, you know, I don't think you can make sense of nearly any death, you know, unless there's, you know
Joyce	Unless they're
Rena	Unless they're, you know, in their 80s or, you know, to me that's how I think death should be
Joyce	die of old age

Rena   Die of old age, but young deaths, you know, like my 6-year-
old niece with the brain tumor, isn't easy. How do you make
sense of death when it's unexpected?

Rena and her mother were interactively making the meaning that
the only deaths that can be made sense of are those of older people
whose deaths are expected. Their point seems to be that one cannot
make sense of young, unexpected deaths.

They arrive at their meanings by using the strategies of comparison
and cooperative interrupting. Comparisons were made between the
deaths of old people and Rena's niece. Joyce interrupts Rena coopera-
tively to help her finish a thought.

One question that this study raised but that was not designed
specifically to answer was how attaching particular meanings to the
death affects the course of bereavement. Some of the clearest answers
about the effect of a particular meaning on bereavement were given
by those who said there is no meaning to be made. For example,
Ronnie's sister-in-law Karrie said that believing the death was meaningless affected her recovery:

Karrie   Well, I think it makes it a lot tougher myself.
Int   Does it, Karrie? And can you say in what way?
Karrie   I think, well, because it, it gives you very little hope, you
know. What, what do you have for hope when you've seen
this real vibrant, vital person in the family just suddenly
disappear? It's very difficult to go on. I think, um, as hard
as it's been to watch, ah, Rena and the two kids, I think
without the two children, it would have been harder. It's
hard as it is. In a way, it makes it harder to have children
because there's so much more responsibility and to know
they're growing up fatherless.

One can hear Karrie trying to find consolation in noticing Ronnie's
children but also that the lack of a meaning that gives hope made the
grief harder. As was typical of most respondents making the "no sense
to be made" meaning, Karrie continued her search for meaning even
after insisting there is no meaning to be made.

Rena, Ronnie's spouse, and Joyce Primo described the effect of
thinking there is no meaning to be made. They compared their

reaction to Ronnie's death to their reaction to the death of Karrie's mother-in-law, Jackie, who had died in the interim between Ronnie's death and the interview:

Rena   Well, I think it makes it a little harder in the sense that, you know, accident, accidental deaths are just really senseless. They're very shocking and they're very quick, rather than disease, you don't have

Joyce   You can prepare.

Rena   Yeah, there's no sense, like in Jackie's death either. Well, she got cancer. You have more time to

Karrie Yeah, I think Tim told me that many times, that at least there's that time to say all those things that you wanted to say. You can spend some time. You can make some memories that you want to make, that you want to have. There's time to do that.

The interactive nature of meaning-making is seen again in this excerpt. This family sees all deaths as senseless, but sees accidental deaths, like Ronnie's, as even more senseless. When there is warning, a time to make memories, the death may make more sense to family members.

Some respondents made the point that the death was senseless by saying that they could not understand it. Dominic Primo's statement serves as an example:

Dominic I guess I don't, ah, I guess I just don't, you know, I don't understand his death at all. I don't understand the, you know, the outside of it, you know, being a master plan and everybody being tested. I, ah, ah, I don't understand it. I don't understand anybody's death, when they're in the prime of life and have so many responsibilities and, ah,

Joyce   Things going for them

Dominic Things going for them, and they're so full of life it's hard to understand. But, ah, I could even say that about my dad. When he passed away, he was in his 80s. It seemed senseless because he was in such good health. Hard to understand that.

Int   Um, huh. So even when someone is older, you could have that same response.

Dominic Sure, I, you know, unless they're in real ill health, you know, the quality of life

Karrie Suffering

Dominic suffering, you know, like that. Outside of that, you know, I can't understand it.

Although the main point to be made with this excerpt is how lack of meaning may be expressed as not understanding, it is a prime example of how the Primo family does family speak. They weave their words together by echoing each other's words, finishing sentences, and interrupting. Dominic starts out by saying he cannot understand how it makes sense for someone in the prime of life to be killed. Others build on his meaning, and he returns to his basic thought, that he does not understand. The only death he sees as making sense is one in which there is suffering. One of Dominic's meanings is that even the death of his 80-year-old father was senseless because he had been in good health.

Members of the Miner family, who lost Anne in midlife from cancer, made the second largest number of statements to the effect that there is no sense to be made of the death. Anne's husband, Rafi, said, "You don't make sense of death. . . . There was no reason . . . it just happened." Anne's son, Toby, said, "There was no purpose to her death." Anne's father and brother each said, "There was no sense to be made," "Death does not make sense," and "You can't figure death out."

In regard to his mother's death, Tom Barlow said, "You don't try to make sense of the death because you don't know." Karrie Primo added her twist to the "no sense to be made" subgroup:

Karrie I don't know if I really have made sense of it. I don't think we really can. Something that tragic and that sudden, I, ah, I don't, have never really made sense of it. But I don't think that's ours to do. I don't think that we can just make sense of things in life. Why do children get cancer? Why do people die in war? I think there's a lot of things we just can't make sense of. We have to accept them. I'm just kind of an accepting person, and I can't really find any answers.

Respondents seemed to interpret the question of making sense of the death as asking whether they have been able to find positive meaning. Of those who said there is no sense to be made, many went on to share their negative meanings. The net result was sets of meanings that seemed incongruent. Rena Primo's response is a good example of these mixed-meaning systems:

Int   Rena, when you go inside yourself, how do you make sense, or do you make sense, of Ronnie's death?

Rena   Uh, I don't make sense of it. I really don't. To me, it was really senseless. It was an accident. I don't feel like, um, he had any big calling to be, you know, up in Heaven, but I guess I don't make sense of it, I just, I really, I'm still a believer of, you know, everybody has their number, and it must have been his number. I can't make sense of why it was. But it must have been his time. And the same with the two other guys. I just, it doesn't make sense to me.

First, Rena said she did not make sense of Ronnie's death. Then, she said his death was an accident. Then, she said what his death was not: It was not God calling Ronnie. Next, she shared a fatalistic meaning: His number was up. When viewed logically, these meanings may appear incongruent. Rena seemed to have been sharing her process as it was happening in her mind. Her process rules for meaning-making did not seem to include a demand for logic or consistency.

Once again, these findings underscore the notion that it is not uncommon for people to make seemingly incongruent meanings.

Category 3: Death Was Unfair or Unjust

The respondents made 85 negative meaning statements. Many of these statements were accompanied by strong feelings of anger, betrayal, and sadness. The existence of these negative meanings supports the contention that meaning-making is not limited to finding positive meaning in the death.

It is not surprising that when all the negative meanings were grouped according to which families made them, the families who had unexpected losses of relatively young members accounted for most of

them: the Primo family lost Ronnie at age 39 in an airplane crash, the
Miner family lost Anne at age 45 from cancer, and the Smith family
lost Bob at age 49 of a heart attack in his sleep. The types in this group
include "From Day 1, the whole thing sucks," "Bad things should not
happen to good people," "The wrong person died," "Death is bad,"
and "The death was too soon or too late."

FROM DAY 1, THE WHOLE THING SUCKS

Of all the respondents in the study, George Miner was probably the
most uninhibited in his expression of the unfairness of it all:

George   . . . you got to have faith, you know, but, ah, the whole thing
from Day 1 sucks! You know, you're just, you're to bed at
night with Anne on your mind, and you're up in the morning
with Anne on your mind, and you're, and during the day whenever you pause to whatever you're into. This is me speaking
personally, I'm into Anne. What's the reason, the why?
What, you know, pick up the papers and read some of the
devastation that different people are putting on other people
with the way they act, and what they do, and relate to Anne
and say, Good Lord, you know. And so you, you think about
all those Hail Marys you said and all the prayers you said, and
all the positive energy you're trying to push that way, you know,
and then it, it just goes down the tube. You think, wow.

You know, where am I at? Am I in a position where I'm
not being heard? Why? Can't figure out why. So I think
religion-wise it, start thinking, well, maybe this is, well,
maybe this is all, I don't know, kind of, I don't know, maybe
religion is like an insurance policy, you know. You don't
know if you'll ever need it or not, but after you leave this
world, if you got it, you got something to say, hey . . . but,
ah, so I don't really know where, what I'm this kind of
struggling with my religion, you know I always thought, hey,
I raised eight kids and, ah, ah, was very few days that, ah, I
didn't have Mass on Sunday, the holy days, and, of course,
the Catholic faith has changed a lot. We ate more macaroni
and cheese on Friday than any family in Minneapolis. You
know we observed the holy days and, ah, I can remember
when Liz and I were first married, ah, and we never had a

car, and we lived about a mile and a half from church, and, ah, it happened that, ah, during Lent we decided to offer up going to Mass every morning. They had a 5:30 Mass at St. Steven's and we, it was a short Mass, and it was over by 6:00. So we could walk to St. Steven's and walk home, and I'd eat breakfast and catch my lunch bucket and a street car and go to work. And ah, ah, the weather at that time of year happened to be, some mornings it was 10, 15 below zero. You know, we're walking over there, we're going to church. So I think about my religion, and I think, hey, you know, geeze, what's happened here? I tried to keep the faith and stuff. I, you know, why did we lose Liz, and why did, now Anne's gone, and, ah, can't figure it out, you know, kind of shakes you up.

George felt angry, indignant, and betrayed by God. His feelings were tied to the way he construed Anne's death. Some of George's sense of unfairness seemed to stem from his assumption that if he and his family fulfilled their religious obligations, God would somehow spare them. As George saw it, God had not kept his part of the bargain.

Statements about how unfair the death was were also made by Jane Smith and her sister, Lisa. Jane and Lisa are responding to the question how they made sense of Bob's death:

Jane   It's still, just once again, his heart quit. And there's nothing any of us could have done about that. It doesn't seem necessarily fair that someone his age, ah, would die, ah, that is everybody said, life isn't fair. . . . And those of us that are left just have to go on. I mean, I just have to get on [pause] you know, and I've, I think, done a reasonable decent job of that.

Lisa   They could have found more wrong with him than they did. You can't say, "What if." I think it's unfair. He's, Jane's left without him, and the kids don't have a father.

Jane and Lisa construed the death in several negative ways. Jane made the meanings that Bob died because his heart quit, that there was nothing any of them could do, that Bob's dying at such a young age was not fair, and that life was unfair. Lisa joined in with the notion, which was a meaning she shared more than once, that the doctors should have found out what was wrong with Bob. Lisa agreed with

Jane that life was not fair. Another of Lisa's meanings was that her sister and her children have been left without Bob.

BAD THINGS SHOULD NOT HAPPEN TO GOOD PEOPLE

Statements about how good the deceased was and how those who died did not deserve to die came mostly from the Miner and Primo families, again the young deaths. Among the family members expressing negative meanings, Dwight, one of Anne's brothers, was the most articulate spokesperson. Earlier in the interview, Dwight had commented that some family members felt bitter about Anne's death. Dwight's comments are in response to a probe about his own feelings of bitterness:

Dwight . . . I think Anne was the type of person, and Anne was considerably older than me, so Anne wasn't, was really, wasn't around a lot when I was growing up, certainly in this household when we lived in Minneapolis. But the thing that I always remember about Anne is she, she never got a break, she worked for everything that she ever had in life. She was married to a jerk, her first marriage, you know, raised two kids, literally on her own. Ah, put herself through school. Got herself an education, you know, and it just finally gets to the point in life, meets a good guy in Rafi, you know, the two were just perfect for each other, buys a nice house, the kids are grown, Toby's through college. Finally gets to the point where, geeze, maybe we can start doing some of the things that maybe we want to do, and then this happens. You know, it's just, like I say, it's just a series of all the hard work and stuff, just like to throw it all away. And, ah, what was the use, or what was it for? Well, sometimes you got to, you got to try and reflect and see if you can get some answers for that stuff, but they don't come easy.

Dwight, one of Anne's younger brothers, echoed the family theme: Anne was a saint and did not deserve to die. Anne's sister Laura expected Anne's goodness to protect her from death:

Laura Now when I think of that, I mean, that was so bizarre, because it, what, you know. But I never gave up. I never gave up on her. I always thought that some miracle was going to happen because Anne deserved it, because she was so special. It was just not going to happen. Not like that. Anne would somehow, some miracle, Anne was going to survive this whole thing. I never really believed that it was going to get her.

The meaning was that Anne's specialness should have protected her from death. As we have seen in previous excerpts, the Miner family was pretty much in accord that Anne was special. Laura, however, was the one to expand the meaning to include the notion that Anne's specialness entitled her to a miracle, the miracle of survival.

In the Primo family, Ronnie's brother-in-law Randy commented that, from a religious point of view, Ronnie had done nothing to deserve death. The meaning that Ronnie did not deserve death was constructed partially out of a discussion of the adage "What goes around comes around." Because Ronnie had done so much good, he deserved good, not a tragic death.

THE WRONG PERSON DIED

Meanings in this group tended to be made through comparison, a meaning-making strategy described in Chapter 5. Usually, the comparison was between the person who died and someone else who should have died instead. Statements of this type were made by members from 4 of the 10 families. In the following excerpt, using the Milan way of questioning, I asked Joyce Primo how she thought her son Randy would make sense of Ronnie's death:

Joyce   Well, he'd probably say something like, "It should have been me," or, "I don't have any family," you know, like that. You know, like why wasn't it him [Randy] instead of him [Ronnie] because he [Randy] did a lot of crazy things in his life, took a lot of chances.

The question arises whether this meaning is Randy's or Joyce's. It may belong to both of them. Later, when Randy was interviewed, he did talk about his own history as a risk taker and described Ronnie as being a risk taker as well. But he did not say he should have died in Ronnie's place.

An interesting methodological question arises from this quote: When the Milan method of questioning was used, whose meanings were being revealed? The meanings obtained may have belonged to the person who was sharing them, to the person whose answer was being "guessed" about, or a combination of the two. One suspects, in this instance, that Joyce may have been giving her own meaning, that she had given considerable thought to how things would be different if the family member lost had been one without children.

The use of the Milan method may have been a significant meaning-making stimulator. Meanings may have been created that the family members, had they not been interviewed, would not have created. The Milan method is probably best used to reveal systems dynamics, rather than to collect actual meanings from missing family members.

Another example of the wrong-person-died type is found in the comments of Anne Miner's son, Toby:

Toby   I really haven't done too much with it. I don't know. I guess, you know, it is a tragedy. I guess that's about as far as I can get on it.

Int   And what makes it tragic?

Toby   Well, that she died too young, and I sort of feel cheated, along those lines.

Int   So she was too young, and you feel cheated.

Toby   Yeah, yeah. She was a good person, and there's a lot of jerks in the world.

Toby's comments raise the question, Why would anyone make a point about how the deceased did not deserve to die by saying that someone else should have died instead? Perhaps it has to do with a sense of justice. In a just world, a good, young woman like his mother would not have died, but some person who was not good, some "jerk," as Toby put it, would have died instead.

In the Primo family, one could speculate that, in a just world, the one who had taken all the chances and who had no children, meaning Randy, should have died in Ronnie's place because Ronnie was not as much of a risk taker than Randy and because Ronnie had small children.

Toby's comments about someone dying in Anne's place also raise the question whether people are seen within the culture and, therefore, within families as having relative social value and, in the scheme of things, people with a greater social value should be saved. Perhaps one way that individuals or families attempt to regain a sense of order is to reason that someone of a lesser social value "should" have died in place of their family member. This reasoning then becomes a part of their meaning system about the death.

DEATH IS BAD

Among the negative meanings were a group that consisted of negative characterizations of the death. These were different from the more philosophical statements about death as a human condition. Meanings in this group were about a particular death and were more attached to feelings than were the philosophical death meanings. Statements of this type were plentiful, brief, and nearly all came from families in which younger members had died unexpectedly. A sampling: "His death was unacceptable," "Her death was a sad, angry, bitter experience," "We were cheated," "I feel ripped off," "We didn't gain, we just lost," and the death was "a tragedy," "terrible," "a waste," "an unpleasant experience," "too bad to look at," "scary," "unbelievable," "horrible," "devastating," "shocking," and "unspeakable."

THE DEATH WAS TOO SOON OR TOO LATE

Some family members said the death was premature; others said the death should have occurred sooner. As one might expect, meanings about premature death were made more frequently by families who had lost relatively young family members. Jane Smith and her sister, Lisa, said of Bob Smith's midlife death: "He was too young to die," "It is not supposed to happen that early," "It's not fair because he was so young," and "I thought Bob would always be there."

Ronnie Primo's family members also made meanings about how his death had occurred too soon: "The baby did not know her father," "Ronnie was too healthy," "He was too young," and "It was a waste of young lives."

Anne Miner died of cancer in her mid-40s. Her family's meanings included, "We lost her before we had enough time with her," "Anne was young," and "She could have done lots of good." Both the Barlow and the Owens families, while being interviewed in relation to deaths of older family members, referred back many years to deaths of young people in their families, saying that youthful deaths are not supposed to occur. Some meanings made by families suggest they were linked to the dreams and expectations that family members had for those who had died at early ages.

Some family members made meanings about how the person who died should have died sooner. Most of these meanings emerged in families in which the deceased had suffered before death. The Swan family struggled with why Julius, who died at age 91, had suffered in the nursing home for 12 years without being able to speak. They construed his death to mean that he was out of his suffering and on to his "heavenly reward." The Barlow family members each said in a different way that Vera wanted to die sooner. Much of their meaning-making hinged on the fact that she had talked for years to many of them about wanting to die. When she did die, the family took some solace in the notion that finally she had gotten what she had wanted.

Category 4: Philosophical Meanings

The philosophical meanings group was large and diverse. The types within it include fatalistic meanings, philosophy of death meanings, and meanings having to do with the purpose or reason for the death. Examples are given of each type.

FATALISTIC MEANINGS

Many of the statements in the fatalistic meanings grouping had to do with the notion of death occurring when one's time is up. Some were associated with God's time and God's plan, but most were not. Fatalistic statements of this kind were made by at least one member of each family except the Zeeman family.

Of those making statements with a fatalistic tone, Rafi, from the Miner family, was the most articulate. When asked why he thought his young wife, Anne, had died, he answered as follows:

Rafi   It just happened. There's no reason, there's no reason for it.
        . . . Like I said before, I don't really have, I don't have a
        philosophy of life that has any purpose to it. I suppose, I
        suppose I'd be existentialist or something like that. I don't
        know. I don't know enough about existentialism to be sure, but
        I think that's it. I don't, I don't think there's any innate pur-
        pose to any of this, you know, and I think that things just hap-
        pen, and we try to do our best to fit them into our worldviews
        and our life plans and life views and so on, and I think it was
        really good fortune that we found each other, and that we
        were able to have such a wonderful time together, and that
        we did elevate each other, and so on. And I think it was just
        really bad fortune that she had to die, you know. That's really
        the philosophy of it. You know, sometimes you, I basically. I'm
        basically an atheist. I don't really believe in God, you know.

Rafi's core meaning was that Anne's death was beyond reason and
without purpose: "It just happened." Rafi's search for meaning seems
to have been more in terms of medical causes than ways in which her
death fit into some master plan of the universe. His meanings had
more to do with the good fortune of having had time with Anne and
the bad fortune of her death.

Other respondents not as articulate as Rafi made less elaborate,
fatalistic statements. Some had to do with time: "Whenever it's time, it's
time," "The death time is pre-set," "Everybody has a certain time," "We're
here for a certain amount of time," and "My time is a given." Ten fatalistic
statements having to do with the deceased's number "being up" all came
from the Primo family and included, "We all have a number," "When
your number is up, it's up," and "Everybody has a ticket punched; when
it's up, it's up." The fact that the Primo family could espouse both
fatalistic meanings and those that clearly attribute a cause to the death
illustrates once again how the respondents made meaning statements that
seem contradictory. It is a reminder that research instruments that can
pick up seemingly divergent meanings are needed to collect accurate data
about how families make sense of their experience.

Some respondents considered fatalistic meanings but subsequently
rejected them. Deb Munson, for instance, considered a fatalistic
interpretation of the death but questioned its validity by giving an
instance when it would not fit:

Deb   It's like we said in the other interview. I think there, I think there is something to be said about people having a certain time when they are to go, but also you can't explain the Holocaust that way because it wasn't everybody's time in 1941 through '44.

The fatalistic grouping also contained statements that reflected an attitude of resignation: "What happens, happens," "Things happen," "None of us live forever," "Accidents happen," "It's not important enough in the scheme of things," and "You've got to think about it however you think about it."

The notion of resignation brings up an important point about how meaning statements reflect a tension between mastery and fatalism. Some respondents sought to gain control over events; that is, they attempted to master them. Others seemed to be more resigned to events, believing fatalistically that what will be, will be. In a very real sense, the process of meaning-making itself can be an attempt to regain some sense of control following a death. Perhaps searching for explanations of the death is part of the struggle for mastery, whereas becoming fatalistic constitutes a realization that mastering the loss of loved ones is impossible.

Statements representing the impossibility of mastery came in the form of statements about control. Twelve statements could be seen as representing respondents' coming to terms with their lack of control over the death event. Interestingly, lack-of-control statements were made by members from the four families who unexpectedly lost relatively young members: "It's beyond control," "It's out of our control," "We have not got control of it," "You can't control things," "You have no control over life," and "It's not ours to control." Perhaps the need for control is, in part, a function of the type of death, with young and sudden deaths inducing greater feelings of loss of control than more expected deaths of older family members in which there is adequate time to prepare and at least the illusion of control over some things.

PHILOSOPHY OF DEATH

Respondents made 75 statements characterizing death. No specific questions in the interview guidelines asked about general attitudes toward death, but respondents commented nonetheless. It seems that part of making sense of the loss of a loved one is to draw on broader beliefs common to the family, those beyond the scope of a particular death. All families except the Zeeman family made statements that fall into this grouping. Statements in this group can best be described as a series of death characterizations. Some statements were enough alike to form small clusters within the larger group. The largest of these was a cluster of meaning statements having to do with death as part of the natural order: "Death is natural," "Death is part of life," "Death is a part of a continuum," "Death is perfectly natural," "Death is a fact of life," "It is natural to die," "People live and die," and "Death and taxes are part of life."

Other statements clustered around the notion that death was inescapable: "His death was inevitable; we couldn't have done anything," "Death is inevitable," and "Death is not preventable."

Another small cluster had to do with the finality of death. Statements in this cluster often came up in discussions of the funeral, particularly in regard to the last viewing of the body. The following is a typical example. It comes from the interview with Lisa Smith as she hesitatingly reflected on the loss of her brother-in-law, Bob:

Lisa   It was tough because [pause] ah [pause] the, instead, whether it's your mother, whether it's a friend, it's that final [pause] um [pause] thought of, you know, that this person has finally left. That's kind of a tough one. So the finality of it was what made it rough.

Not everyone railed against the finality of death. Mark Buchanan described how he came to respect death as he hunted with his father as a young man and saw the dead animals they had shot. One of his main meanings was how natural it was for creatures, including people, to die. Mark's mother, Coral, having lost her mother-in-law after a long illness, said, "The finality of death makes me at peace."

Clues about what respondents thought of death in general are found in the descriptors they used for death. Less negative descriptions include "Death is something you learn to face," "Death is a loss of innocence," "Death teaches us," "Death is a beautiful place," "Death is to be looked forward to," "Death is a pleasant experience," and

"Hopefully, death is like birth; you are going to something better."
Families apparently drew on their past philosophical meaning systems
to make sense of their loss in the present.

PURPOSE OF THE DEATH

Respondents made 36 statements assigning a purpose to the death.
The terms *purpose* and *reason* were used by respondents interchangeably. Eight families made purpose statements. A typical purpose
statement comes from a family interview with the Miner family:

Laura   See, now I believe that we are all here for a reason, and for
         this and that, and we all have lessons to learn. Once our
         lessons are learned, and it's, you know, what happened to
         Anne happened for a reason. That's what I believe. Whether
         it's to bring us, like you come here today, and Rafi told me
         that this was going to happen, and my own struggle with
         dying and death. I thought, ah, my higher power has brought
         me a teacher. You're going to tell, you're going to share
         something with me that's going to help me face my own
         struggle with death.

Miner family members talked more than most other families about
how they had searched for purpose. Two other Miner family members
spoke:

Paul   I found myself asking, What did she do to deserve this? Why
         has Anne become one of the statistics of the Cancer Institute,
         1991?

Sally   I guess at one point in time I thought that Anne died now
         because something much more, something really terribly nega-
         tive was going to happen when she was sick . . . it really
         makes me feel badly that Anne is gone. But I do think that
         she, that there is a reason why she, there was a teaching
         somewhere.

Sally, one of Anne's sisters-in-law, shared what she thought initially
and what she had come to think more recently. Anne's son, Toby, said,
"It has to happen for some reason."
Mark, Florence Buchanan's grandson, said:

Mark   To me, there's a purpose. I have faith that there is a purpose
for each and everyone's life, that God has a purpose.

Members from other families said, "Death has a purpose," "We're
not supposed to figure out the purpose," "His suffering must have had
a purpose; everything has a purpose," "There was a purpose to her
dying," and "There is something to be learned from her death." The
search for purpose in the death was one of the most important and
most obvious ways in which the bereaved in this study sought to make
sense of their loss.

Category 5: The Afterlife

The largest classification of meanings contained statements related
to the existence of an afterlife. One interview guideline was to ask
where family members saw the deceased as being after death. Responses varied greatly. As might be expected, most, but not all, afterlife
meanings were part of peoples' religious belief systems. Afterlife
statements were classified according to whether they indicated a belief
in an afterlife, indecision about the existence of an afterlife, or a lack
of belief in an afterlife. Statements indicating a belief in an afterlife
were subclassified according to whether they described where the
deceased was, whom the deceased was with, what the deceased was
doing, and what the deceased's state of being was.

YES TO AN AFTERLIFE

Respondents made 82 statements indicating a belief that the person
who had died continued to exist in some form of afterlife; 50 of these
afterlife statements included the word *Heaven,* and 22 referred to a
"special place." At least one member from each family said he or she
believed the lost family member had gone to Heaven. Some families
agreed about the existence of an afterlife; some did not.

In addition to the 82 direct statements about Heaven, 24 references
were made to the deceased's state of being in the afterlife; they included
that the lost family member was "feeling happy," "resting," "okay,"
"worry free," "not suffering," and "at peace." Also, 27 statements

indicated what family members saw the deceased doing in the afterlife; they included such things as "playing golf," "talking with relatives," "being busy, having fun," "making Heaven a happy place," "watching over us," and "giving God help."

The example below represents those who saw their family member existing in some form of afterlife. Pam Mackey shared what she believed afterlife was like for her father:

Pam   Well, I haven't figured out if he is playing golf with Dr. Henry and his two brother-in-laws, or he is playing cribbage with his friend Ed, who died 3 or 4 years before he did, or he is sitting someplace playing with his dogs and cats. I think he is having a good time. Every now and then he looks down and makes sure Mother is all right, makes sure I am doing okay, and then he goes back. I mean, I don't feel, I feel he is in Heaven, or whatever Heaven is. . . . Ah, I just know he is in a place where there is no pain, his shoulders don't hurt, and he is happy. And if that is Heaven, then that is where he is. And he is with his parents. I mean, maybe he is sitting there catching up with his father, I don't know. Ha, ha. Maybe he is playing with cars, I don't know, but I know he is without pain, and I know he is happy.

Pam's responses included where her father was, whom he was with, how he was doing, and what he was doing.

Among families who believed in an afterlife, most used the word *Heaven,* as Pam did. Many had images of the deceased doing things with others who had died earlier. Pam included friends and relatives and the pets they had lost. It was not uncommon for respondents to characterize Heaven as a place where pain and suffering are nonexistent. Pam saw her father as being happy and without pain. Believing her father was in Heaven with loved ones, doing the things he wanted to do, and being out of pain and feeling happy seemed comforting to Pam.

In terms of family agreement, Pam's mother, Jenny, agreed with Pam about Richard's continued existence in an afterlife but disagreed that Richard looked down to see how they were doing. As the analysis of family sharing patterns in Chapter 4 revealed, families claimed a higher level of agreement than actually obtained when probes were used.

UNDECIDED ABOUT AN AFTERLIFE

Four respondents out of 48 indicated they were unsure or ambivalent about the existence of an afterlife or about the person they had lost being there. Tom Barlow said he could not say whether his mother was in Heaven but hoped she was. Tom said he was sure "she lived on in memory as everyone did." George Miner said if there was a Heaven, his daughter, Anne, would be there because she was a good person. His meanings did not include a description of an afterlife, but George kept looking for a sign from his deceased daughter signifying that she was all right. Jane Smith said, "Who knows where Bob is . . . he is inside my heart." Toby Miner, age 23, who lost his mother, Anne, answered the question where his mother was this way:

Toby   Yeah, I don't know, there's a lot. I think, for me there is a lot of unresolved questions about what I believe. I think part of me wants to believe that things go on. And there's another part of me that says that they don't. You know, that's very scientific and very cold. And that you just die, that's it.

At the time of the interview, Toby's main meaning was that he was the last person to whom his mother had responded. Four hours before her death, she had become momentarily conscious and had kissed Toby on the cheek. Toby clung to this experience, which was concrete and tangible, but was unsure about an afterlife.

Anne's side of the family, which is Catholic, were all in agreement that there was an afterlife. Toby's stepfather, Rafi, who is Jewish, believed that Anne existed only in the memory of those who knew her. To construct his own reality about his mother's death, Toby was involved in meaning-making interactions with both sides of the family.

NO TO AN AFTERLIFE

Toby's stepfather, Rafi, was 1 of the 2 respondents out of 48 who held the belief that the lost family member lived only in the memories of the survivors. Rafi's statements occurred in his individual interview and in the group interview. The following excerpt captures his consistent belief:

Rafi	It does not work for me to believe that she still exists somewhere. . . . When you die, you die. You're gone. . . . I don't believe she is anywhere anymore. . . . I think of her as being inside of me, I guess.

Both Rafi and Darren Munson shared the belief that the loved ones they had lost lived on within them. Darren Munson lost his father, Claude, to a death he construed as a premature death because of a careless lifestyle. Darren was asked where he thought his father was after he died:

Darren	Well, I'm not really into, ah, hereafter or anything. I have a lot of trouble with the concept so [pause] I think he isn't anymore. . . . I mean, we have his memory, and in that sense his spirit is alive.
Int	And when you say "his spirit is alive," do you mean like within people who remember him?
Darren	Sure.

Darren was clearly questioning, if not rejecting, the traditional Catholic beliefs to which the rest of his family subscribed. In the family interview, Darren received strong social pressure from his brother's wife, Deb, to explain how he could be a "good" Catholic and question the existence of Heaven. At another point in the interview, Darren referred to the question of the afterlife as being a "sorrowful mystery," a term he said came from the rosary.

Category 6: Religious Meanings

Many of the meanings that families shared were religious in nature. Religious meanings are divided into the following types: revelation, reunion, and reward; death as a test; God as causing the death; and general statements about faith and God.

REVELATION, REUNION, AND REWARD

The revelation, reunion, and reward type of statement included meanings that had to do with what would occur in the afterlife. The revelation meanings were constructed by the Zeeman, Miner, and Owens families and had to do with what would be revealed to them at some point in the future. For example, Derek Zeeman was tearfully struggling with the "why" of his young wife's death when he said:

Derek   You just can't make sense until some point in time in this life ever after, it will make sense . . . someday, maybe all the pieces will fit together, I don't know.

The expectation of someday having answers seemed to mediate against the unanswered questions of the present and to provide comfort. All three families constructed meanings about how they would learn someday why someone in their family had died at a young age.

The meanings that had to do with reunion contained constructions about how the bereaved family members would be reunited someday with family members who had died. Members from 5 of the 10 families made statements about reunion, for a total of 13 reunion references. The following excerpt combines the notions that an afterlife exists, that answers will be found there, and that a reunion will occur. In this passage, Monnie Swan is referring to her father, Julius, who had been in a nursing home 12 years following a stroke that had left him unable to speak. Monnie was responding to the interview question that asked whether she would like to add anything to what she had already said. She answered no but went on to share the following:

Monnie   No, no. Um, I think that, ah, oh, the only thing that I would add is that Dad is having a marvelous time talking to all his relatives right now. I think that they're just catching up on old news, "Well, it was certainly nice to see you again." Or maybe Grandpa or Grandma are saying to him, "Well, you people certainly lived a different life after we left earth. Ah, the world certainly changed after that." [pause] I can just picture his visiting about, um, and there was so many things Dad didn't know about his family life because he was the youngest of 10 children, and, um, he always used to say to me, "Well, the parents didn't tell the children anything." And [pause] so, but I'm not certain exactly if when a person dies if they have all this knowledge automatically, the minute they get to Heaven, or if they have to talk to their family and get some of these answers. But I know they definitely are talking about, "Well, you remember such and such a day, the day we had so much fun," you know, or something like that, and [pause] and he'll say, "I certainly wish I had some of these answers from Monnie and Virginia because they're writing a family history, and I wish I could tell them these things because they'll still asking." I can just hear him say these things [laughter], "She asked me all these things, and I couldn't tell her; now I know the answers."

Int   Well, I can see that you have well-developed images of what it might be like.

Monnie   Oh, definitely.

Int   . . . what kind of an effect does that have, thinking about where he is in the way that you do?

Monnie   Oh, that makes life much easier.

This example, though chosen because it is about family reunions in Heaven, gives a good picture of how elaborate some respondents' images of the afterlife were, as well as how such pictures affected their grief. Monnie's images were as developed as anyone else's in the study.

Interestingly, Monnie was carrying on both sides of the conversation with her father, just as she had for the 12 years prior to his death when he was unable to speak. This and other data raise the question whether meaning-making can occur in the minds of the bereaved as they imagine interactions with the deceased and others who are alive but not present.

Monnie's comments represent a typical response to the question how meanings affect the course of bereavement. Monnie was clear that thinking of her father's family reunion in Heaven made life much easier for her.

DEATH AS A TEST

Members from 4 of the 10 families construed death as a test. Of the 21 references to death as a test, some saw the person who died as having been tested, others saw those who grieved as being tested, and some saw both the deceased and the bereaved as being tested. The respondent who seemed the most invested in the notion of death as a test was Joyce Primo. She made three comments to this effect, and her daughter, Karrie, joined in meaning-making midway through her answer:

Joyce   I think that, ah, sometimes people die to test the world.

Int   Uh huh. Say some more about that; that's very interesting.

Joyce   To see how strong everyone else is. And how they can handle themselves, you know. . . . I just think that we're probably, um, always tested throughout our lives. And I think that these things happen to, ah, see how

Karrie   Test our faith

Joyce   Test our faith and our strength and courage, you know. I think that way . . . certain times in life, certain people have to be tested, see if they can get through, whatever, I don't know.

Among all the meanings espoused by Joyce, the idea that death occurs to test those left behind was paramount. Although other family members questioned her about it and even helped her say what she meant, none of them adopted this particular meaning.

Some respondents were more tentative about the notion of death as a test. In the following excerpt, Susan Swan, Julius's granddaughter, considered that both the deceased and those left behind were on trial or were being tested by God:

Int   . . . how do you make sense of Grandpa's death?

Susan   [pause] Well, they say everything has a purpose, so his suffering, there must have been some purpose for his suffering. And, um [pause] it was certainly a trial, certainly a trial and a testing for him [pause] and [pause] personal trial and testing for him and maybe, to some extent, a testing for the family, but, I don't know.

Swan family members were very concerned with their Christian witness and maintained throughout the interview that everything that had happened was for a purpose. The notion that death was a test attached a purpose to both Julius's death and the family's grief on losing him.

In the next excerpt, the father, George Miner, and the son Dwight, question whether Anne's death had been a test for their faith:

George   Because she was such a good person and, I'm sure that everybody that loses somebody will say the same thing, "Oh, they were such a good person," but ah, the picture, trying to fit the pieces together, and say, you know, I can't, I don't understand it, you know. And sometimes I say to myself, you're not supposed to. Maybe it's a test of your faith. I'd like to run out on the porch and yell up at God and say why, you know, but [pause]

Dwight   But you know it's just, it's, you know, I mean you certainly don't, you certainly don't run it off to just a bad break, you know. Like Dad says, there maybe, maybe it's a test of all of our faith. Maybe it's the test of the family unit in general. Like Dad says, as big families go, we're as close as anybody. . . . Ah, you know, I just, there again, maybe getting back to the faith part of it, a little bit. Um, you know, maybe it's some sort of big test that we're, that we have to live up to a little bit.

These passages about how death is a test seem to capture how some searched for a religious purpose to the death. Perhaps even a meaning as harsh as the idea of being tested by God is more acceptable to some than the notion that death is meaningless. It is not difficult to imagine that construing the death as a test would affect the way one grieved, perhaps demanding that one "do grief well" and to see one's self and one's family as having failed if expectations were not met.

GOD CAUSED THE DEATH

Although the notion that death is a test implies that God is responsible for causing the death, other statements were more explicit about God's involvement in the loss. Fifty statements indicated that the speakers held God responsible for the death of their family members. At least one member from each family except the Zeeman family made a statement about how God had caused the death—for example, "God wanted Vera," "God decided it was her time," "It was the Lord's time . . . his plan . . . his will," "God took her the way she lived— peacefully, and in no pain," "The Lord called her," "It was God's decision," "God said he wanted him, but he would give a baby to get you through it," and "Your life is over when God calls you home."

Some statements posited that the death was predetermined. In these statements, references were made to God's "master plan" or "God's special plan" calling for the death to occur at a certain time.

Not all respondents found comfort in the meaning that God was responsible for the death. Statements that indicated more negative constructions included, "I wondered if God caused the death to punish me," "God didn't save her . . . God let us down . . . I have been searching for God's purpose in [her] death . . . God did not listen to me," "I blame God," and "I am mad at God." Finding negative meanings such as these calls attention to the notion that although all or most grieving individuals may search for meaning in their suffering, as Frankl (1959) suggested, the meanings found are not always positive.

GENERAL STATEMENTS ABOUT FAITH AND GOD

It is not surprising that asking questions about the meaning of death elicited many statements about respondent's religious faith. A thorough analysis of peoples' faith systems is beyond the scope of this study, but two excerpts from Jake Barlow and Tim Primo are shared to give a flavor for what was commonly said. These two were selected because they represent two different ways that respondents reported their faith struggles. Jake's tone was emphatic; Tim's was more tentative.

Jake   Mine has been a struggle both with myself, like climbing a mountain. My Christianity is one of a growing nature, sliding back down, climbing back, trying to get to the top. And I keep getting closer and closer and slide back once in a while, but as each year goes by, I slip less and less. . . . But I think that there is something to this spiritual, there really is something, it's just that we can't understand it. It's one of those mysteries [pause] I believe, you know, that there is a special place. It's a mystery because God's made it that way, and I believe, I believe literally, as literally as I can, as I can understand it, in the Bible's interpretation. You, and again, that can be interpreted in many ways but, ah, I'm, ah, I think

I told you before, I'm a Christian and I practice my faith and I'm far from perfect as is most Christians.

Tim   I don't know, because I believe, you know, there is a Heaven, I don't have any idea what it is. You know . . . Yeah, he was a great person, and I believe he's there, but I don't have any conception of what it is because I, I have trouble with faith. You know, I go to church and I try, and, you know, you know, envision what they tell me, and I think about it and everything, but I don't have any real, you know, I have trouble figuring things out.

Beside the general faith statements such as those shared by Jake and Tim, many global statements about God were made—for example, "God has a purpose," "God is love," "God has nothing to do with people dying," "Maybe God has lots bigger problems than ours," "God has room for alcoholics," "There has got to be a God," and "Don't question God." Although global statements were attached in some ways to certain deaths, they seemed to belong to a group of meanings that were broader than the specific meanings that respondents attached to a particular death. Therefore, they were grouped as a category of their own.

Summary

One can see from the variety of meanings illustrated how diverse they were. It was shown how family meaning-making may include talk about what the death does *not* mean, as well as the assertion by some that there is no sense to be made of the death. After a sampling of families' philosophical meanings and a demonstration of the intricacies of meanings associated with the afterlife, it was shown how families draw on their religious beliefs to make sense of their loss.

Chapter 8 consists of four more categories of meanings. As in this chapter, major features of family meaning-making are identified as they were found to be associated with particular meanings.

8

Meanings About Death
and Family Change

Category 7: The Nature of the Death

The families made meaning about many features of death. Category 7 includes all the meanings having to do with whether the death could have been prevented and, if so, by whom. Also included are the meanings respondents made on the basis of the medical causes of the death and the way the deceased died. The largest type within Category 7 had to do with the preventability of death.

DEATH WAS PREVENTABLE

It probably comes as no surprise that respondents made meanings having to do with whether *someone* could have done *something* in *some* way to have prevented a family member from dying. As we have seen throughout the analysis, not all meanings made by the families were positive. Meanings having to do with the preventability of a particular death were among the negative meanings found in this study. Meanings of this type were more likely to be made by families in which the person who died was young or died suddenly or both. Meanings included in the death-preventable statements were found in three forms, determined by who was seen as being able to have prevented the death. One form had to do with whether the deceased could have prevented his or her own death. A second form had to do with whether family members could have prevented the death. A third form had to do with whether the health care system could or should have prevented the death.

Preventable by the Deceased

A typical statement about prevention of the death by the deceased came from the interview with the Primo family:

Rena   Well, to me it was very senseless. Um, I don't know, I just, I really, I still, you know, am mad about it. But, what's done is done. What are you gonna, you can't bring him back.

Int   And those feelings of madness, Rena, are they anger? What are they directed toward? Do you have a sense of that?

Rena   Well, just the whole situation was, you know, bad, going up in the plane, going with somebody inexperienced, although, you know, I may have done the same thing myself. I've flown in a small aircraft, you know.

The implication here is that Ronnie's death could have been prevented by Ronnie himself if he had not taken the flight.

Some statements dealing with how the deceased had responsibility for his or her own death were related to lifestyle choices. Members of the Munson family made more than a dozen such references in relation to Claude's lifestyle. Darren, the older son, said this:

Darren It made me real angry that he treated himself that way, and it could have been so much different if he hadn't. He would have been healthy, and he could have been closer to, ah, kids and to me, and, ah [pause] it's really hard when there is somebody you love that much as I did when I was a kid, and you have to reject him and move on to other things. . . . Well, I think it's a perfectly natural [pause] thing and we got to accept it [pause] ah [pause] he [pause] I have trouble with the fact that he shortened his life so much and, ah, [pause] physically, and, you know, and I just wish he had done some different things.

Shorter comments from other Munson family members included "He could have lived longer if he stopped smoking," "Claude couldn't keep up with his lifestyle," "He didn't take care of his body," "He shortened his life by the continued use of alcohol," and "From the many years of abusing himself, he wore out too soon."

Derek and Andy Zeeman made references to Debbie's smoking and to pollutants at work as the causes of Debbie's premature death from cancer. She could have prevented her own death had she not smoked and had she changed jobs.

Preventable by a Family Member

Some Primo family members made statements about how they might have prevented Ronnie from getting on the airplane. Dominic, Ronnie's father-in-law, was asked about any unfinished business between Ronnie and himself:

Dominic Ah, I don't, I don't, I kind of think about that and, sometimes, I think, you know, that morning he told me he was going to go fly, I kind of, I didn't know that about it. I guess he had the day planned ahead of time, you know, like 2 or 3 or 4 days or a week or whatever. I didn't know about it. The fact of the matter is, I don't think I knew about it until that morning, until I talked to him. Had I heard about it, I'm sure I would have mentioned something. I don't think I would have told him, ah, ah, don't fly, but I'm sure I would have told him that, ah, he has, he should be real careful with things that he does because he's got a family you know, especially with that little baby. You know, the little baby was only 3 weeks old. I think I might have told him that, had I known. And I kind of wish, you know, when he told me he's going to fly, and he was leaving right then. I was the last one to talk to him, I'm sure. I kind of wish that I would have said, "Jesus, don't go." But I realize that that wasn't, that wasn't possible. . . . I'm sure that had I talked to him ahead of time, if I would have just said, "Look'it, Ronnie, you got a family to think about, and you oughtn't to be flying. It's a dangerous thing." I'm sure that, had I talked to him ahead of it, ahead of time, he'd think twice because he really, he really did, he really did listen to me.

One of Dominic's core meanings was that he should have prevented Ronnie's death. Ronnie had been killed 21 months before the interview, and as can be seen in this excerpt, Dominic was continuing to wrestle with his own sense that he could have prevented it.

Jane Smith had a similar struggle as she thought about her spouse's death. She was asked whether she would like to change anything about how she thought of Bob's death. She recalled the time of Bob's heart attack, when she had heard him making strange sounds in his sleep and she had felt immobilized:

Jane   Well, as I said, the only thing I'd like to change is, I wish I had taken a CPR class, and I wish I had tried. Um [pause] but at the same time, I'm convinced, and maybe this is another mind game I'm playing, I'm convinced that it wouldn't have done any good. I mean, I know that he died within minutes. [pause] It was very helpful, too, when Mike died, to know that Leanne couldn't, that it didn't occur to Leanne either [pause] umm [pause]. They lived in town. The paramedics were there, you know, instantly, by comparison, and there was nothing they could do.

Jane felt guilty about not knowing how to do CPR and for not being able to react, yet at another level she believed that Bob could not have been resuscitated. Her grief was heavily laced, perhaps even bound, by her struggle with whether she could have done anything that might have saved him.

The reference Jane made to Leanne and Mike had to do with how Mike had also died in his sleep of a heart attack as Bob had, and Leanne, like Jane, had been unable to save him. The incident was all the more poignant because Jane had been engaged to Mike before she married Bob. Leanne and Jane had compared their experiences, and some of Jane's meanings came out of these meaning-making interactions with Leanne.

In the Munson family, some of the adult children blamed their mother, Evelyn, for not calling 911 soon enough at the time of their father's death. Sam, the younger son and the most outspoken on the matter, was being interviewed with his wife, Deb; his brother, Darren; and Darren's wife, Marie.

Sam   One thing that I've always thought, and this came out when we talked, but, ah, I was angry for a long time, and I still haven't completely come to terms with it, although it's much better than it was, was the fact that the night that all this happened, my mother, your mother, called Jeannie first, before 911.

Marie   I was thinking about that the other day.

Sam   It's such a pity thing, but it's so, I think it's so crucial. How you could not have your wits about you enough in, ah, I mean, that's an emergency situation. Don't call Jeannie and wait for her to drive all the way over. Call the doctor right during the, when things were happening. The wake and everything, that was very uncomfortable for me. I found it, that anger was the feeling I felt way more than sadness, or loss, or anything else.

Marie   Don't you think that's part of the dependency? It's codependency, and trying to, I mean Jeannie has probably made her decisions for a long time.

Sam   Well, I'm sure.

Deb   No, Jeannie told her that if anything ever happened, to call 911.

Marie   Yeah, but she couldn't think.

Darren   But clearly she didn't want him to make it.

Deb   Yeah, see that's what I think too.

Marie   I would have trouble believing [pause]

Deb   Really.

Sam   There was a lot of discussion about

Deb   I want you to know that you're not the only one thinking that.

Marie   Seriously, I'm on a different wavelength than a lot of us.

This excerpt is a classic piece of family meaning-making. Sam stated the meaning that his mother failed to call 911. Darren elaborated that their mother did not want their father to make it. Deb agreed. Marie was incredulous. The consequence of such a meaning, at least for Sam, was strong feelings of anger, which he said outweighed his feelings of sadness or loss. It is not difficult to imagine how believing that Evelyn could have saved Claude if she had acted appropriately would affect the family's course of bereavement. Interestingly, Evelyn, in her individual interview, reported that she had called 911 before calling her daughter, Jeannie, but the ambulance did not come.

Preventable by the Medical System

Statements about how the medical system failed to save the deceased were made by members from 5 of the 10 families in the study.

A typical example comes from an interview with Lisa, Jane Smith's sister, as she answered the question how she made sense of Bob's death:

Lisa   [pause] His body just, his heart just gave out. I mean, he was too young to die. [pause] The doctors somehow didn't detect that it was that bad. [pause] I think there should have been some way of detecting that it was that bad. Yeah, or taken more tests. Of course, you can't know what they were thinking about it, or if they had any other ideas about [pause]. I don't know, I'm not a doctor. I can't tell what they see, what they could tell about his symptoms. . . . They could have done more tests and saw that there was more wrong. . . . The other alternative could have been a heart transplant or something, you know. He might have not gone along with that either.

The implied meaning is that the death was preventable if the medical system had done its job. Lisa's sister, Jane, agreed with Lisa and told about a person who had had a transplant and was doing well. Jane questioned why it could not have been Bob. The implicit meaning was that Bob's death could have been prevented.

The following phrases taken from other interviews show a range of the meanings related to medical system failure: "She almost had a chance with an experimental treatment system, if the system had worked as it should have . . . things got screwed up because of the holidays," "He should have been on dialysis sooner," "He should not have died; the medical world failed," "Medical people never asked me; I knew it was a heart attack," "The medical staff was negligent," "The medical procedure was questionable," and "A kidney transplant was never mentioned." For some people, making sense of the death includes holding the health care system responsible.

BIOLOGICAL CAUSE OF DEATH AS MEANING

Some meaning statements were simply about what had caused the death biologically. These were in contrast with the religious and philosophical reasons for death that some chose to give. Meaning statements of this type were simple in sentence structure and sounded like attempts to be matter-of-fact or practical about the deaths that had occurred. They included statements related to death from old age: "Things quit working," "Her body gave out," "His body was too tired," "He died because he was sick," and "He died because he was worn out."

Some family members, when asked why someone had died, named the affected body part: "His heart quit," "They both had bad hearts," and "It was his kidneys." Still others made more general statements about the cause of the death: "She had a history of medical problems," "It was an act of nature," and "It was just a physical thing."

Meaning statements that had to do with cancer as the cause of death tended to invite additional meaning-making about the cause of the cancer. Miner family members wondered whether Anne's cancer had been caused by something she did, something she ate, something with which she worked, or whether her cancer had been caused by her unfinished, unresolved grief and anger. The same respondents who gave philosophical or religious reasons for the death were likely to give medical reasons as well, revealing once again the multilayered, complex nature of family meaning systems.

MOMENT OF DEATH

The most vivid example of meaning-making about the moment of death came from the individual interview with Rena Primo. The airplane in which her husband was killed had crashed and burned. Although this is a long excerpt, it seems worth including because of the way it reveals the nature of the meaning-making process. The question to which Rena was responding was whether she would like to change anything in regard to the way she thought about Ronnie's death:

Rena   Um, well, I don't particularly care for the way that he died. That doesn't really sit too well with me. But, you know, I don't think you care for, you know, the way anybody dies, what, you know, terminal illness [pause]. You know, to me they're all horrible unless you're a little old lady or a little old man and you go in your sleep. That's so comforting, and I think everybody thinks on those lines.

Int   Sure, sure. Do you have images of, like the burns, and the, you know [pause]

Rena   Um huh.

Int   What all might have gone on there?

Rena   Yeah, I do.

Int   Does that stick in your mind?

Rena   Um, not as bad as it did. Um, I guess the burns, that doesn't
         bother me, once you're dead you're dead. I guess, you know,
         that doesn't bother me too badly. The way they went, the, I
         don't like anybody being traumatized [pause]. You know,
         scared or fearful, I just, you know, that really makes me sad
         thinking about that. You know they had that, so many
         seconds, knowing that, oh, oh, this is death and probably
         screaming, and, you know, terrified out of your mind, you
         know. That really bothers me. Although I was reassured
         when my dad, I think he really checked into it quite thor-
         oughly, and whatever, and found out, you know, how many
         feet they were up, and how many seconds it took to hit the
         ground, and, "Rena it was only, you know, 8 seconds or 6
         seconds or whatever," he told me. Boom, and they died on
         impact. It was over so fast, that as fast as you can blink two
         times. And they were dead before the fire broke out. And
         the, um, the autopsy, you know, told us that. And I was really
         worried about that, that they may have been injured, you
         know, badly and then had to go, burning to death.

Int   Certainly, the autopsy, whether they died from smoke, or
         fire, or whether they died from something else.

Rena   Right, and I was so anxious to get to the, you know, autopsy
         report to confirm that, and the same with the death certifi-
         cate, and I thought, oh, sure, they, my dad said they don't
         lie on those; they don't spare any feelings. "Right," he says,
         you know, "It says it like it is, you know, died of severe
         lacerations due to sudden impact." I'm sure they all basically,
         you know, broke their necks or whatever. I'm not sure, but
         my dad had said he thought when you drop so fast so far
         that your heart disengages or something. He said basically
         you probably have a heart attack before you even hit the
         ground, and that sounded good too.

This excerpt reveals some important features about meanings, the
most important of which is how Rena constructed a meaning related
to Ronnie's final moments: the meaning that Ronnie had not suffered

for more than a few seconds, that his heart probably had "disengaged" as he descended, and that he was dead before the fire began. It is possible to track her thinking as she rules out some possible meanings.

Also noteworthy is that even though Rena is being interviewed alone, her father's role in her meaning construction is very evident. She is reporting on an interactive process of meaning-making that occurred within the family. The data he gathered and his personal meanings became part of her meaning-making. There is also an indication of how Rena's meanings changed over time and what the impact of making different meanings had been. She said that, early on, when she still believed that Ronnie had died of the burns, she was bothered by the images. She reported feeling better as she had learned from her father's information gathering and arguments that Ronnie probably had been dead on impact. We see here the struggle for positive meaning, which characterized most meaning-making episodes.

In terms of the interview process and the influence of the interviewer as meaning-making stimulators, the passage above provides another example of how the probes resulted in the interviewer becoming an active player in the meaning-making process. Yet, without my asking Rena whether she had been bothered by images of Ronnie being burned, it is doubtful she would have been as explicit about what really troubled her. She also might not have told about what she had learned from her father and the autopsy that helped her construe Ronnie's final moments in a different and seemingly less troublesome way.

Other meaning statements related to the final moments of life were made by members from 4 of the 10 study families. The Buchanans made meaning by comparing the final moments of two grandmothers. Florence, the one included in the study, was reported to have had the less peaceful death of the two. Mark, a grandson, described Florence's death, and then Coral, her daughter-in-law, compared it with her mother's death.

Mark   But when she was really at the end there, it was a real ugly thing to see. I'm sure that's a lot of why somebody that's so beautiful and so wonderful, and you see that everyday, and, all of a sudden, you see that, and it's like [pause] there's no resemblance here at all. That's not my grandma. That's not her by any means.

Coral   And something that was real different was my mother, because she had aged so much, and looked so different, and the morning she died, Kathryn, our daughter, Kathy, said to me, "Mom, I can't believe it. She's just radiant." And it was like she was just transposed. She was so beautiful and radiant when she died that it was just, that's the picture I have there. But it's an altogether different thing. It wasn't a suffering. She was just sleeping away. It was very peaceful. I just got up on the bed and gave her permission to die.

Others, like Pam Mackey, cited the notion of dying with dignity, from which she made meaning about the way her father died. Pam spoke about her father's death in the hospital following cardiac bypass surgery:

Pam   I kinda guess I knew that when they came out and told us the first time that they were having problems that he wasn't going to make it through. Up to that point, I really felt very, very confident that he would make it through the second bypass. His will to live was there. I have never seen anybody in my life fight as hard without losing their dignity. You can fight and get down and out and lose your dignity; Father fought and kept his dignity. You couldn't have asked for him to do any more than what he did.

It was a comfort to Pam as she grieved that her father died as he did.

DEATH BEFORE DEATH

The last grouping of meanings dealing with the nature of the death contained 12 statements suggesting that the family member had really died some time before the actual, biological death. This death before death, in some cases, had occurred because of a loss of mental faculties; in other cases, it had occurred because of estrangement from family members. Respondents who made these statements came from families in which the health of the lost family member had been failing gradually over the years.

Some death-before-death meanings were about emotional death or symbolic death. This type of meaning was most clearly made by the

Barlow family as they referred to losing Vera when she had a "mental breakdown" some years before and, more recently, had stopped recognizing some members of the family when they came to the nursing home. Vera's youngest son, Tom, who lived out of state, made the meaning that he had lost his mother years ago. He did so by comparing the loss of his mother with the loss of his father:

Tom   Ah, I get two. I lost my father and my mother. My mother, it was, I was rather distant to my mother because of her state of mind. In my mind, I probably come to the conclusion that my mother died years back [inaudible]. My mother [inaudible] her fault, something happened to her brain cells. So I was a little bit removed from her. . . . I lost my mother gradually over time because of her Alzheimer's [inaudible]. I gradually lost my mother, and had resigned myself, and whether I liked my mother, or disliked my mother, or love/hate, and had problems with my mother. I did lose my mother gradually during life, you know. Whereas, in the case of my father, [he died] before my eyes when I was 21 years old. That was shocking, and the evening before the wake, we all met at his sister's, and we all came together, and that didn't help much. There was a lot of grief because of the suddenness of it.

Later in the interview, Tom said, "She had died emotionally in my mind years before." Construing her death in this way probably affected Tom's bereavement. Interestingly, he had as much to say about his father's death 20 years before as he had to say about the recent death of his mother. The reactivation of his grief over his father's death, which his mother's death occasioned, seemed to stimulate his meaning-making about both.

Darren Munson compared the biological death of his father with the loss of his father, emotionally, years before.

Darren He'd be somebody that I, as a kid, just absolutely idolized. I mean, he was just a great dad. A great hugger, fun, he was just a terrific athlete. He could do things. He was just strong. I mean he was just, I wanted to be just exactly like him. But then when I started to realize that I couldn't be, because I didn't like to drink anymore [pause] I had to reject him. And to me it, I, ah, I started dealing with his death when I had to do that. And that's 30 some years ago. And so I commented all during that time. I wish my father would stop drinking; he's killing himself. That's what he's doing. And that's absolutely the truth. And on the other hand, Jean liked him when he was that way, and had him to her house, and she drank too. . . . It's really hard when there is somebody you love that much, as I did when I was a kid, and you have to reject him and move on to other things.

Int   Would it be an inaccurate statement to say that there was a way in which he died for you way back then?

Darren   Absolutely.

Darren made the meaning that his father had really died to him many years before, when Darren had made the decision that he could not be like his father because of his lifestyle. Most of Darren's story about his father's death was about how things used to be when his father was still his hero.

Category 8: Attitude of the Deceased Toward Death

An interesting finding in the study was that some people made sense of their loss by referring to how the one who died had felt about his or her own death while still alive. Many meanings like this were shared. Some respondents took comfort from the notion that their loved one was ready to die; others clung to the notion that their loved one had tried very hard not to die. Some constructions were based on what family members said they heard the deceased say; others were based on conjecture.

Meanings were classified into types on the basis of how respondents construed the deceased's predeath attitude. As we have seen throughout the analysis, it was not uncommon for meaning statements to be contradictory. Some respondents said at one point in the interview that the deceased had welcomed death, and in another part of the interview that the deceased had resisted death. The incongruence among meanings may have occurred because of the way the respondent construed the deceased's meanings, or it may have been a reflection of the deceased's own ambivalence. It is not uncommon for people who are dying to vacillate between accepting death and fighting it.

Possibly, the contradictory meanings were strictly a function of the changing needs of the grieving person. It is possible the reflection of the deceased's attitude toward death was not based on the deceased's attitudes at all, but rather totally on constructions of the bereaved family member.

The many meaning statements having to do with the deceased's predeath attitudes were divided into types. Each type is illustrated below.

THE DECEASED DID NOT WANT TO DIE

Twelve meaning statements indicated the deceased had not wanted to die. The following excerpt shows how families made meanings related to the attitude of their lost member toward death. It shows the interactive nature of meaning-making in a subgroup of four Primo family members. Family members, including four in-laws, had just been asked collectively why they thought Ronnie died. It is a good example of how asking questions of the family as a whole elicited interactive data:

Steve   I don't think there's any reason, reason why he died. He just died, you know. Plane crash, and he died.

Tim   It's it for me too.

Steve   It's a terrible accident, that's all.

Tim   Vick?

Vickie   Yeah.

Tim   Yeah, that's the way I feel about it.

Vickie   There was no way he could have survived.

Randy   If there was a way out, he would have found it.

Vickie   That's true, I believe that.

Tim   I know. I know.

Steve   If there was any way of skimming by, or, you know, or beating the odds, Ronnie would have done it.

Randy was the first to say that Ronnie would have found a way out of death if there had been one. Steve elaborated by noting that Ronnie would have "skimmed by" and "beat the odds." We can speculate that it would be unthinkable to these family members, who seemed invested in making Ronnie a hero, that Ronnie gave up easily. By showing that Ronnie's death was unavoidable, that he would have found a way out if there had been one, they co-constructed the meaning that Ronnie did not want to die. The need to make this meaning was at least partially driven by concerns expressed by other family members that, at some level, Ronnie may have wanted to die and, therefore, took risks. These four apparently found such a meaning unacceptable.

Some other families constructed the meaning that their lost members did not want to die. The Munson family used the fact that the hearse got stuck in the snow at the cemetery to make the meaning that their father had fought going to the grave. Dwight Miner, in response to the question whether he had had conversations about death with his sister, said this:

Dwight   Ah, I mean, not I mean the last week or so when she had her last day at [the hospital], ah, you know, we talked a little bit, you know, I mean, I think Anne felt she was coming to the end of the trail, ah, and, and, you know, she consoled me in such a way by saying, you know, I'm okay with it, you know. I'm, I'm, you know, I'm okay that I'm going to die. I know it's, it's getting nearer. Ah, but yet, she still had a lot of fight. I mean, she just wasn't going to close her eyes and let it happen. I mean, someone was going to have to steal the life away from her, you know.

This is a prime example of how respondents made meaning based on what they remembered hearing the deceased say. One central meaning of the Miner family was that Anne had fought for life but that, at the same time, she had become ready to die. The seeming incongruence does not seem so incongruent when thought of in the context of Anne's actual dying process. Family members told how she had fought for life until she realized there was no hope. She then had prepared to die.

THE DECEASED WAS READY TO DIE

Rafi described his wife, Anne Miner, as she prepared to die:

Rafi   . . . I mean, I think that she was ready to die when she heard in the hospital that they couldn't do anything else. I think that she was just ready to let go then. And in a way, it was very brave of her to do that, you know. Rather than just to fight and fight and fight, you know.

Rafi's meaning that Anne was ready to die was based on what he thought Anne's attitude toward her own death had become. To Rafi, Anne's acceptance of death was preferable to her continued fight to live.

Like Rafi, Julie Barlow made meaning in relation to her mother-in-law's readiness to die:

Julie   She was ready. She was comfortable with it. And like I say, she was peaceful. In fact, I think it's the most peaceful I saw Vera in 12 years, you know.

When Julie Barlow was asked how her grief was affected by knowing that Vera was comfortable with death and ready to die, Julie answered instead:

Julie   Oh, it helps. I mean, I can accept it. I can feel good about it. Not, not that I don't miss her and stuff, but it's just . . .

Believing that Vera was ready to die helped Julie accept Vera's death and feel good about it. This type of statement illustrates how the meanings attached to the death affect the course of bereavement.

Any meanings that family members could make about how prepared their loved ones were for death seemed comforting. Jane and Lisa Smith cited evidence that Bob, Jane's husband, who had died at age 49 in his sleep, had prepared for death:

Lisa   I guess a clipping that Bob had cut out about many rooms, God has many rooms, many people, and that he's in one of them.

Jane   That was real interesting. A minister read it and [pause] . . . it was an editorial, and it was a clipping in the paper. It wasn't the passage from the Bible, but it went on to say that there are rooms for people who believe and who don't believe and Buddhists and Muslims and blacks and whites and midgets, and I don't remember exactly. But it was a clipping he had hanging up on his dresser, and maybe I never noticed it before. It was stuck on. He had had it taped, he had a certificate from a trade school or something, and a frame, and had it taped on that. Yeah, it even helped me with our father. He's in a room up there too, regarding all of the things that maybe he shouldn't be there for. There was a place for him too.

Jane and Lisa looked to what they thought Bob believed as the basis for constructing meaning for themselves: Bob is in one of the heavenly rooms, and so is their father. The inference is that if Bob had cut out such a clipping, he had done some thinking about his death. Interestingly, the clipping had not been mentioned in an individual interview with Jane; her sister, Lisa, remembered it.

Other evidence helped make a case for Bob's preparedness. Jane discovered a list of things she should do if Bob died. She said he had made the list and placed it carefully in a bureau drawer where she would be sure to find it.

THE DECEASED DESIRED DEATH

Three families made the meaning that the deceased had desired to die: the Barlows, the Swans, and the Owenses. In each instance, the one who died had been in a nursing home and incapacitated for a period of time. Vera Barlow was 85 and had required nursing home care for several years. Her youngest son, Tom, reported that for many years she had daily expressed a wish to die.

Tom's brother Ben and Ben's wife, Julie, agreed with Tom that Vera had wished to die. Ben's and Julie's comments below were in response to the interview question how they had reacted when they heard the news of Vera's death:

Ben   My immediate reaction was probably [pause] obviously sorrow, but along with that [pause] ah, [pause] happiness for my mother because I knew that [pause] ah [pause] she wanted to go home.

Int   How about you, Julie?

Julie   I feel the same way he did. I mean, it hit me hard when I answered, 'cause I knew what the phone call was about. But, at

the same time, we knew it was, you know, she is finally where
she wanted to be. You know, that made it, that made it easier.

Int   You had the sense that she had wanted to die, or was ready to
die?

Julie   Oh, ya.

Ben   Not just months . . . I'm talking, she talked about dying years
before that. For as long as I, she had always made the comment
that she only wanted to live as long as her parents lived. And
she was a woman who lived quite a bit in the past, so [pause]

Here, the emphasis is on how Vera desired death, rather than on
how prepared she was. Also seen here is how the pain of grief can be
assuaged when survivors believe that the deceased desired death. Ben
said he felt sorrow but at the same time happiness for his mother. Julie
said the news of Vera's death had hit her hard but that she knew Vera
was finally where she wanted to be. Their constructions were based
on the belief that Vera had wished to die.

It is interesting to note that, in the case of the Barlow family, all
five members interviewed agreed on this meaning—a rarity in this
study.

The Swan family also constructed the meaning that death was
desired. Julius had been in a nursing home for 12 years following a
stroke. He was unable to speak but understood what was said to him.
His family members made meaning based on their perception that he
wanted to die. In the following excerpt, his daughter, Monnie, and his
granddaughter, Susan, had just been asked whether they had ever had
family conversations about death:

Monnie   Oh, yes. My mother looked forward to it. Dad considered
it just a matter of course, and I think he was anxious to go.

Int   Um huh. Um huh. You mean when? Before he even had the
stroke, you mean death was something he would have
welcomed, or do you mean more after he

Monnie   Well, I think both. I think as a Christian you realize Heaven
is a lot better than this earth, and Christians kind of look
for- ward to it [pause]. But after his stroke, yes, yes, he
definitely wanted to go. And I think he was disgusted that
he laid so long.

Monnie saw her father as anxious to die. She cried a great deal during the interview and on several occasions consoled herself with the meaning that her father had been anxious to be out of his suffering.

This excerpt also reveals the interplay between religious meanings and meanings based on the perceived attitudes of the deceased toward death. Monnie had two meanings that seemed to help her accept her father's death: "He wanted to go" and "Christians look forward to death." The Swan family was characterized in an earlier chapter as feeling a responsibility to be Christian witnesses through the experience of their bereavement. Their comments about how Julius had seen death seemed to be at least partially influenced by their responsibility to witness.

In each of the three families who reported the deceased had desired death, the deceased was elderly, in a nursing home, and ill.

THE DECEASED BROUGHT DEATH ON HIM- OR HERSELF

Statements about how the person who died brought death on him- or herself were few, but they tended to be qualitatively different from statements that referenced the deceased's desire for death. Certainly, a case can be made for a difference between the deceased's desiring death and his or her instrumentality in causing death.

An extreme form of desiring death is to do something to bring death on. Ben Barlow and Dusty Miner each spoke of the family members they lost in a way suggestive of their instrumentality. Ben Barlow used the word *willed* in considering whether his mother brought on her own death:

Ben   I think, I think there is such a thing as you can will yourself to die if you are along with the physical [pause] ah [pause] if you don't have a will to live, you're not gonna live. If you have a will to live, you're gonna live a lot longer.

Int   And you are saying that she lacked the will?

Ben   Oh, I don't, I don't know if she called it will, I think she had, she [pause] okay, for all purposes she lacked the will but she didn't, she didn't want to, so in essence she, I can't say she lacked it, she just, she didn't want to live, so . . .

It is difficult to understand exactly what Ben meant to say about his mother's will to live or will to die. He may have wanted to say she had been suicidal, or he may have wanted to avoid the implication that she was mentally ill in any way. Only his older brother Jake addressed his mother's mental illness directly. Jake told about her mental condition and how he had gotten her into a mental institution following his parents' divorce.

Dusty Miner made meaning around the question of whether Anne had done anything to cause her own death. Dusty struggled to make sense of the death of his oldest sister, Anne, and by extension, the death of his mother:

Dusty   It's my sister, you know. God! Maybe I didn't have all of the stuff I believe and think about in terms of my sister. Maybe my sister was so goddamned angry that she cancered herself right out of this world, here. Maybe I didn't know my sister as well as I thought I did . . . My mother must have done that to herself. This, I'd like to look at this. She's got two lungs with cancer, there's got to be something genetically or emotionally wrong. Yeah, and I struggle with that.

Dusty vacillated between the notion of self-caused death stemming from an emotional problem and death because of genetics. Others in the Miner family had mentioned genetics. Dusty was sharing his thoughts in the presence of seven other family members. No one else in the family made meanings that were in any way suggestive of the notion that Anne brought on her own death.

Making the meaning that the deceased had done something to bring on death may have been a way for the bereaved families to instill some sense of order into the chaos. The extreme of not wanting to believe that the deceased was caught unexpectedly by death may be to consider that the deceased brought death on him- or herself. Making such meanings may help families come to terms with the ineffable.

THE DECEASED KNEW HE OR SHE WAS DYING

Included in this type of meaning statements were some based on things the deceased family member had done to prepare for death; others were based on things the deceased had said. The largest number of statements that fit this type were made by members of the Primo family, who had lost Ronnie in an airplane crash. Much family meaning-making revolved around what death had been like for Ronnie. It was also the most dramatic death in the study. Statements in the Primo family included "He had things prepared before he died," "He said he was not going to live a long life," "He expected to die young," "He said he wasn't going to live forever," "He said he wouldn't live to be 50," and "He joked about death halfway serious." The Primo family seemed to have a need to make what was a tragic, totally unexpected death seem somehow predictable.

The family making the second largest number of meaning statements indicating that the deceased knew he might die was the Smith family. Bob, like Ronnie, had died suddenly, with no warning. Jane, Bob's wife, said, "He didn't leave anything unfinished. . . . Bob tried to talk to me about death, but I wasn't interested. . . . He considered himself at risk." As was mentioned earlier, Jane also told about how Bob had left a list of things she should do in the event of his death and a newspaper clipping, hanging above his bureau, about Heaven.

In the Munson family, Evelyn cited the fact that, just before his death, her husband, Claude, had had a dream about his mother in Heaven. Evelyn thought the dream meant he had known he was about to join his mother in death. Claude's younger son, Sam, referred to how his father had said he did not have much time, that his time was running out.

Other statements from a variety of families included references to how arrangements that had been made for survivors were signs that the deceased had expected death. The Mackey family reported that Richard had left money in a checking account where it was easily accessible and had taught his daughter to do maintenance things around the house for her mother. The Miner family cited how Anne had made sure that her sister Linda was committed to mothering Anne's daughter, Edna. Some families had more evidence than others that the deceased had known he or she was going to die, but even the slightest evidence seemed to be comforting.

THE DECEASED DIED AS HE OR SHE WISHED

Passages from the Primo and Mackey families dominate and exemplify the group of meanings about how the deceased died as he or she wished. Primo family members said Ronnie's death in an airplane crash was consistent with his fast-track life and that if he had to die, he would have liked having a front-page story about his death.

A fair number of statements had to do with how the deceased had both lived and died his or her own way. The Mackey family was clearest about this type of meaning. They identified "I Did It My Way" as Richard's theme song, citing how he smoked his cigars and ate his eggs in order to enjoy life, at the risk of hastening his death.

Jane Smith talked about how her spouse would have wanted to go as he did, suddenly, in his sleep. Fran, one of Claude Munson's granddaughters, talked about how Claude had chosen to risk dying, rather than to give up what was satisfying to him: food, alcohol, and cigarettes. Family members seemed to take comfort from thinking that the person they lost died as he or she would have wanted.

THE DECEASED SAID NO
TO A COMPROMISED LIFE

This type of meaning statement was another large group. Evelyn Munson, referring to her husband's need for dialysis, said, "He didn't want to live on a machine the rest of his life." Claude's oldest son, Darren, referred to the fact that his father's quality of life had not been good of late, and two other family members made statements about how he did not want to be on dialysis and did not want to suffer. Somehow, Claude's death was made more acceptable to the family when seen in contrast to his living a compromised, pain-filled life, not of his choosing.

Jane Smith noted that her husband "would not want a half-life, or to cut back on anything." Jenny Mackey said it would have been terrible for Richard "to have lived without being able to do what he wanted" and that a compromised life "would have killed their relationship," meaning that Jenny could not see herself giving him physical care. Monnie Swan, whose father had already lived for 12 years unable to speak, said her father had been "sick and tired of being in that condition."

Category 9: How the Death Changed the Family

At least one person from each of the 10 families made meaning about how the death had changed them. Types include how individuals were changed, how the family was changed, and how death became more real.

HOW INDIVIDUALS WERE CHANGED

Someone in each of the 10 families made statements of this type. In the first family interviewed, Pam Mackey, a young adult whose father died during cardiac bypass surgery, made meaning about how she had grown as a result of her father's death:

Pam　　Handling things myself totally [pause] things I could help Mom with that I never realized I could. Stick with things like that. Ya, I'd say there is a lot of growth. Both Mother has, I have. Ah, it's kind of like a spreading wings type situation. . . . You really know how to fly, but you are really, really flying more.

Pam's meaning became part of the way she construed the loss of her father, and it affected the way she grieved. The notion that she had grown as a result of her father's death seemed to sustain her. She mourned him, but she appreciated what she had discovered about herself as a result.

Evelyn Munson, widowed after nearly 50 years of marriage, made meaning about how she had changed since her husband's death. She had just been asked why she thought Claude had died:

Evelyn　I don't know. I think maybe, well, maybe it was so I would be able to stand on my own two feet again. Because I became very dependent on him, you know. Because I let myself. Like Jeannie says, you spent your life taking care of our kids, of us, and taking care of Dad. Now you got to start all over and take care of Evey [Evelyn's nickname]. And so now, suddenly, after me everybody else comes first. You know, that's kind of hard to do. It is new for me.

Interestingly, Tom Barlow, because of his mother's death, revealed how he had been changed by his father's death more than 20 years before. At one point in the conversation, Tom made the statement, "Death happens to everybody." When asked whether his statement was in reference to his parents, he answered this way:

Tom   No. I think in terms of me . . . I, for some time, because of being faced with my father's death so suddenly, there was a time that it may have popped up in my thought process periodically, particularly before I got married. I never wanted to get married. I figured if I got that close to someone again, I'm gonna lose them. Well, I ended up marrying a girl that was younger, so I'll be the first to go.

Tom shared the meaning he had made at the age of 21: When he gets close to someone, the person dies. Meanings attached to the deaths of family members have consequences for the course of bereavement—in Tom's case, perhaps for the course of his life.

In two interviews, five members of the Primo family talked about how their behavior had changed as a result of Ronnie's young death. Three of the in-laws—Randy, Tim, and Vickie—who had been like best friends to Ronnie, made meaning interactively about how Ronnie's death had caused them to think twice about taking risks. Randy spoke first:

Randy   I'm not as dangerous as I used to be. I really think [I] have been, slightly. There are times, you know, when I could have gotten motorcycles or stuff, or done [pause]. I don't even want to take a jump. I wanted to jump out of an airplane, parachute jump and stuff like that, and now I have second thoughts about that. I mean, it's just, you take a little more thought into what you're doing.

Tim   That's exactly what I've done. That's exactly what he's saying. It's the exact same thing. I, even with the parachute, that, and with a lot of things I felt that same way.

Randy   See, I always thrived on doing exciting, you know, death-defying stuff . . drugs and everything and, you know, the whole works, I like that stuff. I like dangerous living. I just have second thoughts about all that stuff. So it's helped me somewhat.

Tim   I do not. I think that same way, except I don't, not for myself, but because now I got two kids, and Ronnie had two kids and Peep [nickname for 3-year-old daughter]. It's just, you know, too many kids, you know, to screw around with anything, you know, now. That's how I feel anyway, you know. Yeah, whenever I hear people going in planes or doing like, you know, jumping or those parasailing, any of that stuff, I think, yeah, maybe it's fun, but the risk is too great now. You know, not like I'm going to shelter myself, but just not going to take stupid risks, you know, whereas I would have, I think.

Vickie   I think the same thing, you know. I mean, we're about to go on vacation in a couple weeks, and we're going to get on a plane, and every time I think about anybody in the family . . . and Dominic just went on vacation. I think of them getting on a plane. That part of it, you know, I think there's some danger there, you know what I mean? But I think, like, Rena is one who always says, "Vickie, it happened to Ronnie. It's not going to happen to any of us, you know."

In an interview with three other members of the Primo family, Ronnie's younger sister, Dolly, and her husband, Leo, spoke of how they tended to take fewer risks since Ronnie's death:

Leo   I don't know if this will answer your question, but something that's kind of struck my mind. I was always, always willing to, any moment, to take the opportunity to fly in an airplane, in a small aircraft, and now I guess I would, might take the time, the time to think about flying a small plane. I don't, I, I probably, I think even on a commercial line, although I think we'll take a plane trip just to experience what it's like, once or not. But I wouldn't think about a small plane. I'd have flown a small plane at any time if I had the opportunity because I don't have those opportunities to fly in a small craft. I wouldn't even have thought about it. . . .

Dolly   I got a good one for that one. I've never been on a plane in my life, and then that happened and then I, I basically think positive in life, but, um, I was scared for a long time. I thought about taking, me and Leo going to Chicago just to see what it's like, like maybe a year ago, and then I let it slide. I'm just taking my time, but I'm very interested in going on a big plane, but then they're scary, you know. Get in an accident on a big plane, but I try to think positive. I'll probably be a little shaky at first, but I think it will be kind of exciting to get somewhere faster, you know. So, if planes weren't faster, I probably wouldn't. But that's one thing that I had a hard time thinking about for awhile. Gosh.

The meaning these five young people seemed to be making was that they could also get killed if they took risks. Prior to Ronnie's death, they had all taken risks quite readily. After his death, they either did not take the same risks or were more reticent. One could speculate that Ronnie's death dispelled the sense of invincibility that the young family members had and that is generally thought to characterize youth. Leo, one of Ronnie's brothers-in-law, expressed the notion of feeling less invincible this way:

Leo   One thing this, not just their death, but their death and all these other people's death, they'd maybe just grown older. But, I think I mentioned this earlier, when I was a kid, I never thought, saw myself ever going to the hospital, never getting sick. Never dying, really. I mean, I guess I kind of knew I was invincible, and even through my teen years I was kind of thinking that way. I guess by that time I knew it could happen, but not like I say I'm getting older, experience things, you know. Now I still don't want to go to the hospital. You know, I've been lucky all my life. I've stayed out of it, but I can't see how I can avoid it some time. How can I be that lucky never to get into the hospital? Now, definitely, I know death is there, you know.

Linda Miner, who lost her older sister, Anne, after having taken care of her for a year, described changes in herself. Linda talked about how losing Anne had meant losing her purpose:

Linda   I feel like there's a void. I had a really intense purpose in where I was moving last year, and that was to try to get Anne through cancer, so right now I don't feel like I'm moving . . . . I keep telling myself that isn't where Anne wants me to be, and I know Anne always, you know, Anne was a pusher. Anne was a supporter. Yeah, you can do that. Now c'mon, get your ass together, you can do that. Um [pause] yeah, well, because I just miss her. It's not like having her here, and tell me, we'll do it, you know.

Myra Owens talked about how she experienced confusion in her own identity after her mother's death. Myra, of all the respondents in the study, said the most about the need to redefine herself after losing someone close:

Myra   But I'm just thankful that I told her I loved her, and I am. I meant it, and I'm glad that we did have a wonderful father, and I felt that, when my mother died, that closed the door, and that's why I had a real problem with identifying myself. Like, who am I now? And when she died, that was it, period. We're done now. Now we're on our own. Now we're the head of our own families.

Myra's meanings included a redefinition of herself.

HOW THE FAMILY WAS CHANGED

Some family members talked about changes in the family as a result of the death. A Barlow grandson, not officially in the study, said the family had become closer as a result of his grandmother's death. He made reference to how the family had to work together to prepare for the funeral and how he and his brothers had been pall bearers. Laura, Anne Miner's youngest sister, said their family had also been brought closer by Anne's death.

In the interview with the Smith family, Lisa explained what had changed in their family:

Lisa   I would say it, Jane and I are closer. I think that many years between us, you know, we haven't been doing the same thing. [pause] You know, she moved out when I was 10 years old. [pause] Distance. [pause] We lived a couple of hours away from each other in those days. [pause] We haven't really been as close as we are, so I think . . .

Lisa indicated that one outcome of Bob's death was that she and her sister had become closer. One got the sense that Lisa liked that her older sister needed her and that the difference in their ages meant less now than it had in their growing-up years.

The Munson family talked about how members were less close because Claude, the person who had kept them connected, was gone. Darren Munson compared how it was before and after his father's death:

Darren   Yeah, it's really, it really did surprise me. And, um, sometimes, you know, he'd come to my office and just kind of sit there. He wouldn't have anything to say, and I would be busy, and I'd kind of wish that he would go, really, you know. And, ah, those sorts of things that, towards the end, he wasn't as interesting as he was. I mean, to spend some time with him was really, it didn't take very long, and you didn't have anything more to say, and you go, that's the reality of it. But what I miss about him [are] the connections that he made, and, ah, you know, that's not there anymore [pause, teary].

Darren's meanings included the notion that, with his father's death, important connections within the family were lost. Darren's description provides a glimpse of how, when family members are lost, the roles they play in the family are lost as well. The family structure is changed.

HOW DEATH BECAME MORE REAL

Many family members made statements about how losing a family member made death more real: It changed or affected their attitudes about losing other family members and made them consider their own deaths. Jane Smith talked about how she wanted to die in the same manner as her spouse had died:

Jane   Yeah, I hope if, I hope when I go it's as quick as Bob went. [pause] I think we all want to go that way. [pause] And I had this awful fear that, when it's time for me, I'm going to hang around for years, sick. You know, nobody wants that.

At another point in the interview, Jane had compared Bob's sudden death with her father's slow death and decided for herself that she preferred sudden death.

Julie Barlow made meaning about how Vera's death prepared her for future losses:

Julie   So, really, she did a lot, you know, a lot for me in that respect. Not that the next one is gonna be easier, you know. My parents aren't going to be easy. But something's different. She has made it more peaceful, more acceptable for me.

Vera's dying had made Julie feel more peaceful and accepting of the anticipated loss of her parents.

Fran Munson, Claude's college-age granddaughter, shared her meaning-making about death. Part of her process of making sense of his death was considering death in general and considering her own death in particular:

Fran   . . . And just through talking to people and reading books, and just growing up, and becoming more aware of things, I think I've, I've finally realized that, if somebody dies, it's not my fault, and death is a natural thing and it happens. It's hard and, um, personally, I'm not afraid of dying. Because I have the feeling that it will be a peaceful place. And I'll be comfortable and I'll be happy, and I just have, I know that it will be hard on my family, and, um, I guess I'm more afraid of people I'm close to dying.

One of Fran's meanings is that someone close to her might die, and she fears that occurring. Fran's meanings may have been influenced by her being in nursing school at the time of the interview. She perhaps is trying to sort out her responsibility for the deaths of others, including both patients and family. Fran described her expectation that death for herself will be peaceful, comfortable, and happy.

Claude Munson's death caused his younger son, Sam, to think about his death. Sam Munson made meaning by comparing his life choices with those his father had made. One meaning Sam made was that he had done things differently from his father by choosing to change his lifestyle. His father had resisted alcohol treatment, which supposedly resulted in an earlier death than what he would have had if he had stopped drinking.

Sam   . . . And I think this just shows that people can understand
           that this is what long-term abuse can do to you. It affects the
           different organs in different ways, and pretty soon you're
           sick and pretty soon you're in trouble. It's, ah, it's a sad thing
           for me to look at because it's close that way. I was lucky
           enough to go through treatment. He just didn't. He thought
           it was great that I did, but old guys like him don't need that.

Implicit in Sam's remarks is the notion that Sam could have
expected the same type of death as his father's if he had not gone to
treatment and that his father's death could have been prevented if he,
too, had chosen treatment.

Another meaning that Claude's death had for Sam was how it
caused him to envision his own funeral. Sam compared his 72-year-old
father's funeral with what his own might be like. He started by
discussing how his funeral would be different because he and his wife,
Deb, have no children:

Sam   And no plans to have. She doesn't want them. I want kids.
           It's been an ongoing thing. If I ever get old, there will be
           nobody there, for me. 'Cause I should help with my brother
           and sister. . . . Ah, there will be nobody, of course, I'll be
           dead, so it won't matter, but I mean, there's, there's no
           [pause] there's nothing carrying it on. I don't know how to
           explain that longer. [pause] My [pause] when Grandpa died,
           I was a pall bearer and Dad was, and when Dad dies, I'm
           there, and the grandkids are the pall bearers, but I don't
           have, there's not any of my kids, you know. [pause] But there
           was, but there was none of my kids there.

Sam appeared very sad as he talked. One of Sam's meanings, made
by comparison, was that his father was mourned by offspring. Sam
would not be. The reality of his father's death caused Sam to reevaluate his own life and the decisions he had made in regard to having
children. These meanings seemed to influence Sam's experience of his
father's death, and Sam's constructions about his father's death had
direct implications for his own.

One commonly seen family change identified by family members
was their fear that someone else was likely to die. Fran Munson is

quoted as saying so in the passage above. Jane Smith talked about the added pressure of thinking that someone else could be lost at any time. The question to which Jane was responding in the next excerpt was whether she thought she had changed as a result of her husband's death:

Jane   Oh, I suppose. I feel like hell. [she and her sister both chuckle] Physically, I'm fine. Um [pause] I just have never before had so many down times. You know, I can't think [pause] I can't think of any times, anything that has been so difficult to get over. Um [pause] I try to be more appreciative of people, but that's difficult too. I'm very close to my boss. I've worked at the same place for 29 years. He's 20 years older than I am. I know that the time is coming when he won't be here, and that seems unfathomable too. Ah [pause] I try to be more appreciative of our relationship, but still you live your normal, everyday life, and he irritated me today. I mean, you know, by the time I left, who cares, but, you know [pause] you just can't, you also can't walk around thinking that everybody you know may die tomorrow. I mean, what a morbid way to exist.

Jane made the meaning that the way she had changed was in how she felt. She could not believe how hard it had been to get over Bob's death and dreaded losing her boss as well. Jane said she was trying to appreciate people more but that it was difficult. It seems that Bob's death had made her more aware that others, including her boss, could die. As she said, however, she still had to live her normal life. Asking Jane how she had changed resulted in her sharing both her meanings and her emotional struggles, which seemed inextricably bound.

Category 10: Lessons Learned and Truths Realized

Statements in this category had a strong existential flavor. Respondents said a great deal about what they had learned from having someone in their family die. Some of what they said was in direct response to being asked whether they had gained any life lessons or truths. Other comments were made more spontaneously. For some, pointing to what they had learned seemed to be an attempt to put a positive spin on their experience.

The meaning statements having to do with life lessons learned or truths realized were divided into five types: (a) don't take others for granted, (b) set priorities, (c) how to live life, (d) live in the moment, and (e) put relationships first. Meanings are included under types where they seemed to fit best, although distinctions among types is relatively arbitrary within this category. To give a sense of these meanings, at least one example of each type is given in full and contexualized. Other quotations fitting each type are given in abbreviated forms.

DON'T TAKE OTHERS FOR GRANTED

The four families who made statements about not taking others for granted were the ones in which the youngest deaths occurred. Respondents from families in which the death was of an older member and in which the death was more or less anticipated did not make statements about taking others for granted. One could theorize that these family members had already stopped taking the person for granted as they had seen the lost person's health fail or as they had seen the person aging.

Toby Miner, age 23, who lost his 45-year-old mother to cancer, said, "You can't take anything for granted." Rena Primo, whose 39-year-old husband was killed, said, "Don't take things for granted," and her mother said, "I don't take things for granted anymore." Jane Smith, who lost her husband to an unexpected heart attack at age 49, noted, "You take people for granted." Jane's sister, Lisa, said, "You don't take for granted how long your spouse will live." Lisa was considering the possibility that she, like her sister, could lose her spouse.

Eighteen-year-old Andy Zeeman lost his mother shortly after his high school graduation. His parents had sought to spare him from the seriousness of his mother's illness so that he would enjoy his senior year of high school. They did not share with him how seriously ill she was. He had been caught unaware. Andy commented, "Um, I guess I just can't take it for granted, ah, the time that you're with somebody." Andy, perhaps for the first time, was contemplating the reality of death. It may be that a sudden, major loss permanently changes how one sees others, relates to others, and experiences oneself.

SET PRIORITIES

Five of the 10 families indicated that they had learned what was most important in life as a result of losing someone in their family. Members of the Buchanan family, who had chosen to bring their 84-year-old mother/grandmother home from the nursing home to die, had the most to say about priorities. Mark seemed to be the major spokesperson for the Buchanan family. As he spoke, his wife, his mother, and his father nodded their heads. Mark, who was 26, was the only one of the nine adult grandchildren to agree to be interviewed. He and his wife were also the only grandchildren present when Florence died. This was how Mark expressed what he had learned:

Mark   I only had one other lesson there [pause] a big lesson for me, another, is just watching from what my parents do. And what you hear and read is that, that emphasis on people, especially those people that are important to you, that emphasis on, you know, having that belief, coming here to visit Grandma, when I was up north, visiting her, taking care of her. For Mom and Dad to bring her home and take care of it, I had to face it. It's important, and it's good. You need to do that. That's important; that's reinforced, reinforced and, then, when she passes away, and then you're at peace with it. You start to finally realize that, you know, that really is important, and it really does pay off, and people really should be the center of your life because you don't have the empty feelings that you hear people write about, talk about on shows. [pause] And that just kind of reinforces to me, it's a big reinforcement, that remember, people are number one. That's the most important. People are close to you, don't forget them.

Mark's wife, Barb, and his mother, Coral, joined Mark in saying what they had learned as a result of Florence's death:

Barb   I would just echo the same thing, um, that both Dad and Mark kind of said as far as learning, you know. It can be so easy to put so many things off that really matter and, um, and then, you know, do. Are you prepared to deal with the regret of "Gosh, you know, I could have made the time," or "I should have made the time," or, you know, and just not, that would be the lesson.

Mark   I remember we jumped in the car to go see your dad.

Barb   Yeah, I was feeling really down because we weren't there because I had something going on here in town, and he had just had one of his big surgeries that day, and I got home from, I had a big graduate school exam, and Mark said, let's go.

Mark   Yeah, jumped in the car and drove to Madison.

Barb   Let's go. Let's go. That's where he was at the hospital.

Mark   Came back the next morning bright and early.

Coral   You have to listen to your own heart. Because we know that the doctor said to us, ah, "This is not going to be good for your family. It's not a good decision. You should put your mother in the nursing home. This just can't work."

Barb   Is that right?

Coral   Right, and um, I believe you have to listen to your own heart and know that everything that you choose to do is only a period in your life. It's not your whole life.

As was common with many of the interviews, family members moved back and forth between the family death and making comparisons with other family members who had died or who had been ill. In this excerpt, Mark and Barb were applying what they had learned from Mark's grandmother's death to Barb's father's close call with death.

The meaning this family conveyed seemed to be that people have top priority, that you have to listen to your heart and make the time for people who are important to you if you want to have peace when those you care about die. Interestingly, Mark and Barb were learning for the first time that the physician had advised against taking Florence out of the nursing home to die at home. This is a good example of how the interview was a meaning-making stimulator and how families made meaning interactively.

Members of other families also spoke of priorities. Jane Smith talked about how she had learned that it was important to take time to do things while you can. She and her husband, Bob, had taken an extravagant vacation before his death, for which she was grateful. In the Swan interviews, Susan and Monnie indicated they had learned that possessions did not matter and that a person's faith was most important. The religious flavor of their statements was consistent throughout their interviews. Their family value was that their reaction to a death in the family was to be a Christian witness.

Although the priorities that family members identified varied, those who spoke of priorities were clear that having lost someone caused them to either change their priorities or set priorities for the first time.

HOW TO LIVE LIFE

Six of the 10 families talked about how the death had taught them something about how to live life. Some of what they said was closely linked to the type of death that had occurred. Darren Munson, whose father had died of alcoholism and other excesses, vowed to maintain a lifestyle without excesses. His brother, Sam, said he had learned "you have to do things in order to live long." He was referring to his own choice to seek treatment for alcoholism. Fran Munson, referring to her grandfather's lifestyle, said, "You have to take care of yourself."

Members of the Primo family were mixed in the lessons they took from Ronnie's death. When they were construing Ronnie's death as the result of taking unnecessary risks, the lesson they took from it was not to take risks. Randy, Tim, and Steve Primo were particularly clear about how, having seen what it was like for the little girls to be without their father and Rena to be without her husband, they were taking fewer risks. When the family was construing Ronnie's death as premature and describing how he had lived life to the hilt, the lesson they took from it was that life should be lived to the fullest. Rena, Ronnie's widow, said, "You have to make the best of it." Ronnie's mother-in-law said she had learned it is important to "live life with gusto."

Colleen Barlow was troubled by the notion that anyone could want to die as her mother-in-law had. She hoped she would never feel that way. Colleen told how both her mother and her mother-in-law had given up on life. In this excerpt, Colleen is referring to both of them:

Colleen   I think it really makes me stop and realize how good I have things, and, ah, to enjoy life, you know. I never had a death wish, and I hope I never will. I mean, I know it is going to happen, and when it comes, I hope I can accept that, but right now I want to enjoy what I have and appreciate what I have, ah, not just for myself but for my family. . . . Where with my mother, too, I mean, I don't like when I saw my mother give up after my dad died. That's another thing that affected me. I think it helped [me decide] that I would never, but I guess you don't know until it happens, but [pause].

This excerpt is a good example of how family deaths often swim together in family members' experience. Colleen's meaning was that both her mother and mother-in-law had given up on life. Colleen had experienced abandonment after her dad's death when her mother gave up on life. What Colleen had learned from her experience was that she wanted to avoid ever giving up on life and abandoning her family.

When asked what he had learned, Tom Barlow, Vera's youngest son, also considered Vera's years of asking to die, and he said, "You have to live and be productive." Pam Mackey, whose father had died during heart bypass surgery, said she had learned to "dwell on the better points of life," that "death is not great, but we all have to die."

Lessons the Swan family claimed to have learned combined in an interesting way. Susan, the bereaved granddaughter, said, "You have to keep looking up." Her mother, Monnie, said, "You should try to plan your finances." Susan focused more on the ethereal; Monnie on the mundane. Monnie was angry that her father's nursing home bills had used up her inheritance, and she seemed to be struggling to contain her anger so as not to spoil her Christian witness.

LIVE IN THE MOMENT

Six of the 10 families made statements about the importance of living in the moment. As might be expected, these statements were more common in the families in which family members had died unexpectedly and at early ages. Various members from both generations of the Primo family said, "Don't look at tomorrow," "Enjoy every day," "Life is a short visit," "Life is a short time and precious," "Live each day," and "Live one day at a time."

In the interview with Dwight and George Miner, father and son interacted about the life truths they had realized as a result of Anne's death:

Dwight   Ah, yeah, you know, I think, ah, you know, kind of, there, seize the moment a little bit, you know.

George   Smell the roses, you mean?

Dwight   Yeah. Yeah, enjoy the, enjoy the, enjoy the snow, enjoy when it rains, enjoy when the sun comes up, enjoy, you know, your kids, even when they get on your nerves like crazy, you know. You know, 'cause nothing is going to last forever, you know. So you have to, you have to [trailing off]

George   . . . life is short you know and ah, I, I'm, I look at the fact we did have Anne for all those years, and whether we took advantage of the opportunity that we should have during her life, I'm not certain about that. But she was a positive, wonderful person, and we had her all those years. It's too bad we couldn't have spent some more, but that's the way it goes. You know, there's nothing you can do about that.

Dwight and George told how they had learned that it is important to seize the moment, to smell the roses, to be glad for everyday things, even those that are irritating. George, Anne's father, added some thoughts about whether they took advantage of the time they had with Anne. At another place in the interview, George shared that he had cancer himself and had been most concerned about his death; he had not expected that his daughter would die first. George's impending death adds gravity to his statements about living in the moment.

PUT RELATIONSHIPS FIRST

Of all the statements about what family members had learned as a result of someone in their family dying, meaning statements having to do with relationships were the most plentiful. Some respondents who had lost young family members spoke about time, particularly how they had come to appreciate the value of time. Derek Zeeman, whose wife died at age 42, said in a tight-throated voice:

Derek   Just appreciate the time, appreciate time, that you have with family and friends.

Lisa Smith, in an individual interview, commented on how she was relating her sister's loss of her husband to the possibility that she, too, could lose her partner. Lisa spoke of what she had learned about time:

Lisa   [I learned to] appreciate the time I have with my husband and [pause] not take for granted that we'll live to be 80 or 90.

Interestingly, Lisa said little or nothing about these considerations when her sister was present, as if she did not want to emphasize the fact that her spouse was still alive. Possible interpretations of this finding include the notion that Lisa may have felt guilty that her spouse was still living but her sister's was not. This was also true with sisters in the Primo family: Karrie reported feeling guilty that she still had a spouse and that her sister's spouse had been killed. Lisa spoke little of her own spouse in Jane's presence out of politeness or respect toward Jane or a desire not to cause Jane pain.

In an interview with four members of the Primo family, two of Ronnie's in-laws—Vickie and Tim—spoke of what they had learned as it related to time and relationships:

Vickie   I guess I kind of look at, like you know, ah, like my father in life, says, we're here for a short visit, and I really believe that there's a lot of meaning behind that. And, you know, to spend as much time as you can with your family, you know. 'Cause you just never know.

Tim   Yeah, my dad and I talk about just living every day, because he's always planned so much for, for the time that he's not going to have now with my mom. And he, he thought that I was a good example as for living for today.

Tim and his father had been spending a great deal of time together since the recent death of Tim's mother. Tim was reporting on their interactive meaning-making in regard to time.

Some statements suggested that respondents had learned the importance of settling interpersonal conflicts in the event that death would occur. Fran Munson, when asked whether she had gained any life truths from losing her grandfather, answered like this:

Fran   Just one that, that's kind of evolved [pause] is that you shouldn't be afraid to tell somebody how you feel. Because you never know. How did I know that my grandpa was going to die when I got in a fight with my dad, left home without talking to him, you know? You never know that [pause]. Leave others you care about on good terms [pause]. It is not a good way to leave, fighting [pause]. You shouldn't be afraid to tell someone how you feel [pause]. If we fight, I always make sure it ends good.

Fran was aware of the multiple estrangements that existed in her extended family and had some fears that there would be more. Joyce Primo, echoing Fran's sentiments, said she had learned how important it was to "forgive others before it's too late."

In addition to the statements about time and relationships and leaving on good terms, some respondents shared advice on how to conduct oneself in relationships. Monnie Swan said, "Try to be more forgiving and broad minded. . . . Be kinder to neighbors." Jenny Mackey said she had learned to "accept people . . . don't try to change them." Jane Smith said she had learned it was important to "be honest . . . try to be more appreciative of people . . . knock off the arguments." Toby Miner said, "Treat other people the way you want to be treated." And Mark Buchanan, referring to both his grandmother's death and the death of a cousin years before, said this:

Mark   Then I realized that it really comes in the neat things those people did for you. And how much I appreciate them, and I think in return I kind of have responsibility to do those same things for other people. If I was lucky enough to have those gifts from these people who were only here for a given amount of time, that it's only right that I kind of try and do the same.

Summary

In conclusion, this chapter included meanings about the nature of the death itself, the deceased's meanings, and meanings about how families changed and learned. The variety in categories and types within categories reflects the wide range of the meanings that family members were willing to share.

This typology includes meanings that seemed to be constructions of individuals, highly influenced by family, as well as meanings that were clearly the products of family interactions. Findings included a fair number of negative meanings that have been talked about very little, if at all, in the grief literature. Emphasis has historically been placed on finding positive meaning in trauma, rather than on negative meaning. Little has been written about how negative constructions affect the course of bereavement. Also not discussed in the literature is the notion that, to make sense of a death, some family members need to say what the death does *not* mean.

Finally, major features of the family meaning-making process that emerged included factors that either inhibit and stimulate meaning-making, how meaning-making interacts with family structure and family dynamics, and how certain meanings made by families may influence bereavement.

9

Looking to the Future

Implications for Theory, Research, and Practice

IMPLICATIONS FOR THEORY

This study lays the foundation for substantive grounded theory about family meaning-making in bereavement. It is classified as substantive grounded theory because it is limited to one situational context (Strauss & Corbin, 1990). Formal grounded theory may be generated when family meaning-making is studied in multiple contexts. As is true of qualitative research, the purpose of this study was to show that some phenomenon exists, to reveal the complexity of the data, and to provide readers with illustrations (P. C. Rosenblatt, personal communication, September 1990). Findings in qualitative studies, such as the current study, are viewed as tentative, and although they may sometimes be used in explaining or even predicting some phenomenon, they are not set forth here as explanatory or predictive theory.

Theories to which this study makes contributions are family systems theory, family stress theory, constructionist theory, and grief theory. What was learned in this study of family grief builds on existing theory and suggests some directions that future development of theory might take.

Family Systems Theory

As was predicted in the design of the study, systems concepts were useful in describing family behavior associated with family grief. The study of family meaning-making provides a picture of family structure and demonstrates the reciprocity between family structure and family meanings. Meaning-making occurred within coalitions, within alliances, and within generations. Meanings were made within boundaries, and the meanings that were made helped maintain boundaries.

Much was learned about how individual meaning-making occurs within the boundary of the family. Even when sharing seemingly individual meanings, family members referred to the meanings of other family members, echoed their words, and agreed or disagreed with them in ways that call into serious question the notion of purely individual meaning-making and individual meanings. The ways in which this occurred in this study of families is reminiscent of the way Reiss (1981) described the family process of reality construction. Reality construction becomes a family matter, Reiss contended, as the family builds up a collective view or schema of its informational world.

Findings of the current study illustrate what is meant in family theory by the notion of *family context:* One part of family context seems to be a shared family history. In their efforts to make sense of a death, family members tapped into family past history by comparing the current death with previous family deaths. Context in family meaning-making also was found to include the ways family features affected all levels of meaning-making.

The discovery that meaning was made on all systems levels and that meanings varied, depending on which family members were present, has implications in the ongoing theoretical debate about the interface between individual and family meanings. It does not seem to be simply a matter of individual versus family meanings, but rather that each subsystem of the family has its own meanings. At the very least, the family serves as a crucible for formation of individual meanings. It may be useful in the future to concentrate more on family processes having to do with sharing and ways to promote healthy family sharing than to focus as much on making a distinction between individual and family meanings.

The finding that family members constructed joint meanings interactively also extends theories about family process. *Family speak* is the term given in this study to the way family members spliced their phrases together and arrived at meanings that could not be identified as belonging to any particular member. Although family speak is how some families made sense of a death, it seems likely that families would use similar means to make sense of other family experiences.

The meaning typology may be helpful in future theorizing about meanings because, in its breadth and richness, it could provide a basis of comparison for other studies of family bereavement and of other family phenomena. For example, limited attention has been paid to the notion that the search for meaning following a trauma may yield negative meanings as well as positive. Also new is the finding that family members talked about what the death did *not* mean. It may be possible to develop ways of describing a given family's meaning system in relation to other family phenomena by drawing on the breadth and richness of the meaning typology.

Family Stress Theory

From the inception of this study, questions arose about the ways family bereavement could be construed as one form of family stress. If bereavement can be considered a family stressor, then family stress theory can be applied in much the same way as it has been to chronic illness by using the double ABCX model of family stress (McCubbin & Patterson, 1983). Of particular relevance to this study is the double C part of the ABCX model, which represents the family's perception of the stressful situation. The double C factor includes an assessment of family resources, an assessment of the concomitant strains and stressors, and the families' perceptions of themselves. As it turned out, the meanings shared by grieving families did not include assessments, nor did the families talk much about their own ability to cope with losing a family member. Their meaning statements were more about the meaning of the death and how the families changed as a result of their loss.

Family self-perception may not be as central in bereavement as it is in coping with chronic illness. Something may be notably different about trying to make sense of an event, such as death, that has occurred in the past and an event, such as chronic illness, that is ongoing. Although the lack of appraisal or assessment meanings in the current study may be a function of the methodology or the bias of the researcher, it would seem to be an important enough difference to warrant investigation in future studies.

Another implication for family stress theory has to do with the assumption sometimes expressed in family stress studies that family meaning-making and shared perceptions are generally desirable. Findings in the current study suggest that the desirability of family meaning-making may have more to do with the nature of the meanings constructed. A negative meaning attached to the death, such as that the death was a punishment or that the death could have been prevented if family members, including the deceased, had acted differently, may be a source of distress in the family, not comfort. Perhaps family meaning-making is desirable if family members are capable of coming to meanings that will facilitate mourning. The construction of negative meanings may not promote healthy family grief even if family members agree.

One can always argue, however, that if family members engage in collective meaning-making, they have a greater likelihood of construing the death more positively or, at the very least, of having the comfort of knowing that others share their meanings no matter how negative. At any rate, findings in this study cause us to examine the notion that the ability to attach meaning is always a "good" thing.

Finally, the findings in this study make more explicit the actual processes by which families come together to make sense of what stresses them. Patterson (1988) called this process *shared social construing*. It may be that what was learned in the current study about the processes of meaning-making in bereavement, particularly that meaning-making occurs on all systems levels using a variety of strategies, also occurs in relation to other family traumas. It will be important to study a variety of families experiencing a variety of traumas to see how the processes compare.

Constructionist Theory

This study supports an underlying premise of symbolic interactionist theory: If people define situations as real, they will be real in their consequences (Thomas, in Burr et al., 1979). Family members were able to talk about how their thinking had affected their grieving.

Families who construed the death as welcomed by the one who had died or who saw the death as the best possible death appeared to have less difficulty. From families in which the death was premature, was seen as preventable, or left small children behind came reports of very difficult grieving.

Findings in this study exemplify the symbolic interactionist concepts, definition of the situation, and definition of self. For instance, the Buchanan family made the meaning that they gave Mother a good death, and the mother-in-law in the Primo family said the death of her young son-in-law occurred to test their faith. A family variant of the symbolic interactionist concept, definition of self, emerged in the data when families talked about how they had changed and what they had learned as a result of their loss.

Findings in this study did little to support the notion of a *crisis construct,* which Reiss (1981) described as a construction of families following a death. He defined the crisis as "a shared (although usually implicitly so) conception of the family process itself" (p. 189). He theorized that the crisis construct focuses on the family itself and includes some percept of its disorganization. Family reality construction in this study seemed to be more about the death and about the lost family member than it was about how the family saw itself in a time of crisis.

Some meanings that emerged in this study were reminiscent of what Reiss (1981) referred to as the *family paradigm,* the family's central organizer that consists of the family's assumptions, constructs, fantasies, and sets of expectations. Some philosophical and religious meanings could be seen as organizing the family; other family meanings could be characterized as assumptions, constructs, fantasies, sets, or expectations.

In other ways, findings in this study are congruent with Reiss's (1981) work and possibly build upon it. According to Reiss, the chaos experienced by the family is transcended by a rich and personal meaning attached to the crisis events. This study supports the notion that families do attach meaning to the crisis events; however, they attach many meanings, rather than one meaning, and they attach negative as well as positive meanings. The contention that families "strive for the emergence of a sense of solidity around a common perception of the revealed significance of the crisis" (Reiss, 1981,

p. 194) is not supported by these data. Family members in this study were as invested in differentiating themselves from what other family members believed as they were in striving toward consensus of meaning. It also seemed that the meaning-making process was quite fluid, that meanings were being made and modified in an ongoing manner, and that the level of agreement varied with these changes.

This study clearly corroborates Reiss's finding that families say different things, depending on who is present. Reiss questioned whether the differences were a result of real differences between individual and family meanings or whether they occurred because, being in the process of construing, members got to new meanings by the next interview. Families in this study also said different things, depending on who was present, but in this case family members were asked why they would not share certain meanings with others present. Their answers revealed that differences were relational and had most to do with such factors as members feeling the need to protect others or fear that their meanings were too different from those of others.

Findings in this study build upon Berger and Luckmann's (1966) work on the social construction of reality. Their notion that "everyday reality is ongoingly reaffirmed in the individual's interactions with others" (p. 150) laid the groundwork for thinking about the interactive processes by which families become able to integrate the reality of a death into their everyday reality. Berger and Luckmann theorized that reality maintenance, modification, and reconstruction occur between individuals and society, but they did not address how one would recognize these processes in the everyday conversation of families. This study showed how families integrated the reality of a death into their everyday reality by using certain meaning-making strategies as they talked among themselves.

Grief Theory

Most grief theories focus on individuals. This study expanded grief theory to include interactive family grief processes. Scant work has been done in which family theory and grief theory have been integrated. This study provides an example of what such studies might look like. Findings add to the development of grief theory by providing some detail about the interactive processes by which families make sense of losing a family member and by identifying the wide range of meanings that families make.

When family meaning-making is conceptualized as a critical element of bereavement, other features of family grief can be seen in relation to meaning-making. This study adds to what we know about how family dynamics, family structure, and a variety of family contextual features interact with meaning-making to determine outcomes in bereavement. The findings in this study would lead one to believe that any theory about grief that does not include family meaning-making would be less than adequate.

IMPLICATIONS FOR RESEARCH

It is important to discover whether what was learned about meaning-making in family bereavement can be applied to other family losses. From the onset of this study, I started noticing how families experiencing a variety of events talk among themselves in ways not unlike the way bereaved families talk. For instance, when a divorce occurs, families must construct new meanings to account for what has happened to the marriage and how life will be different. When a family must relocate, members talk among themselves about such things as why the move is occurring and how family life will be carried on in a new place. When family members are added to a family as they are through birth, adoption, or marriage, new meanings are elicited.

Work has been done already in regard to how families construe chronic illness (Patterson, 1988), and this work continues with other cultures. Of major importance in any of these studies will be learning about differences in family meaning-making in diverse cultural, ethnic, and racial groups.

Meaning-making is crucial to family bereavement and warrants continued study. It is paramount that, in the future, the focus continues to be on the family as the unit of analysis and that studies draw on family theory. It is important that we study family meaning-making in relation to types of deaths other than those in this study. How families make sense of deaths such as suicide, homicide, SIDS, AIDS, and childhood deaths deserves close attention. It would be important to investigate further whether families who experience different types of death construct different meanings and use different strategies. In this study, it was seen that the majority of negative meanings and the statements that no sense could be made of the death came from families who had lost relatively young members with little or no warning. Knowledge about how meanings differ, depending on the type of death, would help build theory and improve care to grieving families.

In the purest form of discovering grounded theory, data collection is continued until categories are saturated, which means that nothing new is being learned (Strauss & Corbin, 1990). In this study, it was possible to intensively interview members from 10 families and to interview a significant percentage of the family members more than once. Some new data were still emerging in the last interview. Categorical saturation had apparently not been reached. It would seem promising to study in as many ways as possible more families similar to those in the current study and different from those in the current study.

Benefits can be gained from analyzing the data from the current study from perspectives other than those reported in the findings. Clues in the data suggest that the meaning statements could be looked at developmentally in terms of cognitive, psychological, or moral development of family members. Suggestions were also found that meanings could be considered in terms of whether they represented family attitudes of mastery or fatalism. And although the study focused on cognitions, data about the emotional dimensions of grief were found. Some meanings seem more emotionally charged than others, and negative meanings were expressed along with negative emotions.

In future studies, the amount of systemic data should be increased. One way would be to interview as many different groupings of family members as possible, starting with the family as a whole and interviewing members both together and separately. On the basis of what was learned in this study, the best order of interviewing is to begin with the whole family first, proceed to smaller groupings such as couples, and then interview individuals alone. This procedure could provide data on why what family members say depends on who is present.

Studying more subsystems would also give a better sense of how the meaning-making process occurs on all systems levels, how subsystems differ in the meanings they construct, and how family structure interacts with the meaning-making process. Such study would be important not only for grieving families but also for families experiencing a wide variety of other events.

Systemic data would be increased in future studies of families by using the Milan method of circular questioning as part of intensive interviewing. And as was seen in the current study, more systemic data can be gathered when the interviewer includes the deceased among the missing family members whose meanings are asked about.

More systemic data could be gained by two modifications to the interviewing process as it was carried out in this study. The first modification is to ask more questions about why some people decided to participate and why others did not. In this study, some family members said they consented just to get other family members *to* talk with each other, and some refused to participate in order to keep certain family members *from* talking with each other. The second modification is to structure the interview so that questions are asked of the family as a whole, rather than individuals. In this study, when questions were directed to the family members and they were not interrupted by the interviewer, more interaction occurred and more family process data were collected. The goal should be to allow the family to be as spontaneous as possible, letting the nonparticipants not participate, and then to record the family's most "natural" patterns. Some families cannot or will not talk with others about such a sensitive subject as a family death, and the fact that they cannot is important family data.

More work needs to be done with all types of families in regard to how family meaning-making, family structure, and family dynamics relate to one another. In this study, meaning-making was found to occur at all systems levels, and it was theorized that shared meanings both create and maintain systems boundaries. Analysis showed an interplay between meaning-making and couple and family dynamics. For instance, in many instances, family dynamics such as reciprocity and reactivity within relationships affected the meanings that were made and vice versa.

Findings from the current study about family members' willingness to talk about death should be kept in mind for future studies about death and other sensitive family issues. When asked whether they could talk with each other about the death, family members indicated a higher level of willingness than they actually demonstrated in later interviews. Had there not been multiple interviews, this finding would not have emerged and the initial report of high sharing levels would have been taken as valid.

Some questions that this study raises can only be answered by longitudinal studies. Questions that need answering are, How long does it take to establish family meanings? How much do meanings change over time? What happens when negative meanings prevail? Are there families who cannot make any sense of their experience? How do certain meanings influence family outcomes? Answers to these questions would go a long way toward building our knowledge base about families and meanings.

IMPLICATIONS FOR PRACTICE

From its inception, this study changed the way I practiced psychotherapy. Conversations both in and out of therapy sessions were heard differently. Statements of meaning literally jumped out of people's narratives. It became clear that clients and others felt more heard and cared about when their meanings were acknowledged, even if their meanings were negative. The ways couples and families talked about their experience among themselves became immensely important. Their conversations were found to be quite similar to those of the study families even though they were often talking about experiences other than the loss of a loved one. Giving words to the differences in meanings held by members of couples and of families was found to help them develop more tolerance for each other's reactions and to be less defensive.

One middle-aged couple had construed the accidental death of their college-age son so differently from each other that they could barely discuss their loss outside the therapy office. The husband's meaning was that God had taken his son as punishment for his choosing to leave the seminary. The wife's meaning was that her son died because they had failed to get him help with his alcohol problem and alcohol abuse had caused the accident. Providing a safe environment in which they could explore their divergent meanings became a goal of therapy. Helping them recognize and respect each other's meanings opened the way for them to work through their feelings of guilt and reach some common understandings.

The importance of cultural differences in the meanings that families attach to death was emphasized when a colleague reported that one of her Native American families had construed the suicide death of their daughter in a wooded area as being a matter of the good spirits of the woods calling her away. She had no choice but to go, they said. It is hard to imagine all the ways this family's grief may be affected by that particular meaning, as opposed to one more laced with guilt and shame.

Meanings were seen to be important in family situations other than death. A woman in therapy for depression was wrestling with, among other things, having a teenage daughter with such severe disability that she had to be cared for in an institution. The mother, holding the belief that she herself was defective, had construed her daughter's disability as her fault. Therapy focused on recognizing her meaning and facilitating her talk with her husband about the meaning of their daughter's problems. This joint meaning-making helped her come to some less pejorative meanings, and her level of distress lessened.

What was learned about family meaning-making in this study can be used by a wide variety of helping professionals, not only psychotherapists. Approaching bereaved families from the perspective of how they make sense of their loss can be extremely helpful. Most forms of helping, even just being neighborly, deal with meanings in one way or another. Many findings in this study could be used by health care professionals, clergy, and educators to work more successfully with families in a wide variety of situations.

What are the specifics of how helpers can use a meaning-making perspective to help families? First, no matter what the trauma has been, it is important to listen to the family's story. People make sense of their experience by telling stories over and over again. Listening to the family story helps in collecting family data, helps the therapist join with the family, and is an intervention in itself. It conveys caring. The questions that were used to collect data in this study can be used to elicit family stories in a variety of settings.

Hospice nurses and clergy who conduct bereavement visits to families might gather family members together to participate in rituals that require the retelling of family stories. Meaning-making through retelling the stories could lead both to meanings that are more conducive to the resolution of grief and to helping family members feel less isolated. In disconnected families in which people have not been talking about the death, retelling the story can help reconnect members.

Findings in this study indicate that paying attention to the dreams of grieving families may be useful. Like stories, the dreams that family members report reveal important meanings. Dreams revealed may be the less conscious or more risky meanings that members have not been able to share with each other more directly. Exploring dreams with grieving people can stimulate meaning-making. Not only do dreams give important data and stimulate meaning-making, but the ways in which dreams are talked about in the family can reveal a great deal about the family and important family dynamics.

Listening for meaning-making strategies could help the therapist learn a great deal about coping styles. By listening for how the current death is compared with other deaths in the family, the therapist may be able to identify unresolved losses, sometimes even from past generations, that have an influence on grief about the current loss. Paying attention to what family members make of coincidences could help the therapist learn about belief systems within the family. And noticing how members characterize the deceased could help in identifying conflictual relationships with the deceased that, in turn, may complicate mourning.

When families are viewed through the window of meaning-making, a great deal about families can be assessed. Important structural characteristics such as coalitions, alliances, multigenerational patterns, and boundary problems come into focus. Meaning-making strategies can be seen to interact powerfully with such structural characteristics and family dynamics to produce particular meanings that, in turn, influence how families grieve.

Listening for whether individuals and families can make sense of their experience and whether meanings are positive or negative is helpful in identifying ways of helping families. Some meanings seem to be associated with more distress than are other meanings. In bereaved families, if the way a death is construed seems to be associated with inordinately high levels of distress, then working with the families either to construe the death differently or to live with distressful meanings is indicated. Some deaths may always have negative meanings to some or all family members. A disservice is done to families when they are given the message that they should be able to find positive meaning and purpose in their lives no matter what the loss.

Setting goals to promote factors that stimulate meaning-making and to discourage factors that inhibit meaning-making can provide a grounded approach to intervention. This study demonstrated that the failure to make meanings that will help family members resolve their loss may stem from such meaning-making inhibitors as not talking with each other, having faulty information, a need to protect themselves and others from painful thoughts and feelings, a high level of denial, and high levels of shame about past family events. Working with a family on any of these issues can help members talk to construct meanings that will facilitate their grief, help them be more supportive of each other, or help them find comfort in learning that others in the family are thinking and feeling as they are.

Findings in regard to the role of rituals and meaning have implications for both therapists and helpers other than therapists, particularly those who plan funerals and other death rituals. Not only do rituals help the bereaved make sense of the death, but the reverse may be true: The meaning the death has to the family may indicate what rituals are appropriate. By paying attention to the meanings as they are revealed in the family story and the ways families use certain strategies to make sense of their experience, helpers can learn what rituals would be both appropriate and helpful.

Some implications for family therapists overlap with implications for family life educators. If the ability to make meanings influences how families cope with the death of a family member and perhaps other traumas, then it is important to identify and teach family communication and encourage the building of beliefs and values that will sustain families in times of loss. It would also be important to teach children and parents how to maintain healthy levels of openness, both inside and outside the family, that will facilitate meaning-making. Teaching self-expression and respect for others' views could be a valuable preparation for meaning-making in regard to a variety of life experiences, including the trauma of losing loved ones.

Summary

In Chapter 1, the conceptual frameworks that informed this study were delineated, and definitions were set forth. From symbolic

interaction theory was drawn the notion that reality is socially constructed and that meanings so construed determine consequences.
From the family systems framework came the concepts necessary for
describing the structural changes that occur in the family following a
death—namely, changes in roles, rules, and boundaries. An argument
was given for the need for more studies of family grief because most
of what we know about grief is from an individual perspective.

Family meaning-making was defined as the social act whereby
family members interpret stimuli in the context of the family and
represent the situation to themselves and each other in symbolic terms.
Meanings were construed to be the products of interactions with
others and as being influenced by the context in which they occur,
including the influence of society, culture, and historical time.

In Chapter 2, the empirical and theoretical literature was reviewed,
revealing that the process of family meaning-making in grieving families
had not been studied. In Chapter 3, a description was given of how the
study was conducted, including a rationale for the use of qualitative
methods greatly influenced by grounded theory. Researcher bias was
identified and explored. Emphasis was on the tension between the roles
of therapist and researcher and how that was handled in this study.

In the first three chapters, the conceptual and methodological
groundwork was laid. In Chapters 4 through 8, the findings were
presented. In Chapter 4, the families were introduced and some of
their overall patterns of meaning-making were described, including
the identification of factors that either stimulated or inhibited family
meaning-making. Families with the greatest number of meaning-making stimulators were shown to be the most willing to talk with each
other about the death. True family consensus was shown to be less
likely than agreement among some groups of family members. Excerpts of interviews demonstrated that meaning-making occured at all
systems levels and that meanings both created and maintained systems
boundaries. The differences between what was shared in individual
interviews and what was shared in family interviews were used to
demonstrate that family members shared different meanings, depending on who was present. The notion that meanings attached to the
death affected the course of bereavement was stressed.

Chapter 5 began the descriptions of the strategies that families used
to make sense of their experience. Families were shown to use stories

and stories within stories to reorder their worlds following their loss. A wealth of meanings were found embedded within their stories, and stories helped characterize families. It was theorized that dreams help families make sense of the death, especially if members talk about the dreams among themselves. Families were shown to make sense of their experience by comparing the death with previous deaths inside and outside the family and, in doing so, perhaps were establishing themselves within the reference group of all bereaved. The term *coincidancing* was coined to capture the way families noticed so-called coincidances associated with the death and attached meanings to them.

In Chapter 6, the meaning-making strategies of characterization and family speak were described. Families seemed to need to make sense of their lost member's life in order to make sense of his or her death. *Family speak* was the name given to the way family members co-constructed meaning by weaving their phrases together. Family speak consisted of members finishing each other's sentences, asking questions, agreeing, disagreeing, and interrupting each other.

In Chapters 7 and 8, all the meanings found in the transcripts were organized into a typology. In Chapter 7, the meaning statements of a negative and ultimate nature were shared. Meanings ranged from statements about what the death did *not* mean to some very specific meanings about what the death *did* mean. Emphasis was placed on the notion that families do make negative meanings and that they may insist there is no sense to be made of a death, particularly if the family member is relatively young and dies unexpectedly.

Ultimate meanings described in Chapter 7 included a wide range of more commonly discussed philosophical and religious meanings. Many meanings were shared that related to whether the person the family had lost continued on in some sort of afterlife.

In Chapter 8, meanings were more substantively related to the nature of the death itself or to the family. Of special importance were the things families said about how losing someone had changed them and caused them to think about relationships, to set priorities, and to realize life truths.

Some features of family meaning-making cut across all the findings chapters. These mainly consisted of interactions among family structure, family dynamics, and the meaning-making process. These intricate relationships were noted and speculated about as they emerged in each chapter.

Conclusions

In this book, a study of how 10 multigenerational families made sense of the loss of a family has been shared. This close examination of how families made sense of a death provided important information about the process by which families constructed reality. The strategies by which family members constructed their meanings were identified and illustrated with multiple examples. New terms were coined to capture two of the strategies: *coincidancing* and *family speak*. Factors that either stimulated or inhibited family meaning-making were identified. Important family patterns, including patterns of sharing and patterns of agreeing, were traced. The profusion of meaning statements found in family stories about the death were captured and classified. Previously unstudied features of family bereavement were identified: making negative meanings and saying what the death was not.

This study of family bereavement is unique because it was totally qualitative. Qualitative research is still rare (Gilgun, in press). In recent years, less than 1% of articles appearing in the *Journal of Marriage and the Family* were purely qualitative (Ambert, Adler, Adler, & Detzner, 1995).

This study is unique in that it was about *family* grief, rather than *individual* grief, as most studies have been. In few studies have what we know about families and what we know about grief been integrated in any meaningful way. This study provided a beginning.

This study is unique in that it focused on the interactive, microprocesses of family construing. It did so by collecting data from multiple generations at multiple systems levels, including large family groups, and by interviewing family members both separately and together. Although family members may agree in some way about the meaning of a death, meanings differ, depending on who is asked and who is present in the room during the interview. Asking only one member about individual or family meanings gives a seriously limited view of family meanings, leads to false conclusions, and may lead to misdirected interventions.

This study is unique in its use of the modified Milan family therapy method. It was used to "mind read" missing and deceased family members in order to expand the amount of systemic data collected.

This study is unique because it described the relationship between meaning-making and other family variables. It identified factors that either inhibit or stimulate the process of meaning-making. It demonstrated how meaning-making is influenced by family structure and family dynamics. And it suggested how certain meanings may influence the course of bereavement.

Although not unique in this regard, this study expanded the meaning of meanings. The study explored what constitutes individual and family meanings and proposed that, by using family speak, family meanings are constructed. It is important to note that the meaning typology consisted mostly of meanings that were products of family interactions, rather than individual meanings. Even those meanings that seemed on the surface to be constructions of individuals were shown to be, at the least, highly dependent on the family context.

Emphasis has historically been placed on finding positive, rather than negative, meaning in trauma. This study suggests that families who lose younger members unexpectedly are more likely to have negative meanings and to say that there is no sense to be made of their loss. Especially well studied has been the notion that, through suffering, people can find a sense of purpose and meaning in life (Frankl, 1959), but very few meaning statements have been made about how family members found a sense of personal purpose as a result of their loss experience. This study expanded the definition of *meaning* to include negative meanings and idiosyncratic meanings closely attached to the death itself.

The definition of what constitutes a meaning may also have been expanded by the finding that, to make sense of a death, some family members needed to say what the death did *not* mean. It could be reasonably argued, however, that saying what the death did *not* mean is really a meaning-making strategy, rather than a type of meaning. It may be a strategy employed by families as one means of ferreting out what the death *does* mean.

An attempt has been made in this book to show what can be learned about the process of family meaning-making by studying grieving families. What bereaved families can teach us is useful in understanding not only family grief but also other family phenomena. Virtually any family event that has the potential to upset the family's status quo is likely to invoke meaning-making processes not unlike those identified in this study. Speculation has been made that what was learned may be applied to families experiencing marriage, remarriage, chronic illness, mental illness, divorce, geographic relocation, adoption, and birth, to name but a few. If the constructionists are correct, then the way families construe events determines the consequences of the events. It behooves those who care about family outcomes to understand this meaning-making process at the family level.

Some strategies that grieving families use may be used by all families no matter what challenge they face. Some family traumas will trigger a flurry of meaning-making activity at the family level. The meanings that families make may be as varied as those that grieving families make, and they may be as attached to the nature of the event as they were attached to the nature of the death. The families in this study have given us a window into how this meaning-making process occurs.

When someone dies, family members struggle to make sense of the death by talking among themselves. The meanings they make have a great deal to do with how they will grieve. Bereaved families make meaning in couples, dyads, and family groups. Their meaning-making is inhibited or stimulated by such family characteristics as family rules, family structure, family rituals, and the nature of the death. Bereaved families make a myriad of meanings by using multiple strategies: They tell stories, they dream, they make comparisons, they make something of coincidences, they characterize the deceased, they use common daily discourse, and they talk about what the death does *not* mean. The meanings that families make may be positive or negative and range from the most substantive to the most abstract, from those closely associated to the current death to those about life in general. The meanings that bereaved families make greatly affect the way they grieve.

A great deal about family grief can be seen by focusing on family meaning-making. And a great deal can be learned about family meaning-making in general by studying family meaning-making in bereavement. At the very least, meaning-making is important to family life, and, at the very most, it is the core.

Epilogue

During the writing of this book, there has been a "strange encounter" with time. Since the data from the study were originally analyzed, time has passed and a fair amount of theoretical, empirical, and methodological work has been done. These newer works, of course, had no influence on the design of the study or on the original analysis. To present them in the earlier chapters as if they had been available at the time of the study would be misleading. The solution, though somewhat unconventional and perhaps awkward, was to save the discussion of newer works for presentation here. During the intervening years, there has been an ongoing interaction with the findings as they have been prepared for presentation to a wide range of students, scholars, and clinicians, to say nothing of the immersion in the data that has been necessary to writing this book. These newer works are reviewed here as they relate to the ongoing exploration of family meaning-making.

When the study was designed, nothing in the literature dealt directly with the intersection of family processes, meanings, and grief. Such is still the case. A recent extensive search of the relevant literature did not turn up any study or theoretical work dedicated primarily to how family members interactively make sense of the loss of a family member. What was found were studies and theoretical works that in some way corroborate or further illuminate certain dimensions of family meaning-making or point to better methods for the study of such phenomena.

For the most part, examples come from the family literature, particularly family stress theory and the grief literature that tends to cut across disciplines. In addition, some significant advances in qualitative methods and methodology have been made. Those that show promise for studies of family meaning-making in the future are highlighted.

The Family Literature

Studies of family meanings continue to be rare. Rarer still are studies of family meanings associated with death. Studies about family grief focus on processes other than meaning-making, and studies about meaning focus on meaning and purpose in life such as Frankl (1959) defined it, not on meanings attached to the death itself. Theoretical and empirical work that does address family meanings in ways most similar to the current study has been done by Patterson and Garwick (1994a, 1994b, 1994c), who address family construction of meaning in relation to chronic illness. These authors make a case for how meaning attribution is necessary to the family's adaptation to chronic illness. The current study assumed that the way a family construes a death is critical to how they will grieve.

Patterson and Garwick (1994b) developed the notion of three levels of family meanings: situational meanings, family identity, and family worldview. Although a more detailed classification was used in the current study, some meanings shared by families could be seen as fitting the Patterson and Garwick levels of meanings. For example, meanings such as "the death was preventable" could be construed as a situational meaning. Meanings in the "philosophical" category could be seen as reflecting the family's worldview. Meanings about how the family changed could be thought of as family identity. Interestingly, meanings reflecting family identity were the least common. This finding may reveal something important about the differences between family meanings associated with chronic illness and those associated with death. One could speculate about the relative importance of family identity in coping with the ongoing challenge of chronic illness versus coping with the finality of death.

As in the current study, Patterson and Garwick (1994b) conceptualize meanings as co-constructions of family members. Patterson and Garwick (1994a, 1994b, 1994c) discuss in a limited way how family meanings come about, but they do not focus on the actual processes by which family members co-construct meaning. Rather, they call for more research on how families share and construct meanings (1994c). This study described both family sharing patterns and meaning construction patterns in relation to death and has implications for other family phenomena.

Some theoretical work done since the completion of this study addresses the issue of individual versus family meanings, an ongoing family research debate set forth early in this book. Patterson and Garwick (1994c) describe family meanings as distinctly different from meanings held by individual family members and even different from consensus between family members. They describe family meanings as

> the interpretations, images, and views that have been collectively constructed by family members as they share time, space, and life experiences; and as they talk with each other and dialogue about these experiences. They are the family social constructions, the product of their interactions. They belong to no one member, but to the family as a whole. (pp. 80-81)

Other researchers question whether family meanings exist. Broderick (1993) contends that we make a "serious logical error" when we speak of family beliefs because "only an individual can have a belief or value or world view or understanding" (p. 186). Broderick stresses that, in any group of individuals, there are as many realities as there are people. His concern seems to be that when meanings are attributed to the family, it is assumed that everyone in the family agrees when they do not agree. Although it is important not to assume agreement where agreement does not exist, the notion that family meanings do not exist is challenged by the findings in this study. It would seem that at least the products of family speak constitute family meanings, evidenced by the fact that such meanings arose out of family discourse and could not be traced to any single family member. And if the symbolic interactionists are correct, all meanings are constructed interactively. In the current study, the reason behind interviewing multiple family members both together and apart was to learn more about patterns of family meaning construction and to shed light on the very questions raised by Patterson and Garwick (1994c) and Broderick (1993).

The Grief Literature

At the time the current study was being analyzed, an internationally recognized grief researcher, Margaret Stroebe, called for the refinement of what we know about meanings and grief. In a paper challenging the importance of grief work theory, Stroebe (1992) pointed out that no clear theoretical statement has been made to clarify what constitutes "meaning" and, more important, when investigating the search for meaning as a dimension of grief work, no distinction has been made between positive and negative meanings and their consequences. This study helps illuminate what is meant by "meanings" in relation to a death and demonstrate that negative meanings are not uncommon. As nearly all grief researchers do, Stroebe seemed to be referring to individual meanings, not family meanings, which are even rarer in the discourse of grief theorists and researchers.

In 1993, Margaret Stroebe, Wolfgang Stroebe, and Robert Hansson edited the *Handbook of Bereavement*. Archer (1995), in his review of the handbook, described it as a collection of writings of well-known authors in the grief field and characterized the text as "a landmark for researchers and practitioners interested in grief" (p. 477). With the exception of a chapter by Rosenblatt (Chapter 7) on the social context of private feelings, the book had a conspicuous lack of empirical and theoretical work on family grief as a phenomenon in its own right and as a critical dimension of grief theory. My own search of the literature suggests that the absence of coverage of family grief in the *Handbook of Bereavement* was a true reflection of the literature, not an oversight on the part of the editors.

Some of what has been learned about meanings associated with death comes from the field of construct psychology. About the time this study was completed, Holcomb and Neimeyer (1993) reported their study of 504 university students who were asked to write free-form for 5 minutes about their personal meanings of death as a complement to standardized measures of death fear, threat, and anxiety. The free-form writing data were content analyzed by using codes developed in previous work on death anxiety. This work investigated meanings attached to death, albeit death in general, not a specific death as in my study. They compared constructions of death with a variety of other respondent characteristics and shared a constructivist's perspective. The constructivist perspective underlying the Holcomb and Neimeyer study (see Neimeyer, 1993, 1995; and Neimeyer & Neimeyer, 1994, for a description of personal construct psychology) is compatible with symbolic interactionist theory and holds promise for future studies that would bridge individual meaning systems and family meaning systems. Personal construct psychology, particularly as articulated by Neimeyer, recognizes the social construction of meaning but emphasizes systems of meaning within the minds of individuals. A body of work has developed around how to "measure" and assess meanings and their impact on life course (Neimeyer, 1993). This work has included ways to work therapeutically with individual meaning systems, and it holds promise for working with families who have experienced a death or other impactful family events.

Within the grief literature itself, a few studies were found that examined the relationship between meanings and grief. Generally speaking, what has been investigated was a search for meaning or purpose in life as Frankl first described it in 1959. Without exception, studies focused on individual meanings, not on how bereaved family members interactively construct meanings. Two examples from a family developmental perspective were found. In a text entirely devoted to family grief, Shapiro (1994) contends that adults, children, and families search for the cause of death in an attempt to integrate the death into their lives and to regain a sense of safety and order in the world. Shapiro uses clinical examples of accidental deaths and the case of murder to show how some people struggle to find cause. She does not discuss the process by which family members make meaning, only that they try to attribute cause. She suggests ways that clinicians can help them do so. She does not deal with meanings other than those related to the cause of the death.

DeVries, Lana, and Falck (1994), writing as Shapiro did from the family developmental perspective, reviewed the parental bereavement literature and concluded that the meaning of the loss differs, depending on the family's developmental stage. Clearly, one way to analyze the meaning statements collected in this study would be from a developmental perspective, asking how the developmental stage of a given family influenced the meanings they made and vice versa. DeVries et al. focused on factors that influence the parental grief experience at various family developmental stages, rather than the meanings themselves or the processes by which families construct meaning.

In some other studies of parental bereavement (Heil, 1993; Lang, Gottlieb, & Amsel, 1996; Wheeler, 1993-94), couples were interviewed and were asked about meaning associated with the death of their child. With the exception of Heil (1993), meaning or meaninglessness was seen through Frankl's lens (1959) as meaning or purpose in life, not the meaning attached to a particular death. Heil investigated personal meanings attached to the loss of a child as they were discovered in the diaries of grieving mothers. Although the types of meanings that Heil was interested in were similar to those in the current study, her focus was not on the co-construction of meaning by bereaved couples. She did, however, interview couples.

In another study of parental bereavement that shared grounded theory methodology and social constructionist thinking with the current study, Braun and Berg (1994) broadened the definition of meaning and described phases in the process by which people make meaning. In their definition of what constitutes meaning, these authors included not only meaning and purpose in life (Frankl, 1959) but also meanings attributed to the death itself and previous meaning structures. They used the term *re-construction of meaning* to characterize the process by which parents make sense of the death of a child. The process of reconstruction has three phases that they called *discontinuity, disorientation,* and *adjustment.* Although these authors expanded grief theory by describing phases of meaning construction, their use of the term *re-construction* may in some ways be limiting. The term implies rebuilding something already in existence. In the current study, the majority of meanings shared by family members seemed to be new. New constructions arose out of the special circumstances of the death and the ways family members used strategies to co-construct the meaning of a particular death. Braun and Berg spoke of meaning construction as an individual process, rather than as a family process, but they did emphasize, as did the current study, that current grief models are not adequate to explain the importance of meaning construction in the experience of loss.

In a small grounded theory study modeled to some degree on the current study and using a definition of meaning as broad as that of Braun and Berg (1994), Brown (1996) interviewed five bereaved adolescents regarding how they made sense of the death of a significant person in their lives. Although Brown's emphasis was not on family interactive patterns of meaning-making, but rather on individual meanings, she discovered a broad range of meaning categories, some similar to those shared by the family members in this study. She also found themes that characterized each adolescent. Her findings corroborated the findings of the current study in that meanings were often found, not in directly articulated statements, but embedded within the stories that respondents told about the death. With an eye to application of her findings to psychotherapy, Brown identified the relationship between meaning-making in response to loss and the adolescent developmental tasks of identity formation, emancipation, and establishing peer relationships.

Some recent work on grief and meaning that has relevance to the application of the current study comes from clinical theory. Sedney, Baker, and Gross (1994) drew on their experience as family therapists to present the notion that bereaved families make sense of their experience by telling the story of the death. These authors made a case for how listening to families' stories is a means to assess families and to gauge their progress as they grieve the loss of a family member. These ideas are entirely congruent with the findings of this study, in which, when multiple family interviews were content analyzed, telling the story of the death emerged as a major strategy used by families to make sense of what had happened to them. Sedney et al.'s ideas have relevance to how the findings in the study of family meaning-making may be applied to family therapy. They asserted that asking families to tell the story of the death helps them gain emotional support, makes their experience meaningful, and brings the family together.

Also coming out of the clinical practice arena, Brown (1993) developed a model of intervention for bereaved women who had experienced perinatal loss. Her arch-shaped model has as its "keystone" the meaning of the loss. Her work has relevance to the current study in that it construes the meaning of the loss as central to bereavement. To Brown, the keystone is understanding what the pregnancy loss means to the woman, her partner, the family, the community, and society. Although Brown's emphasis is on understanding meanings, rather than on how meanings are constructed, her wide lens allowed her to see more types of meanings than most. Brown's meanings included loss of the child as a possession, loss of the mother's self-esteem, loss of her self-image as a parent, loss of a dream, and loss of the ability to create. Brown insisted that knowing the meaning that the loss has to the bereaved is critical to the integrity and value of interventions, also a major practice implication of the study reported in this book.

At the time the current study was being finished, Harvey, Orbuch, Weber, Merbach, and Alt (1992), drawing heavily on previous research, discussed meanings and the meaning-making processes in ways similar to the current study. Harvey et al. used the term *account-making* to capture the meaning construction process. Their thesis was that "account-making is a central healing force in stress reaction sequences" (p. 103). Additionally, they made the point that account-making is critical not only in grieving the loss of a loved one but also in response to any major stressor, including divorce, dissolution of a major relationship, and other forms of personal devastation. Harvey et al. also identified determinants of successful account-making that correspond roughly to the meaning inhibitors and stimulators in this study. These authors also identified a "social interaction component" (p. 104) in account-making but, unlike the current study, suggested that interaction occurs after private account-making when the injured party "confides" in another. In this study, the meaning construction process is seen as interactive from its inception.

Advances in Methods and Methodology

In 1992, Jane Gilgun, Kerry Daly, and Gerald Handel edited the text *Qualitative Methods in Family Research*. Their book grew out of the Qualitative Family Research Network of the National Council on Family Relations and reviewed studies that used innovative methods. Although their text contained no studies of family bereavement, the studies reported have more in common with the current study than most coming out of other disciplines, and this reference would have informed the current study had it been available at the time this study was designed. The similarities among most of the studies in the Gilgun et al. text and the current study are that they dealt with interactions within families and involved interviewing multiple family members. Gilgun et al. identified the common thread of qualitative family research as being a focus on meaning construction. In her introductory chapter, Gilgun called attention to the emerging diversity in family research, diversity of methods, and the diversity found in definitions of the family.

In the *Handbook of Qualitative Research,* Norman Denzin and Yvonna Lincoln (1994) captured some of the emerging family methods and ways of looking at families that Gilgun et al. noted in 1992. Some of the edited works in that text are particularly relevant to the study of meaning-making in family bereavement and are summarized here. Coming out of the ethnomethodological school, Holstein and Gubrium (1994) noted that the range of qualitative research approaches with phenomenological sensibilities has grown considerably. Using language somewhat different from the symbolic interactionists cited in this work, these authors pointed to new analytic resources that have been developed to more fully explicate the "roles of discourse, conversational structure, and the content and context of interactional exchanges" (p. 270). At the time the current study was being designed, such analytic resources were not as accessible as they have become since that time. Holstein and Gubrium's more recent work addresses this gap in the literature.

In a later article, Holstein and Gubrium (1995) applied some of these analytic resources to the study of the deprivatization and construction of domestic life. Using the term *meaning-making,* they contended that the essence of family is found, not in idealized social forms, but rather in interpretive practice. By *interpretive practice,* they meant the "situationally sensitive procedures through which experience is represented, organized, reproduced and understood" (p. 896). They construed family, not as a distinct entity secluded in households, but as "a socially constructed, situationally contingent cluster of meanings . . . a constellation of ideas, images, or terminology which is used to assign meaning to everyday life" (p. 896). Holstein and Gubrium contended that, by family discourse, domestic order is created, thereby making family "an interactional accomplishment" (p. 896). Although they did not explicitly mention making sense of death as a part of creating domestic order, it seems reasonable to think it would be. More important, their emphasis on family discourse and their notion that family is interactionally accomplished is evidenced by the current study.

In terms of the "hows" and "whats" of interpretive practice, Holstein and Gubrium (1994) used a combination of audiotapes and field notes, as was done in this study. Their analysis consisted of examining transcripts, using their field notes for context, just as the current study did. Also, as in the current study, they focused on the construction of everyday meanings. They resisted, as they put it, the "invidious comparison of the constructed comparisons of everyday life and some scientific, objective or transcendental standards for what reality 'should be' or 'really is' " (p. 900). In their view, the meanings that are constructed stand on their own, context dependent as they are.

No review of relevant, recent work would be complete without heralding Gilgun's chapter in the 3rd edition of *Handbook of Marriage and the Family* (in press). Gilgun does a masterful job of reviewing the history of qualitative family research in a way that helps situate the current study squarely within the traditions of The Chicago School of Sociology. Symbolic interactionism, which influenced the design of this study, has its roots in the Chicago school. The early Chicago sociologists, Znaniecki and Thomas in particular, emphasized personal meanings from the beginning. They were interested in understanding persons in historical situations and in developing theories that illuminate social processes. Glaser and Strauss (1967), who were trained in the Chicago school, went on to develop grounded theory, which uses inductive methods to discover core concepts underlying everyday experience. Grounded theory is the major methodology underlying this study.

Advances in Computerized Data Analysis

Thomas Richards and Lyn Richards (1994) did an excellent review of newer computer software packages, called *Q.D.A.s,* designed specifically for the analysis of qualitative data. Although apologetically discussing the software they developed, NUD•IST 3.0, these authors did an even-handed review of other analysis packages and the advantages and disadvantages of Q.D.A.s in general. Indeed, much of what was done by hand and by improvised word processing functions in the current study could now be done with Q.D.A.s, particularly NUD•IST 3.0.

NUD•IST 3.0 provides for advanced textual analysis. Both the interview data and the memos could be automatically indexed by code. Multiple windows could be used to select the best exemplars of each analytic point. All instances of a given code could be retrieved simultaneously. Qualitative matrices could be built to facilitate answering such questions as how the type of death, age of the deceased, meaning-making strategies, and meanings relate to one another. These factors could be compared within and across families. Concepts could be displayed in the form of trees on the screen. Furthermore, steps in the analysis could be tracked by NUD•IST 3.0, which might facilitate reporting of data and replication.

Software such as NUD•IST 3.0 is purported to go beyond the early software in providing conceptual analysis functions. This means that it has theory-finding, theory-building, and theory-testing capacity. Richards and Richards (1994) would likely describe the method of coding used in the current study as coding for retrieval. Although they did not see coding for retrieval as atheoretical, they contended that it is possible to expand analysis to the conceptual level by using certain specialized software. Newer, computerized Q.D.A. methods are purported to provide for the building of networks of concepts, relationships between concepts, evidence, coordination of data, and "hierarchies of theory/data/explanation chunks" (p. 448). In the current study, concepts and the data to support them emerged from within the clusters of codes. Exemplars of the codes had to be retrieved one at a time from the data and from the memos and then be combined with analytic thoughts in writing packets. The notion of arranging data in ways that show relationships among concepts is appealing, especially in relation to displaying axial coding. Also appealing is the notion that Q.D.A.s can be used to find co-occurrences in the data—for example, to search for co-occurrences of certain strategies used by families, types of meanings, types of deaths, family structure, and family dynamics. This could have helped build more substantive theory.

Even advances in general purpose software, though not designed specifically for qualitative researchers, could be helpful in studies of family meaning-making. Some of the most promising are the word processing programs that offer such features as publish/subscribe, linking, and the incorporation of video and audio data (Richards & Richards, 1994). The analysis of data in the current study would have been greatly enhanced by the ability to work simultaneously with both written text and audio- or videotape of family interactions and to display visually the levels of the meaning typology.

Q.D.A.s are not without their risks, risks that may have been averted in the current study by doing so much by hand. One risk is that of the Q.D.A. "machinery" overpowering the message or over-powering the researcher. Richards and Richards (1994) pointed out one difficulty with using such software: So many different ways to examine the data are possible that it becomes difficult for some researchers to end the analysis. Some have argued that Q.D.A. software may coerce a project along a certain direction, but Richards and Richards (1994) argue that even the simpler software packages can coerce the project simply by the lack of support for various analyses. At any rate, "qualitative data analysis is probably the most subtle and intuitive of human epistemological enterprises, and therefore likely to be the last to achieve satisfactory computerization" (p. 461).

Appendix

Interview Guidelines

Code _____   Date _____

1. Who in your family died?
   When?
   Did you live in the same household?
2. How did _____ die? Probes: diagnosis? length of illness? whether respondent gave care (type and frequency)? events leading up to the death?
3. How did you learn of _____'s death? Probes: present at time of death? saw and touched the body?
4. What ceremonies were there? Probes: funeral? wake? memorial service? preparation of the body?
5. (Milan) Did you talk about _____'s dying and death? If so, what stands out in your memory about that talk or those talks?
6. (Milan) How did you and _____ get along? (meaning quality of relationship)
7. (Milan) Was there any "unfinished business" between you and _____ when _____ died? (may need to say, "anything left unsettled between you"?)
8. (Milan) Did you have any kind of "good-bye" interaction with _____?
9. (Milan) Where do you think _____ is now? What do you believe about an afterlife?

260

10. (Milan) In what ways do you think about _____'s death now? When you go inside yourself, how do you make sense of _____'s death, or do you make sense of it?

11. (Milan) Why do you think _____ died?

12. (Milan) What beliefs do you hold that relate to _____'s death? Do you have a sense of where your beliefs come from?

13. (Milan) Do you talk with other family members about _____'s death? Do you see it the same way as they do, or differently? What do they believe, compared with what you believe? (same or different views, beliefs, meanings, interpretations) Who in the family thinks of _____'s death most like you do? Who most unlike you?

14. What is there about _____'s death or your reaction to it that you would not share with family members? What would keep you from sharing?

15. If you don't talk with family members about _____'s death, do you think you still share certain beliefs (as in #14) about _____'s death? Which ones do you think you share? Not share? With whom?

16. (Milan) Do you have a sense of _____'s presence still being with you? Do you talk to _____? Do you have interactions with _____?

17. Are there ways you think about _____'s death that hinder you from living with the loss of _____? Help you live?

18. Has the way you think about _____'s death changed over time? Can you say how it has changed? Probes: what believed at first? what over time as compared to now?

19. Would you like to change the way you think about _____'s death? If yes, why would it be good to think about _____'s death in this other way?

20. What other significant losses have you had in your life? Who or what? When? How? How did you respond? (same or different from this loss)

21. Are there any "life lessons" or "life truths" that have come to you as the result of _____'s death? Probes: have you changed? If yes, in what ways?

22. Personal belongings/room: What became of them? How divided? What about _____'s room? What meaning do belongings/room hold for you?

23. If not already revealed, ask about coincidences noticed. Meaning given?

24. Is there anything else you would like to say about what the event of _____'s death means to you?

25. Anything else you would like to say in general?

NOTE: At the close of the interview, ask questions about how they feel now, how the interview was for them, a reminder about the grief counselor contacting them if they wish, and an offer of printed information on grief support.

Genograms

The Mackey Family

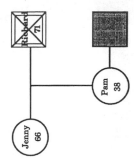

KEY

☐ = male
○ = female
✕ = deceased
⊗ = subject of interviews
● = not interviewed

⊠
▨

Three Interviews:

- Cause of Richard's death – heart disease
- Interviewed 5 months after Richard's death

1. Jenny
2. Pam
3. Jenny and Pam

FAMILY 1

263

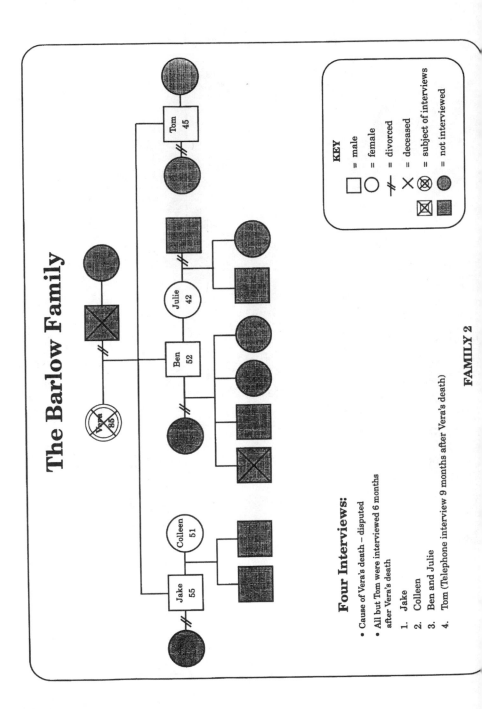

The Barlow Family

KEY

☐ = male

◯ = female

⫽ = divorced

✕ = deceased

⊗ = subject of interviews

▨ = not interviewed

Vera 86

Tom 45

Julie 42

Ben 52

Colleen 51

Jake 55

Four Interviews:

- Cause of Vera's death – disputed
- All but Tom were interviewed 6 months after Vera's death

1. Jake
2. Colleen
3. Ben and Julie
4. Tom (Telephone interview 9 months after Vera's death)

FAMILY 2

The Munson Family

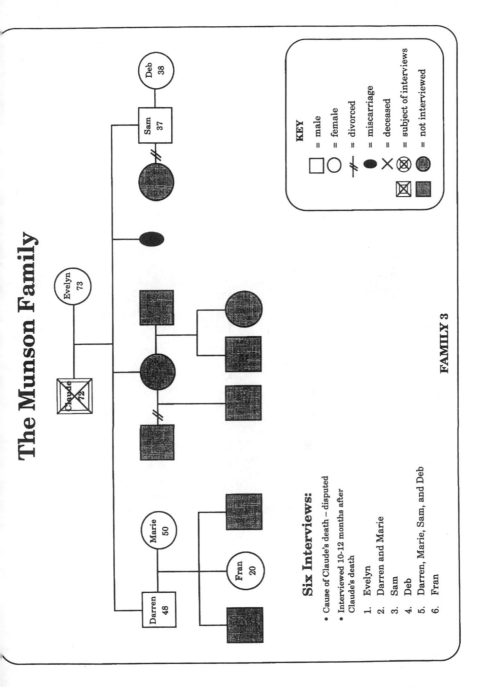

Six Interviews:

- Cause of Claude's death – disputed
- Interviewed 10-12 months after Claude's death

1. Evelyn
2. Darren and Marie
3. Sam
4. Deb
5. Darren, Marie, Sam, and Deb
6. Fran

KEY

□	= male
○	= female
⫫	= divorced
⬬	= miscarriage
✕	= deceased
⊗	= subject of interviews
⬤	= not interviewed

FAMILY 3

The Swan Family

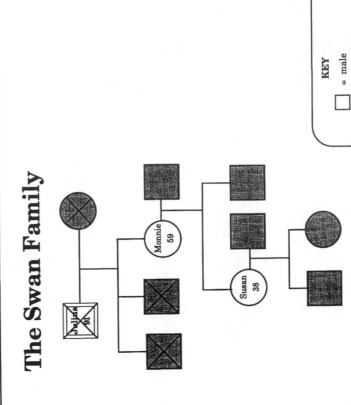

FAMILY 4

Three Interviews:

- Cause of Julius' death – pneumonia
- Interviewed 8 months after Julius' death

1. Monnie
2. Susan
3. Monnie and Susan

The Smith Family

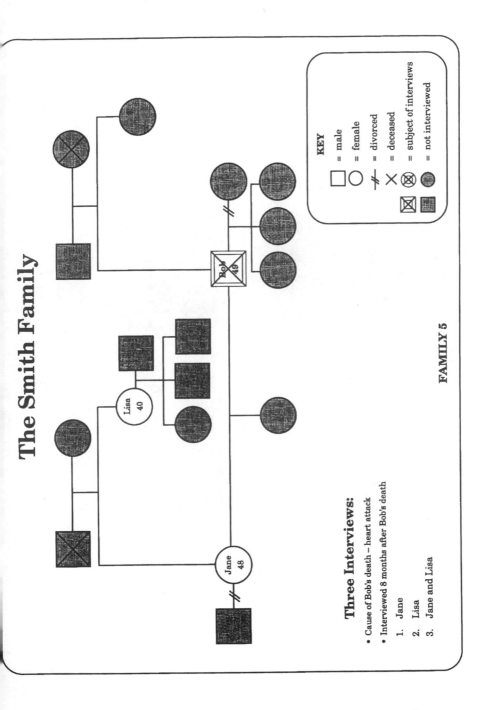

Three Interviews:

- Cause of Bob's death – heart attack
- Interviewed 8 months after Bob's death

1. Jane
2. Lisa
3. Jane and Lisa

KEY

□	= male
○	= female
⫽	= divorced
✕	= deceased
⊗	= subject of interviews
●	= not interviewed
⊠	
▦	

FAMILY 5

The Primo Family

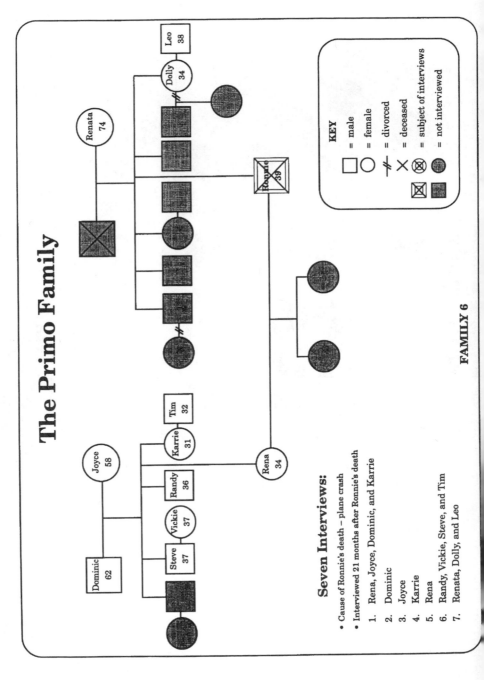

Seven Interviews:

- Cause of Ronnie's death – plane crash
- Interviewed 21 months after Ronnie's death

1. Rena, Joyce, Dominic, and Karrie
2. Dominic
3. Joyce
4. Karrie
5. Rena
6. Randy, Vickie, Steve, and Tim
7. Renata, Dolly, and Leo

KEY

☐ = male
◯ = female
⚊̸ = divorced
✕ = deceased
⊗ = subject of interviews
⬤ = not interviewed

⊠ ▦

FAMILY 6

The Zeeman Family

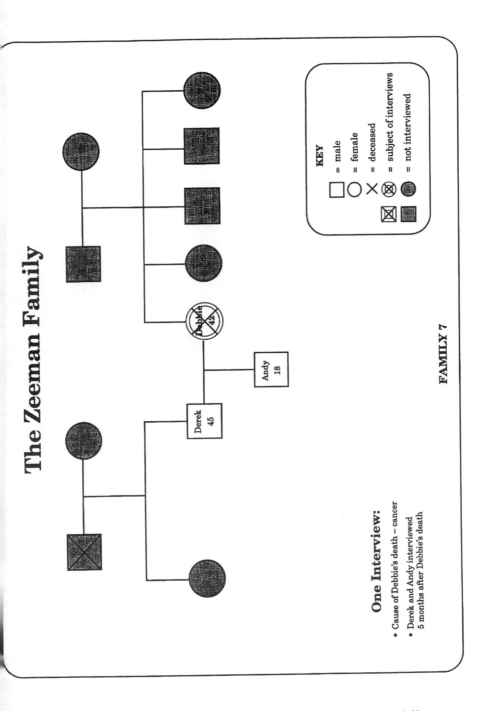

KEY

□ = male
○ = female
✕ = deceased
⊗ = subject of interviews
◉ = not interviewed
⊠ ▨

One Interview:

- Cause of Debbie's death – cancer
- Derek and Andy interviewed 5 months after Debbie's death

FAMILY 7

The Miner Family

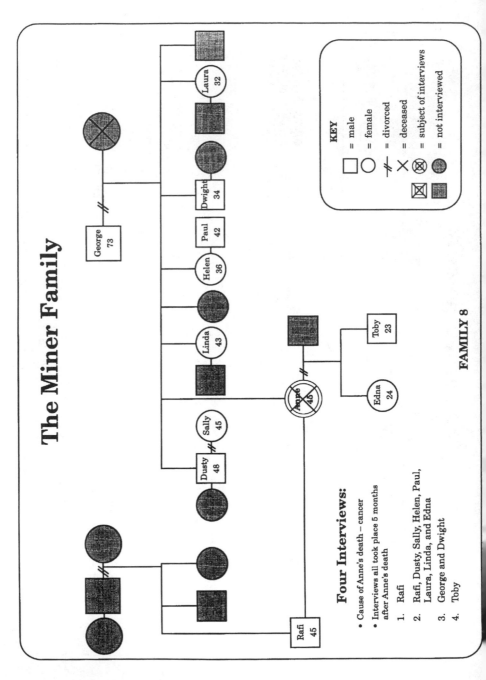

FAMILY 8

Four Interviews:

- Cause of Anne's death – cancer
- Interviews all took place 5 months after Anne's death

1. Rafi
2. Rafi, Dusty, Sally, Helen, Paul, Laura, Linda, and Edna
3. George and Dwight
4. Toby

KEY

☐ ◯ = male

◯ = female

⫫ = divorced

✕ = deceased

⊗ = subject of interviews

▦ = not interviewed

270

The Owens Family

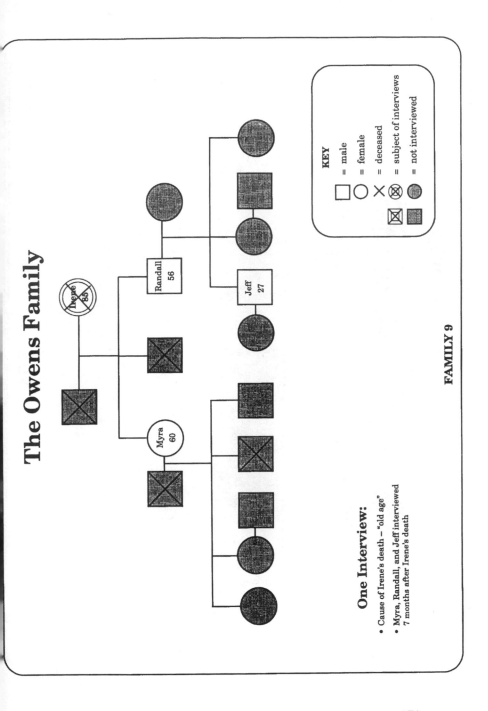

One Interview:

- Cause of Irene's death – "old age"
- Myra, Randall, and Jeff interviewed 7 months after Irene's death

KEY

□	= male	
○	= female	
✕	= deceased	
⊗	= subject of interviews	
●	= not interviewed	
⊠		
▨		

Irene 88

Randall 56

Myra 60

Jeff 27

FAMILY 9

The Buchanan Family

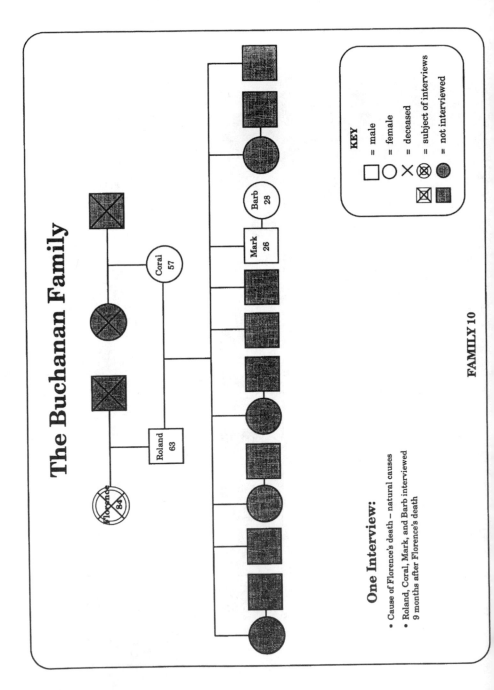

FAMILY 10

One Interview:

- Cause of Florence's death – natural causes
- Roland, Coral, Mark, and Barb interviewed 9 months after Florence's death

KEY

□	= male
○	= female
✕	= deceased
⊗	= subject of interviews
●	= not interviewed

272

References

Adler, A. (1958). *What life should mean to you.* New York: Capricorn.

Ambert, A., Adler, P. A., Adler, P., & Detzner, D. F. (1995). Understanding and evaluating qualitative research. *Journal of Marriage and the Family, 57*(4), 879-893.

Antonovsky, A. (1979). *Health, stress, and coping.* San Francisco: Jossey-Bass.

Antonovsky, A., & Sourani, T. (1988). Family sense of coherence and adaptation. *Journal of Marriage and the Family, 60,* 79-82.

Archer, J. (1995). Book review of M. S. Stroebe, W. Stroebe, & R. O. Hansson (Eds.) (1993). *Handbook of bereavement: Theory, research, and intervention. Journal of Social and Personal Relationships, 12*(3), 474-477.

Babbie, E. (1983). *The practice of social research* (3rd ed.). Belmont, CA: Wadsworth.

Berger, P. L., & Luckmann, T. (1966). *The social construction of reality.* Garden City, NY: Doubleday.

Boscolo, L., Cecchin, G., Hoffman, L., & Penn, P. (1987). *Milan systemic family therapy.* New York: Basic Books.

Boss, P. (1987). Family stress. In M. B. Sussman & S. K. Steinmetz (Eds.), *Handbook of marriage and the family* (pp. 695-723). New York: Plenum.

Braun, M. J., & Berg, D. H. (1994). Meaning reconstruction in the experience of parental bereavement. *Death Studies, 18,* 105-129.

Broderick, C., & Smith, J. (1979). General systems approach to the family. In W. Burr, R. Hill, F. I. Nye, & I. L. Reiss (Eds.), *Contemporary theories about the family* (Vol. 2, pp. 112-128). New York: Free Press.

Broderick, C. B. (1993). *Understanding family process: Basics of family systems theory.* Newbury Park, CA: Sage.

Brown, J. M. (1996). *Adolescent bereavement and meaning-making.* Unpublished doctoral dissertation, Minnesota School of Professional Psychology, St. Paul.

Brown, Y. (1993). Perinatal loss: A framework for practice. *Health Care for Women International, 14*(5), 469-479.

Bruner, J. (1990). *Acts of meaning.* Cambridge, MA: Harvard University Press.

Buckley, W. (1967). *Sociology and modern systems theory.* Upper Saddle River, NJ: Prentice Hall.

Burr, W. R., Leigh, G. K., Day, R. D., & Constantine, J. (1979). Symbolic interaction in the family. In W. R. Burr, R. Hill, I. F. Nye, & I. L. Reiss (Eds.), *Contemporary theories about the family* (Vol. 2, pp. 42-111). New York: Free Press.

Constantine, L. L. (1986). *Family paradigms.* New York: Guilford.

Cooley, C. H. (1902). *Human nature and the social order.* New York: Scribner.

Cooley, C. H. (1909). *Social organization.* New York: Scribner.

Davies, B. (1987). Family responses to the death of a child: The meaning of memories. *Journal of Palliative Care, 3*(4), 9-15.

Denzin, N. K., & Lincoln, Y. S. (1994). *Handbook of qualitative research.* Thousand Oaks, CA: Sage.

DeVries, B., Lana, R. D., & Falck, V. T. (1994). Parental bereavement over the life course: A theoretical intersection and empirical review. *Omega, 29*(1), 47-69.

Dewey, J. (1922). *Human nature and conduct.* New York: Scribner.

Frankl, V. E. (1959). *Man's search for meaning.* New York: Washington Square.

Gilgun, J. F. (in press). Methodological pluralism and qualitative family research. In S. Steinmetz, M. Sussman, & G. Peterson (Eds.), *Handbook of marriage and the family* (3rd ed.). New York: Plenum.

Gilgun, J. F., Daly, K., & Handel, G. (Eds.). (1992). *Qualitative methods in family research.* Newbury Park, CA: Sage.

Glaser, B. G., & Strauss, A. L. (1967). *The discovery of grounded theory: Strategies for qualitative research.* Hawthorne, NY: Aldine.

Hall, A. D., & Fagan, R. E. (1956). Definition of systems [Revised introductory chapter of *General systems*]. New York: Bell Telephone Laboratories. (Reprinted from *General Systems, 1,* 18-28).

Harvey, J. H., Orbuch, T. L., Weber, A. L., Merbach, N., & Alt, R. (1992). House of pain and hope: Accounts of loss. *Death Studies, 16,* 99-124.

Heil, J. L. (1993). The grief recovery process after the death of a baby: Inner experiences and personal meanings. *Dissertation Abstracts International, A: The Humanities and Social Sciences, 54*(2), 695.

Hess, R. D., & Handel, G. (1959). *Family worlds: A psychological approach to family life.* Chicago: University of Chicago Press.

Hill, R. (1958). Generic features of families under stress. *Social Casework, 39,* 2-3.

Holcomb, L. E., & Neimeyer, R. A. (1993). Personal meanings of death: A content analysis of free-response narratives. *Death Studies, 17,* 299-318.

Holstein, J. A., & Gubrium, J. F. (1994). Phenomenology, ethnomethodology, and interpretive practice. In N. K. Denzin & Y. S. Lincoln (Eds.), *Handbook of qualitative research* (pp. 262-272). Thousand Oaks, CA: Sage.

Holstein, J. A., & Gubrium, J. F. (1995). Deprivatization and the construction of domestic life. *Journal of Marriage and the Family, 57,* 894-908.

James, W. (1890). *Principles of psychology* (Vol. 2). New York: Holt.

Kantor, D., & Lehr, W. (1975). *Inside the family.* San Francisco: Jossey-Bass.

Lang, A. G., Gottlieb, N., & Amsel, R. (1996). Predictors of husbands' and wives' grief reactions following infant death: The role of marital intimacy. *Death Studies, 20,* 33-57.

LaRossa, R., Bennett, L., & Gelles, R. (1987). Ethical dilemmas in qualitative family research. In D. Olson, *Family research methodology I and II* (Vol. 2, pp. 303-313). St. Paul: University of Minnesota Press.

Lazarus, R. S. (1966). *Psychological stress and the coping process.* New York: McGraw-Hill.

Lofland, J., & Lofland, L. H. (1984). *Analyzing social settings.* Belmont, CA: Wadsworth.

Lopata, H. Z. (1981, May). Widowhood and husband sanctification. *Journal of Marriage and the Family, 43,* 439-450.

McCubbin, H. L., & Patterson, J. M. (1983). The family stress process: The double ABCX model of family adjustment and adaptation. In H. I. McCubbin, M. Sussman, & J. M. Patterson (Eds.), *Social stress and the family: Advances and developments in family stress theory and research* (pp. 7-37). New York: Haworth.

McLain, R., & Weigert, A. (1979). Toward a phenomenological sociology of family: A programmatic essay. In W. Burr, R. Hill, F. I. Nye, & I. L. Reiss (Eds.), *Contemporary theories about the family* (Vol. 2, pp. 160-205). New York: Free Press.

Mead, G. H. (1932). *The philosophy of the present* (A. E. Murphy, Ed., with prefatory remarks by J. Dewey). Chicago: Open Court.

Mead, G. H. (1934). *Mind, self, and society.* Chicago: University of Chicago Press.

Mead, G. H. (1936). *Movements of thought in the 19th century.* Chicago: University of Chicago Press.

Mead, G. H. (1938). *The philosophy of the act.* Chicago: University of Chicago Press.

Miles, M. B., & Huberman, M. A. (1984). *Qualitative data analysis.* Beverly Hills, CA: Sage.

Moon, S. M., Dillon, D. R., & Sprenkle, D. H. (1990). Family therapy and qualitative research. *Journal of Marital and Family Therapy, 16*(4), 357-373.

Muxen, M. (1991). *Making sense of sibling loss in adulthood: An experimental analysis.* Unpublished doctoral dissertation, University of Minnesota.

Nadeau, J. W. (1980). *Walking and dying.* Unpublished manuscript.

Nadeau, J. W., & Johnson, P. V. (1983). *Social support as a health determinant in conjugal bereavement.* Paper presented at the National Hospice Symposium, Minneapolis, MN.

Neimeyer, G., & Neimeyer, R. A. (1994). Constructivist methods of marital and family therapy: A practical précis. *Journal of Mental Health Counseling, 16*(1), 85-104.

Neimeyer, R. A. (1993). Constructivist approaches to the measurement of meaning. In G. J. Neimeyer (Ed.), *Counseling psychologist casebook: Vol. 2. Constructive assessment: A casebook* (pp. 58-103). Newbury Park, CA: Sage.

Neimeyer, R. A. (1995). Limits and lessons of constructivism: Some critical reflections. *Journal of Constructivist Psychology, 8*(4), 339-361.

Parkes, C. M., & Weiss, R. (1983). *Recovery from bereavement.* New York: Basic Books.

Patterson, J. M. (1988). Families experiencing stress: The family adjustment and adaptation model, Applying the FAAR model to health-related issues for intervention and research. *Family Medicine, 6*(2), 202-237.

Patterson, J. M., & Garwick, A. W. (1994a). The impact of chronic illness on families: A family systems perspective. *Annals of Behavioral Medicine, 16*(2), 131-142.

Patterson, J. M., & Garwick, A. W. (1994b). Levels of meaning in family stress theory. *Family Process, 33,* 287-304.

Patterson, J. M., & Garwick, A. W. (1994c). Theoretical linkages: Family meanings and sense of coherence. In H. McCubbin, E. Thompson, A. Thompson, L. Thompson,

& J. Fromer (Eds.), *Sense of coherence and resiliency, stress, coping, and health* (pp. 71-89). Madison: University of Wisconsin System.

Piaget, J. (1953). *The origins of intelligence in children.* New York: International Universities Press.

Reiss, D. (1981). *The family's construction of reality.* Cambridge, MA: Harvard University Press.

Richards, T. J., & Richards, L. (1994). Using computers in qualitative research. In N. K. Denzin & Y. S. Lincoln (Eds.), *Handbook of qualitative research* (pp. 445-462). Thousand Oaks, CA: Sage.

Rose, A. M. (Ed.). (1962). *Behavior and social processes.* Boston: Houghton Mifflin.

Rosenblatt, P. C. (1983). *Bitter, bitter tears.* Minneapolis: University of Minnesota Press.

Rosenblatt, P. C., & Fischer, L. R. (1993). Qualitative family research. In P. B. Boss, W. J. Doherty, R. LaRossa, W. R. Schumm, & S. K. Steinmetz (Eds.), *Source book of family theories and methods: A contextual approach.* New York: Plenum.

Schoenberg, B., Carr, A., Peretz, D., & Kutscher, A. (Eds.). (1970). *Loss and grief: Psychological management in medical practice.* New York: Columbia University Press.

Schvaneveldt, J. D. (1981). The interactional framework in the study of the family. In I. F. Nye & F. M. Berardo (Eds.), *Emerging conceptual frameworks in family analysis.* New York: Praeger.

Sedney, M. A., Baker, J. E., & Gross, E. (1994). The story of a death: Therapeutic considerations with bereaved families. *Journal of Marital and Family Therapy, 20*(3), 287-296.

Shapiro, E. R. (1994). *Grief as a family process: A developmental approach to clinical practice.* New York: Guilford.

Shapiro, J. (1989). Stress, depression, and support group participation. *Family Relations, 2,* 169-173.

Strauss, A., & Corbin, J. (1990). *Basics of qualitative research.* Newbury Park, CA: Sage.

Stroebe, M. (1992). Coping with bereavement: A review of the grief work hypothesis. *Omega, 26,* 19-42.

Stroebe, M. S., Stroebe, W., & Hansson, R. (Eds.). (1993). *Handbook of bereavement theory research and intervention.* Cambridge, UK: Press Syndicate of the University of Cambridge.

Stryker, S. (1972). Symbolic interaction theory: A review and some suggestions for comparative family research. *Journal of Comparative Family Studies, 3*(1), 17-32.

Tannen, D. (1990). *You just don't understand.* New York: William Morrow.

Taylor, S. E. (1983). Adjustment to threatening events: A theory of cognitive adaptation. *American Psychologist, 38,* 1161-1173.

Thomas, W. I. (1923). *The unadjusted girl.* Boston: Little, Brown.

Thompson, S. C. (1985). Finding positive meaning in a stressful event and coping. *Basic and Applied Social Psychology, 6*(4), 279-295.

Thompson, S. C., & Janigian, A. S. (1988). Life schemes: A framework for understanding the search for meaning. *Journal of Social and Clinical Psychology, 7,* 260-280.

Van Manen, M. (1990). *Researching lived experience.* New York: State University of New York Press.

Waller, W., & Hill, R. (1951). *The family.* New York: Dryden.

Weitzman, E., & Miles, M. B. (1994). *Computer programs for qualitative data analysis.* Thousand Oaks, CA: Sage.

Wheeler, I. (1993-1994). The role of meaning and purpose in life in bereaved parents associated with a self-help group: Compassionate friends. *Omega, 28*(4), 261-271.

Worden, J. W. (1982). *Grief counseling and grief therapy: A handbook for the mental health professional.* New York: Springer.

Wright, S. (n.d.). *Adapting Milan style systemic therapy from family therapy to family research.* Unpublished manuscript.

Index

ABCX model of family stress, 232
  C factor of, 39
  double, 33
  double C factor, 232
Accunt-making, 255
Adjustment, 253
Adler, A., 3, 273
Adler, P., 245, 273
Adler, P. A., 245, 273
Advances:
  in computerized data analysis,
    257-259
  in methods and methodology,
    255-257
Afterlife:
  belief in, 181-182
  indecision about, 183
  no belief in, 183-184
  statements about, 181-184
Agreeing/disagreeing, 148-151
AIDS, 236
Alt, R., 255, 274
Ambert, A., 245, 273
Amsel, R., 253, 274
Anonymity, 63-64
Antonovsky, A., 33, 273

Appraisal meanings, 30, 36
Archer, J., 251, 273
Articulation, 68
Assumptions, 13-14
Attitude toward death, 202-211
Attribution theory, 38
Axial coding, 55
  applications, 55
  definition of, 54

Babbie, E., 19, 58-60, 64, 67, 273
"Bad things should not happen to good
    people" statement, 172-173
Baker, J. E., 254, 276
Barlow family, 70, 264f
  afterlife statements, 183
  attitude of the deceased toward
    death, 205-209
  characterization of the deceased,
    143-144
  coincidancing, 126-128, 134
  comparison, 118-119, 121
  consensus, 105-106
  family change, 216, 224-225
  individual change, 212-213, 217

EDITOR'S NOTE: Page references followed by *t* or *f* indicate tables or figures, respectively.

interview excerpts, 71-72, 87-89, 103, 118, 126-127, 143-144, 168, 189-190, 201, 205-206, 208, 213, 218, 224-225
meaning statements, 201
negative statements, 168, 176, 189-190
shared meanings, 103-104
sharing patterns, 87-89
theme, 114
willingness to share, 100-101
Beliefs:
in afterlife, 181-184
See also Meanings
Bennett, L., 64, 274
Berg, D. H., 253-254, 273
Berger, P. L., 5-8, 35, 235, 273
Bias:
researcher, 65-66
self-presentation, 68
Boscolo, L., 43-44, 273
Boss, P., 5, 9, 14, 17-18, 273
Boundaries, 11
Braun, M. J., 253-254, 273
Broderick, C., 2, 11-12, 273
Broderick, C. B., 250-251, 273
Brown, J. M., 254, 273
Brown, Y., 254-255, 273
Bruner, J., 15, 273
Buchanan family, 71, 272f
coincidancing, 125-126, 132
comparison, 121
family change, 222-223
individual change, 228
interview excerpts, 94, 181, 199-200, 222-223, 228
meaning statements, 199-200
negative statements, 179
purpose statements, 180-181
shared meanings, 104
sharing patterns, 94
story, 111-112
Buckley, W., 11, 274
Burr, W. R., 5, 8-10, 13, 72, 233, 274

Campbell, Joseph, 111
Carr, A., 47, 276
Cecchin, G., 43, 273

C factor, 39
double, 232
Characterizations of the deceased, 85, 94-95, 136-148
excessively positive, 145-148
positive, 142-144
typical, 137-142
Circularity, 44
Circular questioning, 43-45
Milan method, 43-44
Code book, 55-57
Coding:
axial, 54-55
examples, 54, 54t
open, 53-55
Coherence:
definition of, 33
sense of, 33
Coherence of family life, perceived, 33
Coincidancing, 110-135, 245
definition of, 110, 126
reluctant, 126-130
Coincidences, 125-126
as acts of deceased, 134-135
as acts of God, 134-135
as physical symptoms, 130-132
as premonitions, 132-134
Comparative evaluations, 58
Comparison(s), 110-125
definition of, 76
interactive, 123-124
negative *versus* positive, 121-123
simile as form of, 124-125
with other family deaths, 118-121
Compromised life, "deceased said no to" statements, 211
Computerized data analysis, advances in, 257-259
Conceptual frameworks, 4-13
Confidentiality, 64
Constantine, J., 5, 274
Constantine, L. L., 11-12, 274
Constructionist theory, 233-235
Construction of meaning:
individual, 29-32
re-construction, 253
See also Meaning-making
Construction of reality, 7, 15, 22, 29
social, 35

Constructs, 27
  crisis, 23-26, 30, 234
Construing, shared social, 233
Cooley, C. H., 274
Cooperative interrupting, 152
Corbin, J., 18, 40-41, 52, 54-55, 59, 67,
  230, 237, 276
Couple level of meaning-making, 72,
  76-78
Crisis construct, 23, 30, 234
  definition of, 25
  description of, 24
  features of, 26
Cultural differences, 240
Culture. See Meaning

Daly, K., 255, 274
Data:
  demographic, 45-46
  verification of, 57-62
Data analysis, 52-57
  computerized, 257-259
  interpretive practice, 257
Data collection, 49-52
  techniques of, 41-49
Davies, B., 20, 22, 31, 35-36, 38-39, 274
Day, R. D., 5, 274
Death:
  as test, 186-188
  as too soon or too late, 175-176
  as unfair or unjust, 169-176
  as wished, 210-211
  before death, 200-202
  biological cause of, 196-197
  family change due to, 211-220
  God as cause of, 188-189
  individual change due to, 212-216
  knowledge of the deceased of,
    209-210
  meanings about, 191-229
  moment of, 197-200
  nature of, 191-202
  other family deaths, 118-121
  philosophy of, 178-180
  preventability of, 191-196
  purpose of, 180-181
  reality of, 217-220

  self-caused, 208-209
  the deceased as knowing of, 209-210
  the deceased as ready for, 204-206
  the deceased's attitude toward,
    202-211
  "The Dying" (substory), 112-113
  with dignity, 200
"Death is bad" statement, 175
Deceased:
  as ready to die, 204-206
  attitude toward death, 202-211
  characterization of, 85, 94-95,
    136-148
  coincidences as acts of, 134-135
  death as preventable by, 192-193
  death as wished by, 210-211
  knowledge of death, 209-210
  "said no to compromised life"
    statements, 211
  sanctification of, 136, 145
  self-caused death, 208-209
  "The Deceased's Life" (substory),
    112
  "The wrong person died" statements,
    173-175
Definition of self, 10
Definitions of situations, 8, 15
  See also Meaning
Demographic data, 45-46
Denzin, N. K., 257, 274
Detzner, D. F., 245, 273
DeVries, B., 252-253, 274
Dewey, J., 274
Dialectic of society, essential, 6
Dignity, dying with, 200
Dillon, D. R., 61, 275
Discontinuity, 253
Disorientation, 253
Double ABCX model, 33
Double C factor, 232
Double factors, 33
Dreams, 110-118, 135
Dyadic level of meaning-making, 78-81
Dying:
  the deceased as knowing of, 209-210
  "The Dying" (substory), 112-113
  with dignity, 200
  See also Death

Echoing, 151-154
Elaborating, 154-155
Elemental strategy, 56
Essential dialectic of society, 6
Ethical considerations, 64-65
Evaluations, comparative, 58

FAAR. *See* Family adjustment and
    adaptation response model
Fagan, R. E., 11, 274
Fairness, death as unfair or unjust,
    169-176
Faith, general statements about, 189-190
Falck, V. T., 252, 274
Family:
    balancing, 142-144
    construction of reality, 39
    context of, 231
    definition of, 16
    definition of the event, 25
    information processing phases, 24
    meanings about change in, 211-220
    perceived coherence of life in, 33
    reorganization templates, 25
    respondent families, 70-71
    restructuring, 11-12
    "The Family History" (substory), 112
    See also specific families
Family adjustment and adaptation
    response model, 34
Family consensus, 104-106
    definition of, 73, 86, 105
    pure, 109
Family grief, 245
Family literature, 249-251
Family meaning-making, 1-4, 81-85
    capturing, 40-69
    definition of, 15, 243
    in-law effect of, 83
    past attempts to understand, 19-39
    rationale for study of, 1-4
    research studies on, 32-38
    strategies of, 56, 71, 107, 110
Family meanings, 1, 250
    definition of, 23
    shared, 23
    versus individual meanings, 27

Family members:
    change in, 212-216
    death as preventable by, 193-195
    grief of, 245
    individual meaning-making, 29-32,
        73-76
    individual meanings, 27
Family paradigm, 23, 30, 234
Family schema, 34
Family shared meanings, 101-104, 109
    definition of, 86
Family sharing, 86-101, 107
    comparison of willingness for, 99-101
    conditions necessary for, 92-99
    definition of, 86
    I Would Share If I Had Something to
        Share pattern, 93-94
    I Would Share If Others Would Listen
        pattern, 93
    No, I Would Not Share pattern, 87
    patterns of, 73, 86-106
    We Would Share If It Did Not Make
        Us Uncomfortable pattern, 94
    We Would Share If It Were About Life
        pattern, 94-95
    We Would Share If It Were Not
        Negative About the One Who
        Died pattern, 96
    We Would Share If It Were Positive
        pattern, 95
    We Would Share If My Meaning Is
        Not Too Different From That of
        Others pattern, 96-99
    Yes, I Will Share; No, I Will Not
        pattern, 88-91
    Yes, I Would Share pattern, 86-87
    Yes, We Will Share, 91-92
Family speak, 135, 148-157, 231-232,
    244-245
    definition of, 110, 148, 153
Family stress:
    ABCX model of, 39, 232
    double ABCX model of, 33
    research studies on, 32-38
Family stress theory, 232-233
Family systems theory, 11-13, 231-232
Family worlds, 1, 6
Fatalistic meanings, 176-178

Finishing sentences, 154-155
Fischer, L. R., 5, 14, 16-19, 57-58, 61,
    64, 67-68, 276
Found meanings, 30-31, 36
Frankl, V. E., 16, 77, 189, 246, 249,
    252-253, 274
Friedkin family, 28
"From Day 1, the whole thing sucks"
    statement, 170-172
Funerals, 112-113

Garwick, A. W., 249-251, 275
Gelles, R., 64, 274
Genograms, 45-46, 263-272
Gilgun, J. F., 245, 255-257, 274
Glaser, B. G., 18, 40-41, 46, 257, 274
Global strategy, 56
God:
    as cause of death, 188-189
    coincidences as acts of, 134-135
    general statements about, 189-190
Gottlieb, N., 253, 274
Grief:
    and meaning, 20-22
    family, 245
    individual, 245
Grief literature, 251-255
Grief theory, 235-236
Gross, E., 276
Grounded theory, 40
Gubrium, J. F., 257, 274

Hall, A. D., 11, 274
Handbook of Bereavement (Stroebe,
    Stroebe, and Hansson, eds.), 251
Handel, G., 255, 274
Handle, 1, 6
Hansson, R., 251, 276
Harvey, J. H., 255, 274
Heil, J. L., 253, 274
Hess, R. D., 1, 6, 274
Hill, R., 16, 25, 33, 274, 276
History substory, 112
Hoffman, L., 43, 273
Holcomb, L. E., 251-252, 274
Holstein, J. A., 257, 274
Homeostasis, 12

Homo narrus, 111
Homo sapiens, 111
Huberman, M. A., 57-59, 275

Ideology. See Meaning
Illnesses, 112, 121
Implicit meanings, 30, 36
Inarticulation, 68
Individual change, 212-216
Individual concordance rates, 108
Individual grief, 245
Individual meaning-making, 73-76
    research studies on, 29-32
Individual meanings, 27
In-law effect, 83
Interaction, synbolic, 4
Intermediate strategy, 56
Interpretive practice, 257
Interrupting, 151-154
    cooperative, 152
Intervening conditions, 56
Interviews:
    guidelines for, 42-43
    intensive, 41
    multiple member, 42
    structured, 42
    study, 260-261
    unstructured, 41

James, W., 274
Janigian, A. S., 20, 29-31, 34, 36, 39,
    276
Johnson, P. V., 21-23, 47, 51, 53, 275
Journal of Marriage and the Family,
    245
Justice, death as unfair or unjust,
    169-176

Kantor, D., 12, 274
Kutscher, A., 47, 276

Lana, R. D., 252, 274
Lang, A. G., 253, 274
LaRossa, R., 64, 274
Latent typifications, 77, 160, 165

definition of, 15
Lazarus, R. S., 18, 30, 34, 275
Lehr, W., 12, 274
Leigh, G. K., 5, 274
Lessons learned, 220-228
Life:
    compromised, 211
    how to live, 224-225
    living in the moment, 225-226
    quality of, 211
Life scheme, 30
Lincoln, Y. S., 257, 274
Literature:
    family, 249-251
    grief, 251-255
    See also Research
Lofland, J., 14-16, 18, 41-42, 47,
    52-53, 77, 160, 165, 275
Lofland, L. H., 14-16, 18, 41-42, 47,
    52-53, 77, 160, 165, 275
Lopata, H. Z., 136, 145, 275
Luckmann, T., 5-8, 35, 235, 273

Mackey family, 70, 263f
    afterlife statements, 182
    attitude of the deceased toward
        death, 210-211
    coincidancing, 134
    comparisons, 122-124
    family change, 225, 228
    individual change in, 212
    interview excerpts, 102, 122, 124,
        182, 200, 212
    meaning statements, 200
    shared meanings, 101-104
    theme, 114
McCubbin, H. L., 33, 36, 39, 232, 275
McLain, R., 17, 275
Mead, G. H., 275
Meaning(s), 37
    about death, 191-229
    about family change, 211-220
    appraisal, 30, 36
    attachment of, 15
    cultural differences in, 240
    definition of, 14-15, 159, 243, 246
    family, 1, 23, 27, 250
    family shared, 86, 101-104, 109

fatalistic, 176-178
found, 30-31, 36
grief and, 20-22
implicit, 30, 36
individual vs family, 27
meaning of, 246
negative, 159-190
philosophical, 176-181
re-construction of, 253
religious, 184-190
search for, 29
shared, 1, 73
situational, 34
ultimate, 159-190
Meaning-making, 257
    as family process, 1-18
    couple level of, 72, 76-78
    definition of, 15-16
    dyadic level of, 78-81
    family, 1-4, 15, 81-85, 243
    individual, 29-32, 73-76
    inhibitors of, 75, 107
    patterns of, 70-109
    process of, 22-29
    re-construction of meaning, 253
    stimulators of, 75, 84, 107
    strategies of, 56, 71, 107, 110
Meaning statements, 159
    about afterlife, 181-184
    about faith and God, 189-190
    about not taking others for granted,
        221-222
    about purpose of death, 180-181
    death was preventable, 191-196
    negative, 169-176
    no sense to be made, 164-169
    not statements, 161-164
    revelation, reunion, and reward,
        184-186
Medical system, death as preventable by,
    195-196
Memory, selective, 68
Mentalistic variables, 5
Merbach, N., 255, 274
Methods and methodology:
    advances in, 255-257
    relevance of, 16-18
Milan method of circular questioning,
    43-44

Miles, M. B., 57-59, 275-276
Mind reading, 43-44, 245
Miner family, 71, 270f
    afterlife statements, 183-184
    attitude of the deceased toward
        death, 204-205, 208-210
    characterization of the deceased, 141,
        145-148
    coincidancing, 128-130, 134
    comparisons, 122-123
    dreams, 115-118
    dyadic meaning-making, 78-81
    family change, 216, 226, 228
    individual change in, 215
    individual meaning-making, 75-76
    interview excerpts, 61-62, 74-75,
        78-79, 97, 113, 115-116, 122,
        128-130, 146-147, 162, 170-174,
        177, 180, 183-184, 187, 205,
        209, 215, 226
    meaning-making, 73-74
    meanings, 62, 188
    meaning statements, 197, 221
    negative statements, 162-163, 168,
        170-174, 176-177, 185
    purpose statements, 180
    sharing, 97-98
    story, 113
    theme, 114
    willingness to share, 99-100
Moon, S. M., 61, 65, 67, 275
Morphostasis, 12
Munson family, 70, 265f
    afterlife statements, 184
    attitude of the deceased toward
        death, 204, 210-211
    characterization of the deceased,
        142-143
    coincidancing, 132
    dreams, 117
    family change, 217, 224, 228
    family speak, 153-154
    individual change in, 212, 217-220
    interview excerpts, 81-83, 112-113,
        117, 153-154, 178, 184, 192,
        194-195, 201-202, 204, 217-219,
        228
    meaning-making, 81-85

meaning statements, 192-195,
    201-202, 212
negative statements, 177-178
sharing, 99
story, 112-113
theme, 113-114
willingness to share, 100-101
Muxen, M., 275

Nadeau, J. W., 21-23, 47, 51, 53, 275
National Council on Family Relations:
    Annual Conference, 59
    Qualitative Family Research
        Network, 255
    Theory Construction and Research
        Methods workshop, 59
Native American families, 240
Negative meanings, 159-190
    "Bad things should not happen to
        good people" statements, 172-173
    "Death is bad" statements, 175
    "Death was unfair or unjust"
        statements, 169-176
    "From Day 1, the whole thing sucks"
        statements, 170-172
    "No sense to be made" statements,
        164-169
    not statements, 161-164
    statements, 169-176
    "The death was too soon or too late"
        statements, 175-176
    "The wrong person died" statements,
        173-175
Neimeyer, G., 251-252, 275
Neimeyer, R. A., 252, 274-275
Norms. See Meaning
Not statements, 161-164
NUD·IST 3.0 (software), 258

Open coding, 53-55
Openness, 12
Orbuch, T. L., 255, 274
Other family deaths, 118-121
Owens family, 71, 271f
    characterization of the deceased, 145
    coincidancing, 126

comparison, 119
individual change in, 216
interview excerpts, 95, 216
meaning statements, 206
negative statements, 176
religious meanings, 185
shared meanings, 104
sharing, 95
theme, 114

Paramount reality, 6
Parkes, C. M., 143, 275
Patterson, J. M., 18, 30, 33-36, 39,
    232-233, 236, 249-251, 275
Penn, P., 43, 273
Perception, selective, 20
Perceptual variables, 32
Peretz, D., 47, 276
Perspectives. See Meanings
Philosophical meanings, 176-181
Philosophy of death, 178-180
Physical symptoms, 130-132
Piaget, J., 34, 275
Pilot study, 52
Positive characterizations of the
    deceased, 142-144
    excessive, 145-148
Premonitions, 132-134
Preventability of death, 191-196
    by family member, 193-195
    by medical system, 195-196
    by the deceased, 192-193
Primo family, 71, 268f
    attitude of the deceased toward
        death, 203-204, 210-211
    characterization of the deceased,
        137-141
    coincidancing, 130-132
    comparisons, 119-121, 124-125
    consensus, 105
    couple meaning-making, 76-77
    dreams, 117
    family change, 224-225, 227
    family speak, 150-153, 155-156
    individual change in, 213-215,
        227-228
    interview excerpts, 76-77, 89-90, 96,
        119-121, 124-125, 131, 137-140,

150-152, 155-156, 163-169, 173,
    187, 190, 192-193, 197-198, 203,
    213-215, 227
meaning-making, 76-77
meaning statements, 192-194,
    197-199, 221
negative statements, 163-170,
    172-175, 177, 187, 189-190
sharing, 96-98
sharing patterns, 89-92
theme, 114
willingness to share, 99-100
Priorities:
    relationships first, 226-228
    setting, 222-224
Probes, 42
Protectionism, 91, 121, 141
Psychotherapy, implications of research
    for, 239-242

Q.D.A.s (software), 257-259
Qualitative Family Research Network,
    255
Quality of life, 211
Questioning, 85, 155-157
    circular, 43-45

Reality:
    paramount, 6
    social. See Meaning
Reality construction, 7, 22, 25, 29
    family's, 39
    social, 35
Reality maintenance, 6
Re-construction of meaning, 253
Referencing, 148-151
Reiss, D., 18, 20, 22-31, 35-36, 39,
    231, 234-235, 276
Relationships first, 226-228
Reliability, 59
Religious meanings, 184-190
    coincidences as acts of God, 134-135
    death as test statements, 186-188
    general statements about faith and
        God, 189-190
    "God caused the death" statements,
        188-189

revelation, reunion, and reward
    statements, 184-186
Reorganization templates, 25
Research:
    advances in methods and
        methodology, 255-257
    current studies, 40-69
    family literature, 249-251
    grief literature, 251-255
    implications for, 236-239
    interpretive practice, 257
    locating respondents, 49
    past studies, 19-39
    selecting respondents, 46-49
    studies on family stress and family
        meaning-making, 32-38
    studies on grief and meaning, 20-22
    studies on individual meaning
        construction, 29-32
    studies on meaning-making process,
        22-29
    summary, 38-39
Researchers:
    role and bias, 65-66
    selectivity, 67
Research study:
    assumptions, 13-14
    conclusions, 245-247
    first phase, 53
    implications for practice, 239-242
    implications for research, 236-239
    implications for theory, 230-236
    interview guidelines, 260-261
    limitations, 66-69
    methodology, 16-18
    open coding, 53-55
    participants, 47-49
    pilot study, 52
    respondent families, 70-71
    See also specific families
Revelation, reunion, and reward
    statements, 184-186
Revelations, 27
Richards, L., 258-259, 276
Richards, T. J., 258-259, 276
Roles:
    family, 11
    researcher, 65-66
Rose, A. M., 5, 9, 13, 276

Rosenblatt, P. C., 5, 10, 12, 14, 16-19,
    57-58, 61, 64, 67-68, 230, 251,
    276
Rules, 11

Sanctification of the deceased, 136, 145
Schoenberg, B., 47, 276
Schvaneveldt, J. D., 13, 15, 276
Search for meaning, 29
Sedney, M. A., 254, 276
Selective memory, 68
Selective perception, 20
Self, definition of, 10
Self-caused death, 208-209
Self-presentation bias, 68
Sense of coherence, 33
Sentences, finishing others', 154-155
Shapiro, E. R., 252, 276
Shapiro, J., 36-37, 39, 276
Shared meaning(s), 1
    definition of, 73
    family, 23, 101-104
Shared social construing, 35, 233
Sharing, family, 86-101, 107
    patterns, 73, 86-106
    willingness, 99-101
SIDS, 236
Simile, 124-125
Situational meanings, 34
Situations, definitions of, 8, 15
Smith, J., 2, 11-12, 273
Smith family, 71, 267f
    afterlife statements, 183
    attitude of the deceased toward
        death, 205-206, 210-211
    coincidancing, 132-134
    comparisons, 121, 123
    family change, 216, 223-224, 228
    family speak, 149-150
    individual change in, 217, 220, 227
    interview excerpts, 93, 123, 132-133,
        149, 161, 171, 179, 194, 196,
        205-206, 216-217, 220, 227
    meaning statements, 194, 196, 221
    negative statements, 161-162,
        170-172, 175, 179
    sharing, 93
Social construction of reality, 35

Social construing, 35
  shared, 35, 233
Social reality. *See* Meaning
Sourani, T., 33, 273
Sprenkle, D. H., 61, 275
St. John's Bereavement Study, 47
Stereotypes. *See* Meanings
Stimulators, 107
Stories, 110-114, 135
  substories, 112-113
Strategies of meaning-making, 56, 71,
    107, 110
  elemental strategy, 56
  global, 56
  intermediate, 56
Strauss, A., 18, 40-41, 52, 54-55, 59,
    67, 230, 237, 276
Strauss, A. L., 18, 40-41, 46, 257, 274
Stress, family, 32-38
Stroebe, M., 251, 276
Stroebe, W., 251, 276
Structure, 11
Stryker, S., 10-11, 276
Substories, 112-113
"Surviving the Death" (substory), 112
Swan family, 70, 266f
  attitude of the deceased toward
      death, 206-208
  family change, 224-225, 228
  interview excerpts, 185-187, 207
  meanings, 187
  negative statements, 176
  religious meanings, 185-186
  theme, 114
Symbolic interaction, 4
Symbolic interactionism, 5
Symbolic interaction theory, 4-11
System, definition of, 11

Tannen, D., 152, 276
Taylor, S. E., 14, 18, 20, 36-39, 276
Templates of reorganization, 25
Terminology, 14-16
Test, death as, 186-188
"The death was too soon or too late"
    statement, 175-176
"The Deceased's Life" (substory), 112

"The Dying" (substory), 112
  excerpt, 112-113
"The Family History" (substory), 112
"The Funeral" (substory), 112-113
  excerpt, 113
"The Illness" (substory), 112, 121
Theoretical saturation, 46
Theory, research implications for,
    230-236
Theory Construction and Research
    Methods workshop, 59
"The Relationship" (substory), 112
"The wrong person died" statement,
    173-175
Thomas, W. I., 5, 13, 233, 257, 276
Thompson, S. C., 18, 20, 29-31, 34, 36,
    39, 276
Truths realized, 220-228
Typifications:
  latent, 15, 77, 160, 165
  See also Meanings

Ultimate meanings, 159-190
  "Bad things should not happen to
      good people" statements, 172-173
  "Death was unfair or unjust"
      statements, 169-176
  "No sense to be made" statements,
      164-169
Understandings. *See* Meaning

Van Manen, M., 17, 276
Verification of data, 57-62

Waller, W., 16, 276
Weber, A. L., 255, 274
Weigert, A., 17, 275
Weiner, B., 276
Weiss, R., 143, 275
Weitzman, E., 276
Wheeler, I., 253, 276
Wong, P. T., 276
Worden, J. W., 13, 277
Worldviews. *See* Meanings
Wright, S., 43-44, 277

Zeeman family, 71, 269f
  comparisons, 124
  family change, 226-227
  family speak, 156-157
  interview excerpts, 185, 227

meaning statements, 193, 221-222
negative statements, 160, 176, 179
religious meanings, 185, 188-189
sharing, 93-94, 99
theme, 114

About the Author

Janice Winchester Nadeau, PhD, is a Licensed Psychologist, Licensed Marriage and Family Therapist, and master's prepared nurse. She is in private practice with Minnesota Human Development Consultants, Inc., in Minneapolis.

Dr. Nadeau has more than 20 years of experience working with families in a wide variety of settings. Her doctoral research was funded by a Bush Leadership Fellowship and a 4-year National Institute of Health Grant to study the impact of loss on families. Prior to her doctoral work, she was on the nursing faculty of The College of St. Catherine in St. Paul and was Codirector of the St. John's Hospital Bereavement Study. She is the founder of Growing Through Loss, a community-based grief support program that began in 1985 and has become a model for multiple programs in the Midwest.

In 1996, in Delphi, Greece, Dr. Nadeau was inducted into the International Work Group on Death, Dying, and Bereavement, a group of international grief scholars who meet every 18 months to develop research, knowledge, and practice in the field of death and dying.

She speaks locally and nationally on loss, grief, midlife, and family issues. With Ken Medema, concert artist, she has produced two series of audiotapes: *Where Do I Go From Here?* addresses people who have experienced loss, and *Why Do I Feel Like This?* addresses midlife audiences.